# Amartya Sen and Rational Choice

Are human beings motivated exclusively by self-interest? The orthodox theory of rational choice in economics thinks that they are. Amartya Sen disagrees, and his concept *commitment* is central to his vision of an alternative to mainstream rational choice theory. This book examines commitment as it has evolved in Sen's critique of orthodox rational choice theory.

The in-depth focus on commitment reveals subtleties in the concept itself as well as in its relationships with other concepts which Sen develops in his critique of rational choice theory, for example preference, sympathy, weakness of will, agency, personhood, social norms, rights, self-welfare goal and self-goal choice. The book provides a comprehensive understanding of commitment and offers novel interpretations of the term as a way of strengthening its plausibility. Broadly in support of Sen's conceptualization of rational choice, the book nevertheless reveals ambiguities and weaknesses in Sen's conceptual framework, and it reformulates Sen's concepts when doing so strengthens the claims he makes. The book also engages with critics of Sen and argues for the importance of commitment as a component in the theory of rational choice.

**Mark S. Peacock** was educated at the Universities of Sussex and Cambridge. He worked at the Universities of Witten/Herdecke and Erfurt, Germany, from 1996 to 2006 and is currently a professor in the Department of Social Science, York University, Canada.

# Routledge INEM Advances in Economic Methodology

Series Editor: Esther-Mirjam Sent, the University of Nijmegen, the Netherlands.

The field of economic methodology has expanded rapidly during the last few decades. This expansion has occurred in part because of changes within the discipline of economics, in part because of changes in the prevailing philosophical conception of scientific knowledge, and also because of various transformations within the wider society. Research in economic methodology now reflects not only developments in contemporary economic theory, the history of economic thought, and the philosophy of science; but it also reflects developments in science studies, historical epistemology, and social theorizing more generally. The field of economic methodology still includes the search for rules for the proper conduct of economic science, but it also covers a vast array of other subjects and accommodates a variety of different approaches to those subjects.

The objective of this series is to provide a forum for the publication of significant works in the growing field of economic methodology. Since the series defines methodology quite broadly, it will publish books on a wide range of different methodological subjects. The series is also open to a variety of different types of works: original research monographs, edited collections, as well as republication of significant earlier contributions to the methodological literature. The International Network for Economic Methodology (INEM) is proud to sponsor this important series of contributions to the methodological literature.

**17. The Individual and the Other in Economic Thought**
An Introduction
*Edited by Ragip Ege and Herrade Igersheim*

**18. Economics and Performativity**
Exploring Limits, Theories and Cases
*Nicolas Brisset*

**19. A Structuralist Theory of Economics**
*Adolfo García de la Sienra*

**20. Amartya Sen and Rational Choice**
The Concept of Commitment
*Mark S. Peacock*

For more information about this series, please visit: www.routledge.com/Routledge-INEM-Advances-in-Economic-Methodology/book-series/SE0630

# Amartya Sen and Rational Choice
The Concept of Commitment

**Mark S. Peacock**

LONDON AND NEW YORK

First published 2020 by Routledge

2 Park Square, Milton Park, Abingdon, Oxon, OX14 4RN

605 Third Avenue, New York, NY 10017

*Routledge is an imprint of the Taylor & Francis Group, an informa business*

First issued in paperback 2020

Copyright © 2020 Mark S. Peacock

The right of Mark S. Peacock to be identified as author of this work has been asserted by him in accordance with sections 77 and 78 of the Copyright, Designs and Patents Act 1988.

All rights reserved. No part of this book may be reprinted or reproduced or utilised in any form or by any electronic, mechanical, or other means, now known or hereafter invented, including photocopying and recording, or in any information storage or retrieval system, without permission in writing from the publishers.

Notice:
Product or corporate names may be trademarks or registered trademarks, and are used only for identification and explanation without intent to infringe.

*British Library Cataloguing-in-Publication Data*
A catalogue record for this book is available from the British Library

*Library of Congress Cataloging-in-Publication Data*
A catalog record has been requested for this book

ISBN: 978-0-367-18874-0 (hbk)
ISBN: 978-0-367-77690-9 (pbk)

Typeset in Times New Roman
by Taylor & Francis Books

**I dedicate this book to my parents.**

# Contents

| | |
|---|---|
| *Acknowledgements* | viii |
| Introduction | 1 |
| 1 Choice, consistency and self-interest | 7 |
| 2 Sympathy | 25 |
| 3 Commitment | 39 |
| 4 Commitment and meta-rankings | 59 |
| 5 Norms and commitment | 76 |
| 6 Binding oneself: Self-imposed constraints | 92 |
| 7 Goals | 104 |
| 8 Self-goal choice | 121 |
| Conclusion | 138 |
| *References* | 142 |
| *Index* | 149 |

# Acknowledgements

Parts of Chapters Two and Three of this book have been published previously as: 'On Amartya Sen's Concept of Sympathy', *Journal of Economic Philosophy* XII (2), 2019.

Parts of Chapter Five have previously appeared in the journal *Rationality, Markets and Morals* as: 'Sen's Apples: Commitment, Agent Relativity and Social Norms' (volume 2, 2011) and 'Commitment and Goals: a Comment on Christoph Hanisch, "Negative goals and identity"' (volume 4, 2013).

I would like to thank the journals and their generous permissions policies which have allowed me to incorporate material from these articles into these chapters.

# Introduction

The concept of commitment has proven to be one of the most original, lasting and far-reaching innovations which Amartya Sen has made in the theory of rational choice. Being coined in Sen's essay 'Rational Fools' (1977a), the term commitment has undergone significant reworking in Sen's *oeuvre* of the decades following its *début*. Commitment has also proven to be one of Sen's most controversial concepts, for it asks us to conceive choices which are counter-preferential. Such choices, if they exist, must have a foundation independent of a person's preferences, and, as such, many would deem these choices not to belong to the realm of rational choice at all because the latter, as it is conceived in orthodox economic theory, consists in choosing one's most preferred option which maximizes one's welfare. Commitment has proven to be no less controversial when it is associated with what Sen calls a violation of 'self-goal choice' whereby the agent is conceived to make a choice through which she does not pursue a goal of her own. This idea has raised the eyebrows of even Sen's most sympathetic critics who, despite not being beholden to the orthodox concept of rational choice in economic theory, nevertheless register incredulity towards the idea.

The need for a book-length study of commitment arises from a number of considerations. The first concerns the chronology and development of commitment in Sen's work. The concept, though not in name, can be traced back to Sen's 1973 essay 'Behaviour and the Concept of Preference' and Sen reworks and refines commitment well into the 2000s. The concept does not remain unchanged over nearly four decades, and tracing its trajectory allows one, for instance, to descry a logic in, as well as a pre-history to, Sen's major development of the concept in his 'Goals, Commitment, and Identity' (1985b); without a comprehensive perspective, this development of commitment would come somewhat out of the blue to the student of Sen's work. Commitment, one may say, has enjoyed a veritable *career* in Sen's work, and it therefore deserves thorough treatment.

The second consideration which justifies a book-length study, pertains not only to commitment but to the family of concepts which are related to it. One such is the concept of sympathy, which Sen introduces, along with commitment, in 'Rational Fools'. Sympathy is usually interpreted in a way which would require a relatively straight-forward augmentation of the individual's welfare function, and hence orthodox rational choice theory does not have great difficulty incorporating sympathy, as Sen himself observes. The analysis of Chapter Two, however, reveals that the concept is not as simple as first meets the eye. Many aspects of sympathy have hitherto been passed over, and the claim that sympathy can be easily incorporated into orthodox rational choice theory is subject to challenge. Another concept of relevance to commitment is altruism which, although not a central aspect of Sen's conceptual repertoire, is nevertheless connected to the notion of commitment. Is altruism more closely related to sympathy or commitment? Sen thinks it can be related to both, depending on how one defines altruism, and, in Chapter Three, I tease out the way in which it dovetails with each, something not readily apparent from Sen's rather oblique discussions of altruism.

A book-length study of commitment also allows one to illuminate aspects of Sen's work which, though he introduces them in relation to commitment, usually pass without great elucidation or critical comment in the secondary literature. One example is Sen's lapidary vignette about two boys who are to distribute two apples, one small, the other large, between themselves. Although the short paragraph-long example supposedly illustrates the distinction between sympathy and commitment, the way in which it does so is not obvious, as a treatment of the vignette demonstrates in Chapter Five. A fourth consideration which justifies a book-length study of commitment bears upon the ideas which Sen has developed independently of commitment. Though there are many aspects of his *opus* which have no apparent or at best tangential relevance to commitment, some of these aspects are fruitfully read in light of what he writes about commitment, for there are relationships to be uncovered which Sen himself does not make obvious. One example is Sen's critique of libertarianism. Sen reformulates the libertarian conception of rights, and he does so, I contend in Chapter Six, in a manner analogous to how he would have us conceive commitments. A second example involves Sen's writing on agency and, in particular, on agent-relativity. Having contributed to philosophical debates on agent-relativity in the early 1980s, one can see that what he writes there has significance for the concept if commitment. This matter is explored in Chapter Five. The notion of personhood or personal identity is also one to which Sen has dedicated much attention in his later writings, and it, too, can be fruitfully related to the concept of commitment, as I show in Chapter Four. Finally, a monograph-length study also allows us to identify questions raised in Sen's writings, particularly those of the 1970s, which are not addressed or given satisfactory answers in those works. Such matters resurface in Sen's subsequent works in which he offers further resources for answering them. One example is Sen's need to provide a causal explanation of choices which are not based on preferences. The notion of counter-preferential choices necessitates this causal account. Another example concerns the ability of human beings to act on as-if rankings of the options before them and what motivates them to do so, a theme which crops up in various chapters of this work.

Many aspects of Sen's work are not treated in this book. The reader will, for example, find little on social, as opposed to individual, choice in the pages which follow. Nor will his now well-known capability approach to well-being find an airing save for some references to it in Chapter Seven. These lacunae, if such they be, are inevitable in the treatment of a scholar whose *opus* is as voluminous and far-reaching as Sen's. Fortunately, secondary literature on these and other parts of Sen's work is not thin on the ground, and the reader who is interested in topics not covered in the present book will find rich pickings amongst Sen's interpreters, defenders and critics. I should also note that the following study of commitment is analytical and exegetical. Although I probe Sen's work and, in later chapters, the work of his interpreters with a critical eye, my priority is to establish clarity about what Sen writes. The tasks of analysis and exegesis might seem modest, but the subtlety and sometimes caliginous nature of what Sen writes demand an approach which sets itself the goal of ascertaining what he actually means with the concept of commitment and its attendant concepts. This does not mean that the current study cannot be used as a propaedeutic to a more critical approach to commitment than contained in the pages which follow.

The structure of the monograph is as follows. The primary focus of Chapter One is Sen's 1973 article, 'Behaviour and the Concept of Preference'. After reviewing Sen's critique of one version of rational choice theory, which identifies rationality with the internal consistency of choice, the chapter examines Sen's critique of the role accorded to preferences in the orthodox economic theory of choice. The concept of preference, Sen observes, is related, on the one hand, to welfare by what I call the *normative relationship* and, on the other hand, to choice by what I call the *aetiological relationship*. Being enmeshed in these two relationships is a burden, Sen holds, which the concept of preference struggles to bear. In the context of the prisoners' dilemma, Sen suggests a way to lighten the burden placed on the concept of preference by loosening its bonds with welfare. He suggests that one can do so by broadening the notion of preference to what he refers to as 'ultimate preferences', which would allow preference to liberate itself from its strict relationship with welfare maximization. However, he does little more than mention this idea and does not pursue it in his subsequent work. Instead his focus becomes a dissolution of the aetiological relationship whereby not all choices are based on the causal foundation of an agent's preferences. Sen elucidates the weakening of the relationship in which preference stands to choice with the idea that individuals in a prisoners' dilemma act on a moral ranking which does not represent their true preferences. This theme of acting on an *as-if ranking*, that is, acting as if one ranked the available options in a manner different to that expressed by one's preferences, returns many times in Sen's work.

Chapter Two commences the analysis of 'Rational Fools' (1977a) with an examination of the concept of sympathy. Though often held to be less interesting than its sibling concept, commitment, sympathy, I argue, is worthy of detailed analysis. Sen's exposition suggests that sympathy can be distinguished into two types – *contemplative* and *active* sympathy. Contemplative sympathy is simply a feeling, whereby one's welfare is affected by the welfare of others. Active sympathy, by contrast, is necessarily related to an agent's choices and gives rise to what Sen call 'actions based on sympathy', whereby one individual's choice of action brings about an improvement in the welfare of a second individual, whence the first individual experiences a sympathetic increase in her own welfare. An analysis of active sympathy raises the question concerning the manner in which sympathy may be deemed 'egoistic'. Sen holds sympathy to be egoistic, but my analysis shows that only active sympathy can be so. Furthermore, active sympathy, though egoistic, does not entail welfare-maximizing conduct on the part of the agent who performs actions based on sympathy.

Chapter Three is dedicated to the concept of commitment as Sen expounds it in 'Rational Fools'. Sen gives two definitions of the term, the first in terms of the agent's expectations of the consequences of a choice for her own welfare, the second in terms of the reason for her choice. Commitment, Sen argues, involves counter-preferential choice, that is, choice which has a non-preference-based aetiology: committed choices are causally based, not on the agent's preferences, but on her reason for acting. Sen argues that the nature of the reasons which individuals have when their choices answer to the name of commitment involves the agent's 'morals'. Sen's very broad understanding of the term 'morals' is explored. Chapter Three also examines the concept of altruism and its place in Sen's conceptual framework. Although Sen is not explicit about this, I argue that he conceives altruism in a manner which aligns it with the concept of commitment and has strong affinities with 'psychological' approaches to altruism.

Chapter Four analyses meta-ranking, which Sen discusses in both 'Rational Fools' but also in the prior publication, 'Choice, Orderings and Morality' (1974a). The technique of meta-ranking allows one to conceive morality in terms of a ranking of different rankings of outcomes. Sen puts the technique to use in conceptualizing weakness of will in a way which permits a fine-grained understanding of the phenomenon, whereby choices which deviate from what, one holds, one ought to do may be graded according to the degree of morality which they manifest. Meta-rankings also shed light on the prisoners' dilemma, and we resume the discussion of this dilemma from Chapter One with a discussion of acting on as-if rankings. The chapter enquires into the moral psychology of acting on as-if rankings and compares Sen's understanding of the agent who does so with the way Aristotle conceives of three moral characters – the incontinent person, the continent person and the truly virtuous person. Meta-ranking also opens up the theme of personhood, and I ask if a concept of the person can be located in Sen's work. The superordinate role of reason *vis-à-vis* preference, I argue, holds the key to Sen's understanding of personhood.

Chapter Five offers a detailed analysis of Sen's 'two boys and two apples' example from 'Rational Fools', which, though it is designed to elucidate the difference between sympathy and commitment, leaves much unclear. Geoffrey Brennan's (2007) interpretation of Sen's vignette is, to my knowledge, the only sustained analysis of the example in critical discussions of Sen's *opus*. Brennan argues that the interaction between the boys is based on norm-following behaviour, though Brennan contests Sen's view that the encounter involves counter-preferential choice. The difference between Brennan and Sen turns on their respective understandings of norm following. The peculiarity of Sen's understanding of norm following is highlighted through a comparison with more orthodox accounts of such behaviour in the social sciences. The sense in which Sen may be described as a 'heterodox' economist is also explored. The final part of the chapter takes its inspiration from an example from Brennan and leads to the hypothesis that commitment, as opposed to sympathy, is related to agent-relative evaluations of social situations. Agent relativity is a topic to which Sen has made philosophical contributions largely in abstraction from his forays into commitment, but the role of one's own actions in the pursuit of one's commitments indicates a clear relationship between the two.

Chapter Six continues the theme of norm following and addresses a challenge which Daniel Hausman (2012) poses to Sen's understanding of norm-following conduct. The question is: how can an agent bind or commit herself to adhering to a norm when her preferences urge her to do otherwise? For if, as Hausman asks, commitments are 'purely psychological', what is to stop the agent from breaking them? This question necessitates a discussion about the best way of conceiving norms, and I suggest that Sen's understanding of norms – their binding force and normative status – be conceived in analogy to the way in which he conceives rights. Sen's position on rights is compared with that of Robert Nozick (1974) and from Sen's critique of Nozick I develop an account of the circumstances under which rights may be broken and, by analogy, the circumstances under which commitments may be broken.

Chapter Seven commences the analysis of Sen's post-1970s contributions to the theory of rational choice. In particular, it examines Sen's reformulation of the categories of rational choice theory and his critique of the assumptions of this theory. In his essay 'Goals, Commitment, and Identity' (1985b), Sen enumerates three characteristics of 'privateness' in orthodox rational choice theory, which he calls self-centred welfare, self-welfare goal and self-goal choice. None is essential to rational choice, he holds, and each can thus be violated. Sen claims that each characteristic can be realized or violated independently of the realization or violation of the other two. I call this *Sen's independence claim* regarding the characteristics of privateness. The main purpose of Chapter Seven is to test this claim, though doing so presupposes an interpretation of these characteristics of privateness. I offer a capability-theoretic interpretation of them according to which a violation of each characteristic endows the agent with a particular capability, the capability to feel sympathy in the case of a violation of self-centred welfare, the capability to make commitments in the case of a violation of self-welfare goal and, for a violation of self-goal choice, the capability to make non-teleological choices. Sen's independence claim passes the test rather easily, and I ask whether a different, choice-theoretic, interpretation of the characteristics of privateness be justified. Various aspects of Sen's work point toward such an interpretation which would mean that a violation of the characteristics of privateness does not simply endow the agent with a particular capability but that the relevant capability must be activated in the concrete act of choice. The test is more exacting than its capability-theoretic counterpart and consists in constructing an example for each of the eight possible combinations of realizations and violations of the three characteristics of privateness. Four such combinations are treated in the latter part of Chapter Seven and Sen's independence claim passes the test for each. None of the four combinations, though, involves a violation of self-goal choice. Combinations which involve this violation prove trickier and a treatment thereof is postponed until Chapter Eight.

Chapter Eight asks how Sen conceives the violation of self-goal choice. Through an analysis of his critics' understanding of how he conceives this violation, I ascertain that the critics misrepresent Sen. Textual evidence from Sen strongly suggests that an agent whose choice violates self-goal choice makes a *goalless* choice. Having established this, I turn to the remaining four combinations of realizations and violations of the three characteristics of privateness to complete the test of Sen's independence claim commenced in Chapter Seven. The claim fails to pass the test for these four combinations, though a reformulation of self-welfare goal allows one to approach more closely though not completely fulfil the conditions required in these four combinations. An assessment of the manner in which Sen conceives violations of self-goal choice closes the chapter. My assessment confirms a suspicion which is voiced at various points in the book, namely, that an agent whose choice violates self-goal choice may be held to be pursuing her long-term ability to pursue her own goals. If justified, this suspicion would undermine Sen's claim that a choice which violates self-goal choice is one through which the agent does not pursue a goal.

The book's concluding section offers thoughts on the unifying role which commitment plays in Sen's work on the theory of rational choice over many decades. What is striking, when one begins one's analysis of commitment with Sen's 1973 essay, is that, already with the publication of 'Rational Fools', it is clear that Sen delineates two distinct types of commitment which he only distinguishes explicitly in the 1980s. The various ways in which Sen's work on rational choice combats the assumption that individuals are motivated exclusively by self-interest are reviewed and their implications for choice and the relationships in which the concept stands with preference, welfare and goals are noted.

# 1 Choice, consistency and self-interest

## Introduction

This chapter focuses on the essay, 'Behaviour and the Concept of Preference' (1973), Sen's first sustained critique of the theory of individual rational choice in economics. The essay may be deemed 'foundational' in the sense that it contains a host of ideas, most, though not all, of which have proven to be of lasting significance to Sen's thought on rational choice.

The chapter is structured as follows. Section I examines Sen's scepticism towards an understanding of rationality in terms of the internal consistency of choice. Sen has returned to his criticisms of viewing rationality in these terms many times, the most recent being Sen (2017b), and his consistency in pursuing these criticisms almost suffices to make him a paragon of the theory he is criticizing. Although the focus of this section is primarily on Sen's remarks in his 1973 article, I refer to some of his later writings in the course of the discussion to demonstrate the unity of his work over many years with respect to the notion of internal consistency. Section II analyses Sen's criticism of the concept of preference as it is understood in economic theory. The concept, Sen ascertains, stands in two relationships. In one, it is tied to welfare: if a person prefers $x$ to $y$, this necessarily implies that her welfare is greater when she chooses $x$ than it would be were she to choose $y$. I call this the normative relationship. In the other relationship, preference is connected to choice: all choices are causally generated by a person's preferences, and so no choice can be made which does not reveal the person's preferences. I call this the aetiological relationship. Section III explains why Sen thinks this dual relationship in which preference is embroiled overburdens the concept. The way in which the concept can be relieved of this burden is explored through an analysis of the prisoners' dilemma. Sen's discussion of this dilemma contains his first analysis of an individual acting on an 'as-if' ranking, that is, on a ranking of the options which deviates from the individual's true preference ranking. Acting on an as-if ranking means breaking the causal relationship between preference and choice (the aetiological relationship), for it entails substituting one's actual preference ranking with another as the causal basis for making choices. In his 1973 essay, Sen also entertains the idea that individuals' preferences not merely reflect matters related to their own welfare but are orientated to wider concerns, including social responsibility. This idea leads him to consider the notion of a person's 'ultimate' preferences, a conception which would significantly expand the restrictions placed on preferences in orthodox theories of rational choice by admitting non-self-interested matters into the set of concerns captured by an individual's preferences. Conceived thus, preferences would free themselves from the normative relationship, for acting on preferences would not necessarily lead a person to maximize her welfare. However, Sen gives ultimate preferences short shrift in his 'Behaviour' essay. In the chapter's conclusion, I enumerate the various *motifs* which Sen lays down in his essay of 1973. All of them could have become lasting aspects of the alternative theory of choice he develops after 1973, but only some have transpired to have lasting significance for his subsequent work.

## I Internal consistency

Sen is sceptical of the claim that the criterion for the rationality of choice lies in the 'internal consistency' of choice. A thread which runs through his many critiques of this claim is that neither consistency nor inconsistency can be predicated of choices in the absence of something external, that is, without the specification of a 'non-choice feature' (Sen 1986b: 343; 2017b: 309–12) of the person who makes the choices, to which her choices can be referred and with which they may be deemed consistent or inconsistent. The paradigmatic candidate for internal inconsistency is my choosing $x$ over $y$ in one situation and $y$ over $x$ in another. Such a pattern of choice is inconsistent if, for example, one maps these choices onto my preferences, assuming my preferences are well-ordered and stable (Sen 1973: 56). But preferences are external to choices, and so the move from choices to preferences just described proves Sen's point that we must move beyond choices and hold them against an external yardstick if we are to demonstrate their consistency or inconsistency.

The context for Sen's critique of internal consistency as the criterion of rationality is his examination of revealed preference theory. Revealed preference theory was heralded as a means of studying choice behaviour without recourse to 'mentalistic' concepts, such as utility, a term which Paul Samuelson (1938: 61), in laying down the principles of revealed preference theory, held to be discredited. As Sen describes it, revealed preference theory draws an inference from a person's choices to her preferences: if two items, $x$ and $y$, fall within the person's budget set and she chooses $y$, the inference is that she prefers $y$ to $x$ (1973: 54–5). Samuelson's theory may be deemed guilty of its own inconsistency, for if Sen is right, and one can only ascertain whether choices are inconsistent when one can refer them to an external yardstick like preference, revealed preference theory is already stepping beyond the bounds of mere behaviour, to which it wished to restrict itself in the name of providing a more 'scientific' foundation to the theory of choice than that given by theories which utilize the concept of utility. Samuelson (1948: 243) rather gives the game away when he writes: 'the individual guinea-pig, by his market behaviour, reveals his preference pattern – if there is such a consistent pattern'. What Samuelson's statement reveals is that it is the revelation of choices *in accord with a preference pattern*, not the choices ('market behaviour') alone, which yields judgements about consistency and inconsistency. And although there is a case to be made that preferences are not 'mentalistic', they are not identical with choice, and, as Sen argues, they are not necessarily expressed or manifested in choices people make.

The list of difficulties which Sen associates with the consistency criterion continues:

- *Indifference*: if an agent, $A$, is indifferent between options $x$ and $y$, he might, when offered $x$ or $y$, randomly choose $y$, whence the revealed preference theorist will wrongly infer $A$'s preference for $y$ over $x$ (Sen 1973: 62).
- *Changing preferences*: apparently inconsistent choices, of the kind when $A$ is observed to choose $x$ over $y$ in one situation and $y$ over $x$ in another, might bespeak a change in $A$'s preferences during the time between the first and second choice (Sen 1977a: 89, 91). There is no empirical basis on which to distinguish an alleged inconsistency of choices from choices consistent with changing preferences.
- *Non-comparability of the choice situation: prima facie* inconsistency might result from the observer misdefining the agent's definition of the choice situation. The observer might believe she is observing two equivalent choice situations, in one of which the actor chooses $x$ over $y$, and, in the other, the opposite. From the actor's perspective, the choice situation might be understood differently. Thus, the observer would ascribe inconsistency to person $A$ if $A$ chose mutton over lentils today, but lentils over mutton a day hence. But if the mutton is still in the larder when $A$ chooses lentils tomorrow, the two choice situations are not comparable (Sen 1973: 57) because, on day one, $A$ is choosing between mutton and lentils, having, perhaps, eaten neither for a fortnight; on day two, $A$ is choosing between mutton and lentils having eaten the former the day before. For $A$, these choices are not analogous to one another, but if the revealed preference theorist conceives them to be two instances of the *same* choice situation, she will ascribe inconsistency to $A$ when, in fact, there is none.
- *Variety*: an observer might conceive $A$'s choice behaviour to constitute a succession of discrete choices, whereas $A$ conceives her behaviour to represent one choice situation which reflects her 'love of variety' (Sen 1977a: 91; 1982a: 3). For instance, choosing mutton today and lentils tomorrow might be a single choice situation for $A$, and there cannot be inconsistency within one unit of choice. Interpreting the situation as one which involves two discrete choices, the observer would identify this love of variety as inconsistency. To ascertain $A$'s definition of each situation in

this and in the previous case, the observer would require more information than that yielded by observing *A*'s choice behaviour alone (Sen 1973: 71–2). If it is to make accurate judgements about consistency, revealed preference theory would have to involve a hermeneutics of choice rather than merely observing overt behaviour. A hermeneutics of choice would solicit verbal information relating to the chooser's definition of the situation, so that the theorist would delineate choice situations as the chooser does. But this is what revealed preference theory eschews, relying instead, as it avowedly does, only on *A*'s observable behaviour as a source of information about *A*'s preferences.

In his later work, Sen rather 'goes to town' on his critique of rationality as internal consistency. He offers the following examples:

> If a person does exactly the opposite of what would help achieving what he or she would want to achieve, and does this with flawless internal consistency (always choosing the opposite of what will enhance the occurrence of things he or she wants and values), the person can scarcely be seen as rational, even if that person inspires some kind of an astonished admiration on the part of the observer.
> (Sen 1987a: 13; cf. 1986b: 343; 2002a: 20)

No less facetiously, but equally to the point, Sen asks us to entertain the possibility that:

> my object is precisely to establish that I am 'inconsistent' ... I may want to be taken as unusual, or eccentric, or unfathomable. I may believe that, as an oriental, it is right that I should be immensely inscrutable ... Or – more simply – I could just find inconsistency 'great fun' ('what joy to see the puzzled faces of the wise and the learned – especially decision theorists').
> (Sen 1995a: 21–2)

On the more sober plane of logical argumentation, Sen notes that, from choices such as those of *A* depicted above, one cannot infer inconsistency in the way that one may infer inconsistency between statements which *A* might utter, for example 'I prefer $x$ to $y$' and 'I prefer $y$ to $x$'. This pair of statements is contradictory, but choices do not, as such, entail statements, and so they cannot be held, on analogy with statements, to be mutually contradictory (Sen 1995a: 27; 1993a: 126–7). Mere internal consistency does not get us far as a basis for making judgements of rationality. If we adhere to the internal-consistency view of rational choice, the concept of preference, if it is thematized at all, becomes entirely subordinated to the notion of choice, such that the relationship between the two becomes trivial: what we choose is what we prefer (Sen 1982a: 4–5). The internal-consistency view also tells us nothing about the motivation of individuals.

## II Preference, choice, self-interest

The debate surrounding internal consistency is independent of questions regarding motivation, for, as Sen (1977a: 91) writes, a 'consistent chooser can have any degree of egoism that we care to specify'. Consistency is a 'procedural demand' devoid of substantive content regarding people's preferences; the contention that people are, for example, always and everywhere self-interested, by contrast, endows their preferences with a particular content; it specifies their motivation in substantive terms (Sen 1989: 320). The latter contention forms the basis of an understanding of rational choice which offers an alternative to the internal-consistency view. To make a rational choice, according to this alternative view, the individual must choose that option which promotes his self-interest to a greater degree than any other option. Unlike the consistency view of rationality, the self-interest-maximization conceptualization 'involves a clear external reference' (Sen 2002a: 21), namely, to self-interest, to which a person's choices are related (Sen 1987a: 15). This is why the self-interest approach is a 'correspondence approach' to rationality: there is, in this approach, a 'non-choice feature of the person', namely, her self-interest, to which the choices of a rational chooser are to correspond (Sen 1986b: 343).

A correspondence approach to rationality, whilst distinct from, is compatible with, the internal-consistency approach, for exponents of the latter can supplement the consistency view with the supposition that a rational agent consistently pursue her self-interest and only that (Sen 1982a: 5). There is, however, no necessity that the consistency approach be thus supplemented. The motivational supplement of self-interest rather sneaks itself into economic analysis without much justification and is universalized into the assumption that all human behaviour is motivated by the expectation of benefit to the person whose behaviour is being observed. Sen refers to this motivational assumption as 'the convention [amongst economists] that a preferred position [for a given individual] involves a higher level of welfare of that individual' (1973: 66–7); and since, according to adherents of this convention, whatever is chosen is preferred by the individual, we are inexorably led to the conclusion that the chosen item is that which maximizes the welfare of the person concerned (Sen 1977a: 88). Sen calls this convention 'definitional egoism' (1977a: 89). Though he sees the two approaches – consistency and correspondence – as mutually compatible, he is keen to bring out the conceptual independence of questions of motivation from issues of consistency: '[e]ven if the required consistency were to obtain, it would still leave the question of egoism unresolved except in the purely definitional sense' (Sen 1977a: 91). The phrase 'in the purely definitional sense' is Sen's way of capturing the fact that, in much of economic analysis, it is a mere assumption that a person's choices are held always (definitionally) to redound to his own welfare and thus his motivation cannot but be 'egoistic'. Sen's critique of this 'definitional trick' (1985c: 226) surfaces in many of his writings. Whilst it is a testable empirical hypothesis that an individual pursue her self-interest in every act of choice, the empirical plausibility of that hypothesis is not furthered if one simply posits (definitionally) that 'whatever the person can be seen as maximizing ... will be *called* that person's utility (or interest)' (1985c: 226). On occasion, Sen resorts to parody to criticize the definitional stance: '[y]ou drown with your ship doing your duty but desiring escape, and the choice-based definition of utility declares that you have once again – as always! – succeeded in maximizing your utility' (Sen 1981–2: 206; cf. 1977a: 88). The choice-based definition of rationality declares, in fact, that *whatever* one chooses – whether one goes down with the ship or jumps the queue for a lifeboat – one maximizes one's utility.

Sen (1973: 66–7) might be correct about the 'convention' amongst economists of identifying the maximand of choice with the agent's self-interest, and critics of rational choice theory do not tire of taking orthodox economics to task for adopting this convention. Samuel Bowles and Herbert Gintis (2011: 9), for instance, note that 'while self-interest is not formally implied by the conventional approach [to economics], it is generally assumed in practice'. The assumption, Bowles and Gintis (2011: 10, 45) note, 'has never depended on empirical tests', but has unquestioningly been taken to be 'self-evident'. The allegedly self-evident nature of the assumption in some people's eyes makes it 'definitional', which might explain the laxity about testing it empirically. However, it is not analytic to the concept of choice that the agent maximizes her personal welfare in each and every act of choice, which is why Sen refers to the relationship between choice and welfare as an 'empirical' one (1977a: 94).

Sen has often observed that 'utility' can be defined in two ways, one as the 'magnitude we ... wish to maximise', the second, 'more usual meaning', being synonymous with the 'satisfaction', self-interest or welfare of an agent (Sen 1961: 480). Only the second definition entails egoism, for, on the first definition, 'utility' can stand for whatever variable it might be which we try to maximize, and there is no necessity that this variable have anything to do with self-interest. If the two senses of 'utility' are conflated, rational choice theory produces 'an empirical rabbit out of a definitional hat' (Sen 2002a: 27), for a conflation yields the following train of thought: in each act of choice, a chooser maximizes something; this 'something' is to be called 'utility'; 'utility', in turn, is understood to represent the self-interest of the chooser, that is, what the chooser prefers; therefore each act of choice is egoistically motivated and maximizes self-interest. The 'empirical rabbit' turns out to be rather thin on evidence but plump on definition, for it is through the conceptual identification of the two senses of utility in rational choice theory that human beings are understood, whatever the nature of their choices, to be utility maximizers in an egoistic sense. The definitional work renders empirical investigation of the agent's motivation superfluous, as Bowles and Gintis note, for there is no choice which could conceivably refute the claim that all individuals are egoistic utility maximizers once one has entered the 'enchanted world of definitions' posited by the orthodox theory of rational choice and accepted the conflation between the two senses of 'utility' (Sen 1977a: 89).

The assumption that human motivation is universally egoistic marks the first of two relationships in which the concept of preference stands in orthodox economic theory. This relationship is between preference and welfare, and Sen characterizes it thus: 'if a person prefers *x* to *y* then he must regard himself to be better off with *x* than with *y*' (Sen 1973: 67). I refer to this as the *normative relationship* between preference and welfare; it implies that one's preferences are governed by the principle of what is 'good' for oneself in terms of one's own welfare. The normative relationship entails welfare maximization as the underlying principle of choice, when choice is based on preference. There is a second relationship in which the concept of preference stands in orthodox economic theory. It concerns the relationship between preference and choice, whereby an individual's preferences are ascribed a causal role in generating the choices that the individual makes: preferences are ascribed the role of 'determinants of [choice] behaviour', as Sen (1973: 66) writes. A person's preferences are thus conceived to be the *explananda* of his choices, and there is no choice that is not causally generated by a person's preferences; there can therefore be no gap between what one prefers and what one actually chooses. Because it thematizes the causal dimension of human choice, I call this the *aetiological relationship* between preference and choice.

Some revealed preference theorists abjure the aetiological relationship on the grounds that the relationship between preference and choice is not causal but conceptual (see Binmore 2009: 19; cf. Hands 2013; Hédoin 2016). However, if a theory of choice is to be *explanatory*, it must posit some causal relationship which accounts for the genesis of choices. Economists sometimes manifest diffidence toward the issue of causality in their theories of choice, but, as Daniel Hausman (2012: 15) argues, 'choice determination' should be included amongst the axioms of rational choice theory. According to Hausman's notion of choice determination, '[a]mong the alternatives they believe to be available, agents will choose one that is at the top of their preference ranking'. Only by including some such axiom does preference connect causally to choice, and without such an axiom, a theory of choice would remain in the world of conceptual relationships only. The aetiological relationship implies the following explanation of choice: (i) the starting point of a causal explanation of choice is the individual's preference ranking, which is assumed to have the properties of reflexiveness, completeness and transitivity; (ii) the individual identifies from the options available that which he most prefers; (iii) he then chooses his most preferred option. This is the meaning of a preference being the causal basis of choice, for it is because an option is the most preferred that the individual chooses it. If choices were universally caused in this way, the individual's choices would always be based on his preferences. If, to the aetiological relationship, we add the normative relationship between preference and welfare, we must conclude not only that the individual's choices are always based on his preferences, but also that he maximizes his welfare in each act of choice. If the normative relationship is posited definitionally, as Sen thinks it is in much of orthodox economic theory, then being caused by an agent's preferences means that the choice necessarily maximizes the agent's welfare. This is the agent's motivation for choosing as he does.

Sen doubts 'whether such a heavy weight can be put on the slender shoulders of the concept of preference' (1973: 67, 69), and he urges that either the normative or the aetiological relationship be relinquished. We will explore the abrogation of the normative relationship in the next section, but, to finish this section, I limit the analysis to the aetiological relationship, the abrogation of which would give us cases in which an individual's 'choices are not rigidly bound to his preferences only' (Sen 1973: 66). How are we to conceive of such choices? Sen's 1973 article is not explicit about this but the following account seems implicitly to play a role: if a choice is not causally based on a person's preferences, it must be based on something else, that is, generated via a causal mechanism which is not rooted in preferences. The 'something else', whatever it is, allows an individual to side-step the causal power of her preferences and base her choice on a different causal foundation. For those choices of which the aetiological relationship does not hold, the individual's choices are not caused by her preferences. The aetiology of non-preference-based choices is something to which Sen returns in 'Rational Fools', as we shall see in Chapter Three. But he gives us a glimpse of how non-preference-based choice might work in his 'Behaviour' essay, when he examines an example which has the structure of a prisoners' dilemma. This is the topic of the next section.

## III Bottles, dilemmas and social responsibility

Sen commences his analysis of the prisoners' dilemma in the form which has its origins in the narrative first suggested by A.W. Tucker (Poundstone 1992: 117–18), with two detainees who face the options of confessing or not confessing to a misdemeanour and must make their choice of strategy without knowing how the other will decide. Sen asks what might bring parties to this dilemma to relinquish the welfare-maximizing dominant strategy of confession and instead to choose non-confession. The case which interests Sen is one in which players have no possibility of entering a contract through which mutual cooperation can be mutually enforced. Furthermore, it is a case in which neither player has a concern with the other's prison sentence which is reflected in the welfare function of each. As Sen writes:

> [t]here is nothing extraordinary in assuming that a person may prefer that both go to prison for two years each rather than that the other should suffer twenty years while he himself goes free. The problem arises precisely because this is *not* being assumed.
> (1973: 65; cf. 1977b: 228).

*Choice, consistency and self-interest* 15

To the contrary, Sen continues, each player in the case at hand 'is assumed to be self-centred and interested basically only in his own prison term' (1973: 65). Neither player, that is, feels *sympathy* for the other, as Sen will define that term in his essay 'Rational Fools'. Can even self-centred players be brought to cooperate in prisoners' dilemmas? Sen thinks they can and suggests that 'this is precisely the situation in which moral rules of behaviour have traditionally played an important part', for 'traditional rules of good behaviour' can demand 'the suspension of calculations geared to individual rationality', thus averting the suboptimal outcome of mutual confession (Sen 1973: 64). By hypothesizing that players follow a moral code and thus suspend their rational calculation, Sen does not alter the assumption that players' preferences remain self-centred; only their behaviour changes. They are, as Sen puts it, acting *as if* they had concerns which in fact they do not, at least not in a way which redounds to their welfare. Sen is particularly interested in this account of cooperative behaviour because it demonstrates where revealed preference theory 'goes off the rails' (1973: 66).

It does so because the choices just described do not reveal the preferences of each player and so acting according to social 'mores and rules of behaviour ... will drive a wedge between behaviour and welfare' (1973: 67). Now the revealed preference theorist can retort, Sen observes, by 'defining preference as the underlying relation in terms of which individual choices can be explained' (1973: 67). By doing so, the revealed preference theorist would uphold the aetiological relationship by explaining whatever choices an individual makes in terms of her preference ordering. And if these choices do not maximize the individual's welfare, as in the case discussed by Sen, the revealed preference theorist would thereby relinquish the normative relationship. Sen descries a difficulty with this move, for it subverts the 'usual sense' of the term preference, according to which 'if a person prefers $x$ to $y$ then he must regard himself to be better off with $x$ than with $y$' (1973: 67).

In a further elaboration of the prisoners' dilemma, Sen enumerates four possible accounts of cooperative conduct. His example portrays an individual's decision whether to return his glass bottles to the retailer for re-use. I will follow a slightly altered version of the latter story to elucidate Sen's notion of acting on an as-if ranking. Sen's story of the bottle-returner is more complex than the version which I portray, for Sen depicts the individual's choice to be between using non-re-usable steel cans and re-usable bottles, and, only if he opts for the latter, is he faced with the choice whether to return the bottles after use. The simplified version of the example above portrays the same type of choice as Sen's more complex example.

'Being generally interested in the environment but also being lazy about returning bottles' (Sen 1973: 68), the individual hopes that other people will return their bottles whilst he does not (given the negligible impact of his behaviour on the environment and the minor, though not insubstantial, inconvenience to him of returning them). The second best outcome from the individual's perspective is that all people, including him, return bottles,

16  *Choice, consistency and self-interest*

followed by the third best outcome of nobody returning bottles. The worst outcome is that the individual alone returns his bottle, but nobody else does so. Sen (1973: 68–9) considers four explanations which could account for the individual electing the cooperative strategy of returning his empties.

(1) The individual has a preference for returning glass bottles, and so returning the bottles is an activity from which he derives welfare. The individual here therefore sees intrinsic value in returning bottles.
(2) His welfare function incorporates 'a concern for other people's welfare'. Consequently, the environmental damage he would cause by not returning his bottles would affect his own welfare negatively as a result of reducing the welfare of others. Solicitous about the effects of his actions on the welfare of others (because these effects reduce his own welfare), he returns his empty bottles.
(3) His welfare function, as in (2), incorporates concern for others, but the increase in his welfare which would result from the benefit others would receive if he returned his bottles would not outweigh the inconvenience to him of returning them. Nevertheless, should others notice that he is a non-bottle-returner, he would suffer from the stigma of being deemed an 'environmental lout' or suchlike, and fear of being labelled thus persuades him to return the bottles.
(4) The effects of his actions on others, which redound to his own welfare, are not sufficient to motivate him to return his empties. Furthermore, he could surreptitiously dispose of his bottles without being spotted by the disapproving eyes of others. Nevertheless, he stoically returns them because this, he holds, is the socially responsible thing to do, even though surreptitiously disposing of them in the rubbish would be the welfare-maximizing option.

Explanations (1) to (3) have something in common, namely, that returning bottles for re-use is internalized within the individual's welfare function. That is, the individual derives welfare from returning his bottles, either from the act of returning itself (explanation (1)), from the welfare effects on others (explanation (2)) or from the avoidance of censure from others (explanation (3)). Explanation (4) differs from its predecessors in this respect, for although the individual may derive welfare from returning his bottles, the prospect of deriving this welfare in explanation (4) is insufficient to motivate him to return his empties. This, Sen (1973: 69) observes, constitutes a 'serious difficulty' for the traditional theory of rational choice because the chosen option – returning bottles – is not the most preferred, whereby the 'most preferred' option is to be understood as that from which the individual expects to maximize his welfare.

Sen issues an intriguing comment immediately after he presents this fourth explanation: '[i]t is, of course, perfectly possible to argue that actions based on considerations of social responsibility as opposed to one's own welfare do reflect one's "ultimate" preferences, and in a certain sense this is undoubtedly true' (1973: 69). Sen does not explain the term 'ultimate preferences' but presumably he has the following in mind: the individual's ultimate preferences take into account considerations beyond the welfare consequences of his choices to himself, and hence ultimate preferences are not solely orientated to his self-interest; rather, preferences are 'ultimate' in the sense of 'all encompassing' or 'fully inclusive' – they include concerns for doing the right, or socially responsible, thing, as well as concerns for much else besides, including, but not limited to, the individual's own welfare. The term 'ultimate', in the sense of final, suggests, furthermore, that, in forming such preferences, the individual has given due consideration to all possible concerns he might have and has arrived at his considered or reflective preference ranking which, in the example that Sen considers, transcends a concern for his own welfare alone. This rendition of the term 'ultimate preferences' resembles the notion of all-things-considered preferences put forward by Daniel Hausman in a critique of Sen. Hausman (2005; 2012) recommends that preferences be conceived catholically so that they encompass all interests an individual might pursue – self-interest, other-regarding concerns, social responsibility, respect for social or moral norms, in short, *'everything* relevant to evaluation' (Hausman 2005: 53 emphasis added, cf. 57). Let us, then, explore what such a notion would mean for the theory of rational choice.

If an individual's preferences are taken in their ultimate or all-things-considered form, they have the potential to sever the normative relationship between a person's preference and her welfare (Sen 1973: 69): Sen's environmental pioneer from the bottles example would (ultimately) prefer an option – returning his empty bottles – which does not maximize his welfare, and so the assumption that the preferred option is that which maximizes personal welfare does not hold of the bottle-returner's choice (Sen 1973: 67). It is possible that an individual who acts on her ultimate preferences maximizes something else, for example the level of 'goodness' or the quantum of social responsibility which issues from her choices, and Sen hints at such a possibility in his later work (2002a: 37). What is important in the present context, though, is that explaining the individual's behaviour as the outcome of a choice based on his ultimate preferences would leave the aetiological relationship intact: every choice a person makes would be causally engendered by her preferences, whereby a person's preferences value options in terms of more than their effect on his own welfare. The ultimate-preferences explanation of the individual's decision to return his bottles therefore relieves the concept of preference of the 'dual link-up' between both choice and preference, and preference and welfare by dissolving the latter link. The ultimate-preferences explanation does not assume a necessary relationship between welfare and preference (Sen 1973, 69). But by dissolving this link, the explanation infringes Sen's linguistic sensibilities regarding the 'usual sense' of the term preference, which I cited in the second paragraph of this section (1973: 67). If an option is preferred in the ultimate-preferences sense, it does not entail that the option makes the person personally better off in welfare terms. Sen, however, does not rest content with the ultimate-preferences explanation, and it remains conspicuously absent from his further forays into the theory of rational choice.[1] Immediately after his exploration of ultimate preferences, he continues to investigate the idea of acting on an as-if ranking. Sen's return to this theme marks an abrupt end to the discussion of ultimate preferences, and it represents the opposite strategy for avoiding the 'serious difficulty' which case (4) in the bottles example poses for orthodox rational choice theory.

Before we examine as-if rankings in the section which follows, I would like to offer a further explanation of cooperative behaviour in prisoners' dilemma situations. The explanation posits that, when selecting her strategy, a player has two rankings of the options. One is her preference ranking which, in line with Sen's usual sense of the term preference, ranks the options in terms of their welfare effects on the player. Choosing according to this ranking would prompt the player to select the dominant strategy of non-cooperation. The player, however, has a different, let us call it 'moral', ranking, based on a rule of good behaviour. If the player can persuade herself to choose according to this ranking, she will cooperate. This explanation has the advantage of abiding by the usual sense of preference to which Sen is wedded. But the person's self-interested preference ranking is, as it were, overridden by her moral ranking and hence she cooperates. Sen might be expected to embrace such an explanation but in fact he pooh-poohs it in a collaborative work with Walter Garrison Runciman in which they use the prisoners' dilemma to interpret Jean Jacques Rousseau's distinction, made in *Du Contrat sociale*, between 'the general will' and 'the will of all' (Rousseau 1973/1762). Runciman and Sen (1965) contrast their interpretation of Rousseau's distinction with that of Kenneth Arrow which characterizes Rousseau as a proponent of what he calls the 'idealist position' in social philosophy. The idealist position posits a distinction between the individual's will and the general will on which 'social morality' is based (Arrow 1963: 81). The position in question:

> may be summed up by saying that each individual has two orderings, one which governs him in his everyday actions and one which would be relevant under some ideal conditions and which is in some sense truer than the first ordering.
>
> (Arrow 1963: 82–3)

In contrast to Arrow, Runciman and Sen (1965: 557) disavow the idea that players have more than one ranking and base their choices, when the latter accord with the general will, on a moral ranking which represents players' 'truer' interests. The prisoners' dilemma does not arise, Runciman and Sen argue, because their preference ranking fails to mirror their moral values; rather it arises because of the fissure between individual optimality and the result of 'forced collusion' which would bring about the cooperative outcome to the prisoners' dilemma. To achieve this outcome, players need not therefore change or supplant their self-interested preference ranking so that it accords with a truer one which reflects their ideals. Instead, they must contractually oblige themselves (or have an obligation forced upon them) so that they cooperate. In his work on the prisoners' dilemma after his collaboration with Runciman, Sen does not pay much attention to the contractual solution to overcoming social inoptimality; for he is interested in proposing 'decentralized' means of social cooperation. Nevertheless, one aspect of his work with Runciman reverberates through his subsequent work, namely, he does not assume the individuals have an idealized ranking up their sleeves which is a truer representation of their considered interests. For although Sen, as we will see in Chapter Four, believes that individuals have more than one ranking, the task he sets himself is to explain why individuals might act on a ranking which does not represent their true preferences in the name of achieving a social optimum. This brings us to the theme of as-if rankings to which the section which follows is dedicated.

## IV  As-if rankings

To avoid the suboptimal equilibrium of the prisoners' dilemma which ensues if each player selects the dominant strategy, Sen hypothesizes that the players replace their preferences with a different ranking as a basis for their choices; according to this replacement ranking, they choose the cooperative strategy of non-confession. As Sen observes, 'if both prisoners behave *as if* they are maximizing a different welfare function from the one that they actually have, they will both end up being better off in terms of their *actual* welfare function' (1973: 66). Each thereby stands a chance of improving her or his welfare over and above that which they would attain if both played the non-cooperative strategy, and they would be better off as measured by their actual preferences (the preferences on which they do not base their actions but which represent their actual welfare). 'To take an extreme case, if both prisoners try to maximize the welfare of the other, neither will confess ... since non-confession will be a superior strategy no matter what is assumed about the other person's action' (Sen 1973: 66).

Let us address three issues with respect to acting on as-if rankings:

(i)  the implications of acting on as-if rankings for the aetiological relationship;
(ii) the implications of acting on as-if rankings for the normative relationship;
(iii) the motivation of an agent who acts on as-if rankings.

Acting on an as-if ranking involves an abrogation of the aetiological relationship. An agent who so acts renounces her preferences as a causal basis for making choices and substitutes it with a different ranking.

Sen illustrates the phenomenon with a discussion of attempts to boost productivity during China's Great Leap Forward (1973: 70–1). The problem revolves around work motivation and may be presented as a prisoners' dilemma in which the dominant strategy is to shirk. Though each worker hopes that all but she will exert themselves, each ends up shirking and productivity flounders. The Chinese government has tried variously to counter such proclivities, one attempt being to instil workers with 'socialist consciousness', something akin to the sense of social responsibility evinced by our bottle-returner (Clecak 1969; Riskin 1973; Sen 1997/1973: 94–100).[2] If the sort of 'socialist education' proposed by the Chinese were successful, this could be attributable to two effects, according to Sen:

(1) 'a reorientation of the individual welfare functions of the people involved'.
(2) The establishment of a 'different basis of behaviour emphasizing social responsibility whether or not individual welfare functions are themselves revised'.

(Sen 1973: 71)

Under the first effect, workers would change their preferences and actually come to prefer to exert themselves at work as opposed to shirking; this corresponds to the first explanation of the bottle-returner who has (or develops) a preference for returning bottles and therefore values the activity intrinsicially. This might be sufficient to dissolve the prisoners' dilemma altogether if each party to the situation 'would automatically do his "duty"' by working hard, a solution which Sen (1997/1973: 98) describes as 'hardly interesting' (although generations of Chinese leaders would surely have found it something to write home about). What makes it uninteresting to Sen is that, if workers based their choice to exert themselves at the workplace on such changed preferences, their choices would manifest these preferences and hence revealed preference theory would have no difficulty in accounting for these choices. Sen does not deem a change of preference of the sort envisaged under effect (1) to be implausible, for, writing of the prisoners' dilemma, he holds, as we have already quoted him, that each prisoner might actually prefer that 'both should go to prison for two years each rather than that the other should suffer twenty years while he himself goes free' (1973: 65; cf. 1977b: 228). But the explanation of cooperative behaviour which Sen develops refrains from making such an assumption. Players who act on preferences for being 'nice' or 'cooperative' do not abrogate the aetiological relationship, but Sen seeks an explanation of cooperative behaviour which does abrogate this relationship, for it is this abrogation which poses the 'serious difficulty' for revealed preference theory to which he refers (1973: 69). This brings us to effect (2) listed above.

Under effect (2), the Party's moral education instils workers with an ethic whereby they are prepared to substitute, as a basis for action, their actual preference ordering with a ranking based on socialist consciousness. The phrase 'different basis of behaviour' with which Sen describes the second of the effects of socialist education means *different* from the individuals' actual welfare function. Under effect (2), the nature of the individual's welfare function is actually irrelevant, as Sen makes clear with the phrase 'whether or not individual welfare functions are themselves revised'. For irrespective of its content, the individual's preference function has no causal bearing on the generation of her choices. Her choices therefore have a non-preference-based aetiology because they are based on an as-if ranking that reflects socialist values. A person who acts on such rankings 'suspends' rational calculation based on her welfare function and supplants this welfare-orientated basis for decision making with particular moral codes (Sen 1973: 64–5, 72). By this, Sen means that the individual brackets the question: is it in my self-interest to refrain from shirking at work? Instead, the individual's decision to refrain from shirking is made independently of the beckoning of her self-interested preferences. We shall address the question as to what might motivate individuals to comport themselves in this way forthwith, but first, let us turn to the second question which acting on as-if rankings raises, and this concerns the implications of so acting for the normative relationship.

Acting on as-if rankings represents a *prima facie* abrogation of the normative relationship. It does so because acting on an as-if ranking leads, in the examples which Sen offers, to individuals choosing options which do not maximize their welfare. This would seem to break the relationship between preference and welfare, but in fact this is not a felicitous depiction of these choices. It is more accurate to say that, rather than being abrogated, the normative relationship *does not apply* to choices based on an as-if ranking; the normative relationship is therefore neither abrogated nor fulfilled by such choices. This is because the normative relationship connects a person's welfare with her preferences, and so, according to the normative relationship, a person will maximize her welfare *whenever she acts on her preferences*. Consequently, if one acts on one's preferences *and* one's preferences are defined in terms of welfare maximization, the normative relationship holds. However, when one acts on an as-if ranking, one is not acting on one's preference ranking at all. In the examples of acting on as-if rankings which he discusses, Sen assumes that one's actual preference ranking orders the options according to the welfare one derives from them. But if one does not act on one's actual preference ranking, one cannot vitiate the normative relationship between preference and welfare, for the vitiation of the normative relationship would require that one act on one's preferences but not maximize one's welfare, as, for example, would be the case if one conceived preferences to be 'ultimate' in the sense given in the previous section. Rather, acting on an as-if ranking vitiates the aetiological relationship – between preference and choice. By acting on an as-if ranking, one's preferences play no causal role in the determination of choices, and hence the normative relationship is inapplicable to such choices. Sen differs from orthodox economists, not only by rejecting the view that preferences are to be understood in terms of the self-interest of the person who has them, but also because he contends that not all choices are causally based on one's preference ranking. Those choices which are not based on preference abrogate the aetiological relationship.

Can one ascertain whether acting on an as-if ranking will have a determinate effect on the chooser's welfare? Are, for instance, such choices necessarily non-welfare maximizing on account of their abrogation of the aetiological relationship? The answer is that there is no determinate relationship on the chooser's welfare. It could be that acting on an as-if ranking contingently maximizes one's welfare, though it might be the case that doing so leads to a non-welfare-maximizing outcome for the individual. Sen does not go into this in his 1973 article, and so we will leave the matter until we discuss 'Rational Fools' in which Sen is less reticent about this topic, as will be seen in Chapter Three.

Let us conclude this section by addressing issue (iii) above which concerns the motivation of the agent who acts on an as-if ranking. What might motivate a person to act in opposition to her actual preferences? To answer this question, consider how such a person would answer the question: 'why are you basing your choices on an as-if ranking which does not represent your actual preferences?' She might respond: 'because I am hoping thereby to increase my welfare beyond that which would redound to me if my counterpart and I selected the dominant strategy of non-cooperation'. This response harbours some degree of self-interestedness because the agent aims to attain welfare greater than that which the non-cooperative equilibrium of the prisoners' dilemma will yield. However, an agent who is thus motivated does sacrifice welfare: by choosing the cooperative strategy, she must be tempering any egoistic impulses which prompt her to choose the dominant strategy. Judging the degree of egoism of a person who cooperates because she acts on an as-if ranking, therefore, requires that we be clear about the *comparandum* involved: is the player comparing (i) the welfare she would derive from choosing the cooperative strategy *on the assumption that both players cooperate* with (ii) the welfare she would derive if neither cooperated? If so, the player clearly stands to gain by cooperating, for the welfare derived under (i) exceeds that under (ii). Or is, alternatively, the player comparing (i) above with (ii)', whereby (ii)' is the welfare she would receive if her counterpart cooperated and she did not? Sen suggests that the first comparison is germane to actors' situation in a prisoners' dilemma. When he depicts acting on an as-if moral code which prompts individuals to cooperate, he stresses that the outcome will 'lead to a better situation for each in terms of his own welfare'; 'they will both end up being better off even in terms of their *actual* welfare function' (1973: 66; cf. 1974a: 78). In these passages, Sen is adverting to the consequences of acting on as-if rankings for the welfare of players who do so. But the question remains: what is the motivation of agents for acting thus? Sen does not specify the goal of a person who acts on as-if rankings, and hence the motivational question does not receive a clear answer in his 'Behaviour' essay. In a discussion of as-if rankings from his later *opus*, Sen mentions *karoshi*, the phenomenon of Japanese employees working so hard that they ruin their health, sometimes to the point of death (Sen 1997: 191). This might be looked upon as an extreme version of Chinese workers overcoming any tendency to shirk at work, and, of *karoshi*, Sen writes: '[t]he tendency to do one's "duty" to the point of severely damaging one's health ... is easier to explain as the consequence of adhering to a deontological obligation rather than as the outcome that is actually "preferred" by the hapless worker' (1997: 191). The worker's motivation for exerting himself in this case is not open to the suspicion that he is motivated by the prospect of deriving welfare; though if the norms of hard work are stringent, a worker might feel that failing to (over) exert himself might meet with the disapproval of others, and the avoidance of disapproval might motivate the worker to overdo it. Nevertheless, Sen's hypothesis that duty rather than welfare motivate the worker is plausible, and consequently the outcome from the worker's viewpoint cannot be better in terms of his '*actual* welfare'. But the examples which Sen offers in his 1973 essay are less extreme, and the suspicion that the agent's goal be welfare-related is not so easily banished.

## Conclusion

'Behaviour and the Concept of Preference' offers immensely rich pickings. Conceived primarily as a critique of revealed preference theory, the article contains a wealth of ideas which include:

- a rejection of rational choice defined in terms of consistency of choice;
- a disburdening of the concept of preference from the *ménage à trois* which it forms with welfare and choice;
- the concept of 'ultimate preferences' as a means of such disburdening (which would free the concept of preference from the normative relationship by extending the scope of preferences to include non-self-interested concerns, but maintain the aetiological relationship);
- proposing a 'solution' to the prisoners' dilemma, in which players are conceived to act on an as-if ranking which represents options according to the agent's moral considerations or principles of social responsibility which do not coincide with their actual preferences; this involves making choices which have a non-preference-based aetiology.

Some of these motifs appear in various forms in Sen's post-1973 work. Conspicuous for its absence, though, is the idea of ultimate preferences.

Sen's 'Behaviour' essay also bequeaths two debts for Sen to clear in future work. One is an account of non-preference-based choices, that is, those of which the aetiological relationship does not hold. The other concerns the motivation of a person who acts on an as-if ranking. Although these topics are broached in 'Behaviour and the Concept of Preference', they are not treated in a systematic way, and Sen returns to them in his subsequent work on choice.

## Notes

1 Sen does, in his later work, refer to 'everything considered' preferences (1986b: 347; 1996: 453; 1997: 192), but he does not use it as an explanatory concept in his theory of rational choice.
2 The issue of using 'material' or 'moral' incentives for work has been the subject of much debate in actually existing socialist countries, with the USSR having adopted a material-incentives approach which had its origins in the New Economic Policy (Lenin 1921) which had a lasting influence on Soviet economic policy. Other socialists, for example Che Guevara, make a strong case for the incompatibility of material incentives with socialist principles and hence they advocate moral incentives instead (for a recent discussion of Guevara's thoughts on the matter, see Llorente 2018: chapter 2).

# 2 Sympathy

**Introduction**

We begin, in this chapter, our analysis of 'Rational Fools' (Sen 1977a). The essay is Sen's most influential and far-reaching contribution to the theory of rational choice in the 1970s, and it is the work in which he develops the concepts of sympathy and commitment. Like Sen's 1973 article, 'Rational Fools' criticizes the assumption that all human choices are based on the pursuit of self-interest alone. By conceiving every choice a person makes to be based on her preferences, and by representing the most preferred item with a higher utility number than any other item, then 'no matter whether you are a single-minded egoist or a raving altruist or a class conscious militant, you will appear to be maximizing your own utility in this enchanted world of definitions' (Sen 1977a: 89). It might appear absurd that even a 'raving altruist', whom many would deem to be the epitome of non-self-interestedness, is, like everybody else who comes under the scrutiny of rational choice theory, to be conceived as an egoistic utility maximizer. Some theorists, however, seem to see this as a strength of rational choice theory because it makes the theory universal in applicability: '[t]he postulate that an agent is characterized by preferences rules out neither the saint nor Genghis Khan' (Hahn and Hollis 1979: 4). Sen believes that such a broad characterization is simplistic at best. In 'Rational Fools' he proposes the concepts of sympathy and commitment to provide a richer view of human rationality. The former is treated in this chapter, the latter in the next.

Sympathy involves the causal effect of others' welfare on one's own. As a phenomenon of interest to Sen, sympathy predates 'Rational Fools'. Already in 'Behaviour and the Concept of Preference', as we noted in the previous chapter, Sen offers an explanation of returning bottles for re-use which relies on sympathy, though Sen does not use the term in 1973. The second explanation as to why the individual returns his empties appeals, to recall, to the possibility that the agent is 'worried about the welfare of others' such that 'his own welfare function includes concern for other people's welfare' (1973: 68–9). This makes him capable of feelings of sympathy and of acting on these feelings. Still further back in his *oeuvre*, Sen's model of the allocation of labour in a cooperative enterprise (1966: 363–6) uses the assumption that the welfare of individuals is affected by the welfare of other families in the same cooperative. He uses the term 'sympathy' to describe this relationship, to my knowledge, his first use of the term. Thus, Sen's remarks on sympathy in 'Rational Fools' are to be understood as a development of his previous work.

Sympathy has been treated by Sen's interpreters as the weaker sibling of commitment. Sen himself is partly responsible for sympathy's less-than-glamorous reputation, for he tells us that sympathy, unlike commitment, has been comfortably incorporated into an augmented theory of rational choice, and he cites Gary Becker (1996) as one who has accomplished this incorporation of sympathy (Sen 2002a: 31–7; 2005a: 19–20, 2009b: 42–3). Neither has Sen had cause, since 'Rational Fools', to rework sympathy in the manner which commitment has undergone in Sen's subsequent work. Indeed, we argue in Section IV, that, if sympathy has undergone modification in Sen's work, the concept has become less rather than more seditious *vis-à-vis* orthodox notions of rationality, and in this respect sympathy stands in contrast to commitment. This chapter maintains that sympathy has been underestimated, oversimplified and misunderstood by Sen's interpreters, and the analysis which follows might even lead one to contest Sen's claim that sympathy is 'in some ways, an easier concept to analyse than commitment' (1977a: 92).

The structure of this chapter is as follows. Section I examines depictions of sympathy by Sen's interpreters. These depictions reveal ambiguities and raise questions about sympathy which provide the basis for analysing the concept in the sections thereafter. Section II distinguishes two types of sympathy found in 'Rational Fools', one contemplative, which comprises a feeling, the other active, which motivates action. Though not named as separate types by Sen, he clearly distinguishes these two sorts of sympathy, and being clear about which type one is referring to when discussing sympathy is of import. Section II also identifies two epistemological conditions which Sen imposes on feelings of sympathy, and it examines Sen's claims about the impact of uncertainty on the formulation of sympathy. Section III focuses on active sympathy and scrutinizes a technical term which Sen introduces in 'Rational Fools', namely, *actions based on sympathy*. Sen claims that such actions are 'egoistic' (1977a: 92), and I explore precisely how he understands this term and how it relates to welfare maximization as a goal of individuals' choices. Although actions based on sympathy are egoistic, this does not, I argue, make them congruent with the account of choice offered by orthodox economic analysis. Section IV examines more recent expositions of sympathy in Sen's work and tries to account for the way in which the concept may be deemed in this later work to have become more orthodox *vis-à-vis* mainstream rational choice theory than it was in 1977.

## I Sympathy: Sen's interpreters

Fabienne Peter and Hans Bernhard Schmid discuss three types of motivation which Sen distinguishes: '(narrow) self-interest, sympathy, and commitment'. In what follows we compare what Peter and Schmid say about the first two of these. Commitment will be analysed in the following chapter. 'One acts from self-interest when one aims at maximizing one's own welfare'; and one 'acts from sympathy when one's own welfare is affected by how others are doing, as in the case where helping others makes one feel better' (Peter and Schmid 2007: 4). These depictions are noteworthy for three reasons.

First, that self-interest marks a type of motivation is clear from Peter and Schmid's mention of two things: (i) action (which, as they suggest, issues 'from self-interest'), and (ii) the *aim* of a person who acts from self-interest, namely, to maximize her welfare. Peter and Schmid's description of sympathy also refers to action ('helping others'), but, in contrast to the way they depict self-interested action, they do not state the aim of a person who acts from sympathy. Helping others, they remark, makes the actor 'feel better', but this is a statement about the consequences of the act, not about the aim or goal of the actor. Is the goal of an agent who acts from sympathy to make another person better off, whereby the agent's feeling better is an unintended consequence of helping others? Or is the agent's goal to make herself feel better, whereby her attempt to make others better off is a means to this goal? Both cases are compatible with the description that 'one's own welfare is affected by how others are doing', but they differ with respect to the goal the actor pursues. Daniel Hausman (2005: 40) writes that an action cannot be sympathetic in Sen's sense unless the actor expects to benefit from the action. This also leaves the goal open, for my expectation that I will benefit from acting sympathetically does not entail that obtaining this benefit be my goal. Philip Pettit writes that sympathy 'materializes when one pursues one's own self-interest but that self-interest is positively sensitive to the welfare of others' (2005: 17). The word 'pursues' suggests that what is being pursued – self-interest – constitutes the agent's goal; it is what motivates her to act. This would make sympathy 'egoistic', as Sen (1977a: 92) describes it, but is acting sympathetically always egoistic? The answer depends on the actor's goal, and this remains unclear in some depictions of sympathy. Pettit qualifies the statement just quoted when he discusses what Sen (1997: 177 note 32) calls 'altruism through sympathy', which, writes Pettit:

> is not self-interested in the sense of being pursued with an instrumental eye to securing some personal benefit ... [but] that the person we favor is someone whose welfare matters to us, intuitively, in the same manner as our own; let them fare well and we feel good.
>
> (2005: 17)

Favouring somebody whose welfare is as important to us as our own does not sound egoistic. We return to Pettit's interpretation of Sen at the close of the following chapter, when we examine Sen's comments on altruism. In Section III of this chapter, we will clarify the sense in which Sen understands sympathy to be egoistic, something which involves specifying the goal of a person who acts from sympathy.

The second noteworthy aspect of Peter and Schmid's construal of sympathy follows from the first and concerns the notion that sympathetic action makes the actor 'feel better'. Peter and Schmid, to recall, classify sympathy as a type of motivation and it is its motivational aspect which relates sympathy to action, for example helping others. But is sympathy always a motivation for action? Consider again Peter and Schmid's description of sympathy which refers to three things: one's action, one's welfare being affected by how others are faring and an example of an action ('helping others') which makes the actor 'feel better'. A causal relationship is presumably implied here: because one is affected by others' welfare, one is prompted to act so as to improve the welfare of others whereby one's own welfare increases. Sympathy (being affected by others' welfare) is the first element in this causal chain. But it would be wrong to conclude that sympathy always gives rise to this causal process, for my beholding the happiness of others might make me feel happy without my having caused their happiness. Being affected by others' welfare is a feeling which can remain just that. The relationship between being thus affected and one's actions must be clarified. Ann Cudd (2014: 41–2), for instance, contends that sympathy 'involves one's feelings about the experiences of others', a statement which implies no direct relation to action. But Cudd nevertheless defines sympathy as an 'other-directed' *motivation*, and motivation implies action (cf. Cudd 2017: 411). What is the relationship between feelings of sympathy and the actions which they apparently motivate? We tackle this question in Section II.

The third noteworthy point about Peter and Schmid's portrayal of sympathy is that, whereas they associate self-interest with the *maximization* of one's welfare, sympathy, in the form of helping others, makes one 'feel better'. Feeling better presumably includes cases in which my helping another person maximizes my welfare, but feeling better might also involve increasing, but not necessarily maximizing, my welfare. What is the relationship between sympathy and maximization? If sympathetic action necessarily maximizes the welfare of the actor, as some of Sen's interpreters hold, this would enhance its compatibility with the orthodox theory of rational choice. If, however, there is conceptual room for sympathetic actions which are not based on the goal of maximization, sympathy would be at odds with conceptions of choice which insist that the goal of maximizing one's welfare be an element of rational choice.

## II Two types of sympathy

Five passages from 'Rational Fools', labelled P1, P2, P3, P4 and P5 below, form the basis of my analysis of sympathy:

P1: 'sympathy ... corresponds to the case in which concern for others directly affects one's welfare. If the knowledge of torture of others makes you sick, it is a case of sympathy' (1977a: 91–2).

P2: '[i]t can be argued that behaviour based on sympathy is in an important sense egoistic, for one is oneself pleased at others' pleasure and pained by others' pain, and the pursuit of one's own utility may thus be helped by sympathetic action. It is action based on commitment rather than sympathy which would be non-egoistic in this sense' (1977a: 92).

P3: 'When a person's sense of well-being is psychologically dependent on someone else's welfare, it is a case of sympathy; other things given, the awareness of the increase in the welfare of the other person then makes this person directly better off' (1977a: 92).

P4: 'sympathy relates similar things to each other – namely, welfares of different persons' (1977a: 92).

P5: 'I have not yet referred to uncertainty concerning anticipated welfare. When this is introduced, the concept of sympathy is unaffected, but commitment will require reformulation' (1977a: 93).

Passage P3 directs our attention to what shall henceforth be called *contemplative sympathy*. It states that *A*'s *awareness* of an increase in *B*'s welfare suffices to make *A* better off. The 'psychological dependence' (P3) of *A*'s welfare on *B*'s is independent of *A*'s actions. For instance, the increase in *B*'s welfare might arise through someone's else, *C*'s, agency, or result from an 'act of God', hence the contemplative nature of this type of sympathy from the point of view of the agent who feels it. Because *B*'s happiness is brought about independently of *A*'s actions, it makes no sense, when we analyse the sympathetic increase in *A*'s welfare, to speak of *A*'s *motivation*, for *A*'s actions do not bring about the increase in *B*'s welfare, and where there is no action, there is no motivation. *A* merely experiences a feeling caused by her awareness of the increase in *B*'s welfare. Neither, therefore, can we ascribe the making of a choice to *A*, whereby she decides whether or not to be affected by an increase in the welfare of *B*; for being affected or remaining unmoved by the plight of *B* is not volitional but automatic. Adam Smith makes this point when he claims that the sympathy we feel for others arises 'naturally' and 'instantaneously' (1982/1790: I.i.1.3, I.i.2.2), and Sen gives no indication that he dissents from Smith's opinion. Our first conclusion, then, is that sympathy is not necessarily a type of motivation but can be simply a feeling which exists independently of action. When it is independent of the actions of the person who feels sympathy, we have a case of contemplative sympathy.

Although Sen (1977a: 92) does not attribute 'great merit' to his choice of term 'sympathy' (or 'commitment'), contemplative sympathy is well attuned to quotidian understandings of sympathy as a 'state of being affected by the condition of another with a feeling similar or corresponding to that of the other' ('sympathy', *Oxford English Dictionary*, online edition, definition 3.b.).

This, as we argue in Section III, contrasts with sympathy in its active manifestation. Before we get this far, though, let us draw attention to two epistemological conditions which Sen places on contemplative sympathy and also to the impact which uncertainty has for the formulation of sympathy.

Passage P1 identifies a case of sympathy as one in which *A*'s *knowledge* of *B*'s welfare has an impact on *A*'s own welfare. The term 'knowledge' does the same work that 'awareness' does in P3. It might, however, be the case that *A*'s welfare rises as a result of her *belief* that *B*'s welfare has risen, and hence one might hold that *A*'s belief about, rather than her knowledge of, *B*'s welfare be sufficient to induce feelings of sympathy in *A*. But this is not the case. To see why, consider a case in which *A* mistakenly believes that *B* is very happy, and this belief increases *A*'s happiness. *A*, for instance, believes that today is *B*'s birthday and *A* therefore believes that *B* must be feeling happy. *B*'s birthday was, in fact, a week ago, and *B* has been feeling miserable since then, having received no birthday greeting from *A*. The increase in welfare which *A* experiences as a result of her belief that today is *B*'s birthday is not a case of sympathy *sensu stricto*. The reason for this lies in passage P4 which states that 'sympathy relates *similar things* to each other' (Sen 1977a: 92 emphasis added). The similar things are the welfares of two different people. An increase in *A*'s welfare which results from her mistaken belief that *B*'s welfare has risen because it is *B*'s birthday cannot therefore be a case of sympathy, for in such a case, 'similar things' – *A*'s and *B*'s welfare – are not related; the relation instead is between *A*'s welfare and *A*'s (false) belief about *B*'s welfare. But imagine that *B* is in low spirits because he feels neglected by *A* who failed to wish *B* a happy birthday a week ago. *A*, thinking that today is *B*'s birthday, might feel precisely as she would feel had today actually been *B*'s birthday and *A* knew that this was the case and knew, furthermore, that *B* was feeling very happy. But the erroneous nature of *A*'s belief about today being *B*'s birthday excludes the increase in *A*'s welfare from being sympathetic. Sen's 'similar things' clause thus poses an epistemological criterion for sympathy: *A* must actually know *B*'s state of welfare if *A* is to experience feelings of sympathy with *B*. *A*'s belief, in the example just construed, does not meet this epistemological criterion.

Sen imposes a second epistemological condition on contemplative sympathy. Unlike the foregoing condition, the second condition concerns *B*'s knowledge rather than *A*'s, though like the first condition, it excludes a type of feeling experienced by *A* from being sympathetic. To illustrate, assume that a person becomes aware that another person is being harmed, though the latter is not aware of the harm to which he is being subjected. If Sandeep discovers that Judy, the spouse of Sandeep's best friend, Kim, is being unfaithful to Kim, Sandeep may feel a reduction in his own welfare on account of the wrong being done to his friend. Kim, however, is unaware of Judy's extramarital exploits. Sandeep's feeling of sadness is not a case of sympathy because Kim's ignorance of Judy's infidelity means that Kim is not feeling miserable. Sandeep's knowledge of Judy's escapades might make Sandeep feel miserable, but because Kim is not feeling miserable, 'similar things' (Sandeep's and Kim's welfare) are not related. This cannot therefore be a case of sympathy. Only if Kim were aware of Judy's infidelity and his welfare were thereby reduced, and Sandeep were aware of Kim's reduced welfare could we talk of sympathy.

Let us now look at the influence of uncertainty which Sen introduces in passage P5. 'Uncertainty', for Sen, takes an expected-utility form, whereby possible outcomes, $x_1, x_2, \ldots x_n$, are weighted by the agent's respective subjective probability estimates, $p_1, p_2, \ldots p_n$, of those outcomes occurring. Sen's contention that uncertainty leaves the concept of sympathy unaffected applies to contemplative sympathy; for in a case of contemplative sympathy, the state of affairs – the increase in $B$'s welfare – which increases $A$'s welfare sympathetically, is certain; it has been brought about (though not by $A$), and consequently there is no uncertainty surrounding this outcome. $A$ can therefore derive sympathetic welfare from beholding $B$'s enhanced welfare without having to assign a probability to the increase in $B$'s welfare coming about – the increase has already come to pass.

Matters are different when we turn to a different, non-contemplative, kind of sympathy. In passage P2, Sen mentions 'behaviour based on sympathy' and 'sympathetic action'. These terms refer to actions, performed by $A$, which bring about an increase in $B$'s welfare which, in turn, increases $A$'s welfare. Let us call this *active sympathy* to mark the fact that $A$'s action is the causal initiator of $B$'s enhanced welfare and of the subsequent sympathetic rise in $A$'s welfare. Consider the influence of uncertainty on active sympathy. When $A$ considers performing an action, $\varphi$, which she expects to redound positively to $B$'s welfare, $A$ is uncertain about the outcome of her $\varphi$-ing on $B$'s welfare. As a result of $\varphi$-ing, $A$ anticipates an increase of her own welfare equal to $pW_A$, where $W_A$ is the increase in $A$'s welfare should her $\varphi$-ing bring about the increase in $B$'s welfare, and $p$ is $A$'s subjective probability estimate that the anticipated effect of $\varphi$-ing on $B$'s welfare actually does come about. Uncertainty, here, changes the formulation of active sympathy rather as it changes, *mutatis mutandis*, the formulation of commitment (as Sen states in the same paragraph of 'Rational Fools'). Uncertainty does not leave the formulation of active sympathy untouched because uncertainty places us into the realm of $A$'s '*expected* personal welfare' (Sen 1977a: 93). This contrasts with the formulation of contemplative sympathy which is unaffected by uncertainty, as we ascertained in the previous paragraph.

Why, then, in light of the above, does Sen claim, in P5, that uncertainty impinges only on the formulation of commitment but not on that of sympathy? When he tells us that uncertainty leaves sympathy untouched, he seems to make the claim with regard to sympathy *tout court*, not just for certain types of sympathy. A possible explanation is that, for Sen, contemplative sympathy is the primary type, and when he writes of sympathy *sans phrase*, he means contemplative sympathy but not active sympathy. Is there textual evidence that contemplative sympathy is the primary type?

There is, namely, in the way Sen first introduces sympathy in 'Rational Fools' in passage P1. P1 does not mention the sympathetic person's action but merely that the welfare of a sympathetic person is affected by a concern for and knowledge of others' welfare. This definition identifies contemplative, not active, sympathy. This is underscored in Sen's *official definition* of sympathy. I call this definition 'official' because Sen's subsequent expositions of sympathy quote this passage (1985b: 214; 2002a: 35; 2005a: 7; 2009a: 188): '[s]ympathy ... refers to one person's welfare being affected by the position of others (e.g., feeling depressed at the sight of misery)' (1982a: 7–8). This definition does not specify that the actions which bring about an increase in the welfare of person $B$ must be performed by the same person, $A$, who derives sympathetic welfare from the increase in $B$'s welfare. Rather the definition holds sympathy to consist solely in a feeling brought about by awareness of another person's plight. What causes that plight is left open.

There is a further reason for prioritizing contemplative over active sympathy: active sympathy presupposes its contemplative counterpart but not *vice versa*. One may therefore contend that contemplative sympathy is the foundational type. Having performed an action, $\varphi$, and beholding that $\varphi$-ing has increased $B$'s welfare, $A$'s awareness of the increase in $B$'s welfare causes $A$'s own welfare to increase sympathetically. The awareness part of this operation is contemplative. Hence, the full description of active sympathy has two parts: (i) an active part, whereby $A$ acts in a way which increases $B$'s welfare, and (ii) a contemplative part, whereby $A$ beholds the effect of her action on $B$'s welfare and experiences an increase in her own welfare as a result. Uncertainty applies only to the first, active part and consists in $A$ probabilistically estimating whether her action will increase $B$'s welfare. The contemplative part can exist without the active part, that is when $A$'s welfare rises as a result of her awareness of an increase in $B$'s welfare of which $A$'s action is not the cause. In such a case, $A$'s sympathy is purely contemplative. Questions of motivation have no place in contemplative sympathy because the latter is detached from action. Although Sen does not distinguish the two types of sympathy by name, they are clearly implied in his analysis. The nearest Sen gets to an explicit acknowledgement of the independence of contemplative sympathy from its active counterpart comes over thirty years after 'Rational Fools' when he writes that '[s]ympathy is combinable with self-interested behaviour' (2009a: 189). 'Sympathy', here, refers to contemplative sympathy which Sen defines on the page before with his official definition quoted above; that sympathy be 'combinable with self-interested behaviour' means that the former can but does not have to be combined with the latter, and hence the independence of contemplative sympathy from self-interested behaviour is implied. In the section which follows, we examine active sympathy in more detail.

## III Active sympathy

In passage P2, Sen introduces the concept of actions 'based on sympathy' which appears often in his work (1987b: 28; 1999: 270; 2009b: 43). Only with

Sympathy   33

actions based on sympathy (and not with contemplative sympathy) are questions of motivation raised; and only in the context of motivation can we clarify what Sen means when he refers to sympathetic actions as 'egoistic' (P2). He writes in P2 that a person who performs an action based on sympathy is 'pleased at others' pleasure and pained by others' pain' (1977a: 92). This does not tell us whether a desire to feel pleasure or avoid pain motivates the person to act sympathetically. Sen's clearest statement on the motivational aspect of actions based on sympathy comes in a parenthetic remark which, for ease of analysis, I divide into four parts – [a], [b], [c] and [d]; the italics are Sen's:

> (Note, however, that [a] the *existence* of sympathy [b] does not imply that the action helpful to others must be *based on* sympathy [c] in the sense that the action would not take place had one got less or no comfort from others' welfare. [d] This question of causation is to be taken up presently.)
> (1977a: 92)

The remark is truncated and therefore cryptic, but a periphrasis of it is as follows:

> [a] We have established the existence of active sympathy. [b] We should not be led, however, to hold that an action which is helpful to others must be based on sympathy simply because it is helpful to others. [c] To clarify, a helpful action based on sympathy is one which the actor would not perform if she did not expect to derive welfare by performing it. [d] This raises questions of causation.

Let us clarify two terminological matters as a prelude to interpreting Sen's parenthetic remark further. First, by 'causation', Sen means motivation, that is the question: what motivates the agent to act or what is her goal? Second, *action based on sympathy* is a technical term in Sen's writing. I have reformulated its meaning in clause [c] above and investigate it further below.

Sen could have made his parenthetic remark clearer had he inserted the following sentence between [c] and [d]: *But there are other actions which are helpful to others but not based on sympathy; these actions, unlike those based on sympathy, are not motivated by an expectation that the actor will derive welfare from performing them.* Such actions are based on commitment, though Sen does not label them thus in his parenthetic remark; they are distinguished from actions based on sympathy because, as I explain in the ensuing chapter, a person who performs committed actions does so independently of the expectations she has about the welfare consequences of these actions; in other words, the goal of such a person is not to derive welfare. Having implicitly referred to choices based on commitment in his parenthetic remark, Sen mentions the 'question of causation'. He does not, however, discuss the question in relation to sympathy because actions based on sympathy are motivationally straightforward: such actions are performed only because the actor anticipates that they will confer welfare on her. The goal behind actions based on sympathy, then, is the derivation of welfare. Sen repeats this point in *Development as Freedom* (1999), in which he writes: '[i]f you help a destitute person *because* his destitution makes you very unhappy, that would be a sympathy-based action' (1999: 270 emphasis added). The 'because' in this passage is causal and picks out the actor's motivation. If, that is, one helps a destitute person *because* her misery makes one unhappy, it may be inferred that one's lending help is motivated by the goal of ameliorating one's own disconsolate feelings, whereby relieving the suffering of the destitute person is a means to this end. With this passage, then, Sen is describing an action based on sympathy (or a 'sympathy-based action', as he writes here), and this makes the actor's motivation egoistic.

The foregoing does not, however, offer a full specification of actions based on sympathy and in which way they are 'egoistic'. Recall from Section I of this chapter the ambiguity in Peter and Schmid's depiction of sympathetic actions making the actor 'feel better' (2007: 4). Does the goal of deriving welfare ('feeling better') imply that the actor's goal is to *maximize* her welfare? Elizabeth Anderson thinks it does: sympathy, she writes, 'is a matter of maximizing utility in the narrow, egoistic sense' (2001: 22). Cyril Hédoin (2016: 354) likewise believes that Sen associates sympathy with maximization. There is reason to argue, however, that Sen does not associate egoism uniquely with welfare maximization. Let us examine the terminology with which Sen describes actions based on sympathy.

Sen does not use the term 'maximization' when he describes the effects of actions based on sympathy on the actor's welfare. Instead he uses informal terms, as in P2 – the 'pursuit of one's own utility may thus be *helped* by sympathetic action' (1977a: 92 emphasis added). That which one pursues in and through an action is presumably one's goal, but to state, as Sen does, that one's utility is *helped* by sympathetic action does not necessitate that one's goal is to maximize it. Sen's terminology is too loose to sustain an inference to maximization. Sen also writes that sympathy 'does not require any departure from individual-welfare maximization' (1982a: 8). Requiring no departure from maximization means that sympathy is compatible with but does not necessitate welfare maximization. Elsewhere, Sen describes the effects of sympathetic action on its perpetrator in terms of having 'the net effect of making one feel ... better off' (1987b: 28). Again, the term maximization is absent, Sen preferring the informal *feeling better off*. More recently, Sen writes that 'it is their own welfare that they [actors] continue to pursue' when they perform sympathy-based actions (2009a: 43); once again, he makes clear that the individual pursues his own welfare through actions based on sympathy, but there is no mention of maximization. Sen, therefore, apparently conceives the egoism of actions based on sympathy in terms of the actor pursuing but not necessarily maximizing his own welfare. This understanding of egoism corresponds to a conception of egoism found in both everyday parlance and philosophical discussions – of egoism *qua* acting in one's self-interest, with no mention of the technical concept of maximization (Feinberg 1971: 489–90). This notion of egoism implies that the agent's goal is orientated to deriving welfare but not to the maximization thereof. Sen's agnosticism about maximization means that actions based on sympathy do not fit snugly into the orthodox theory of rational choice if welfare maximization be a necessary feature of that theory. I investigate the implications of the conclusion that actions based on sympathy need not be welfare-maximizing in the following section, but first we offer a formal definition of actions based on sympathy. Each of the following conditions is necessary, and they are, together, sufficient for classifying an action as being based on sympathy:

(1) the action increases the welfare of another person;
(2) the increase in the other's welfare thereby confers welfare on the perpetrator of the action;
(3) the prospect of attaining the welfare specified in (2) is what motivates the actor to perform the action; without this prospect, the actor would not perform the action, and so deriving welfare is the actor's *goal*.

Conditions (1) and (2) are consequential – they relate to the welfare consequences of the action for the person to whom the action is directed and for the actor herself. Condition (3), by contrast, is motivational – it provides information about the actor's goal. Condition (2) allows us to distinguish two types of action based on sympathy – those which *maximize* and those which *increase* the welfare of the actor. Both confer welfare on the actor, and deriving this welfare is the goal of the actor in both cases; but the goal of welfare maximization is not a defining feature of all actions based on sympathy. In our discussions of sympathy and commitment in the chapter which follows, we shall refer to these two types of action as welfare-maximizing and welfare-increasing actions.

Sen leaves no room for actions based on sympathy which are not egoistic. In contrast to his conception of contemplative sympathy, which, as we noted above in Section II, concurs with quotidian understandings of sympathy, Sen's notion of active sympathy deviates rather sharply from everyday parlance. None of the definitions of 'sympathy' in the *Oxford English Dictionary*, for instance, suggests any relation to egoism. Neither does any definition suggest a direct relationship with action, the nearest one comes to a mention of action being definition 3.d., which mentions a 'disposition to agree or approve'; but even if one sees, in agreeing or approving, a type of action, it is not the sort if action which Sen has in mind, namely, helping others or ameliorating their suffering, when he delineates the term actions based on sympathy. We may therefore join Sen (1977a: 92) in his scepticism about there being 'any very great merit' to his choice of the term with which he describes what he calls actions based on sympathy.

## IV Active sympathy and maximization

We concluded from Sen's depiction of sympathy in the previous section that a person who performs an action based on sympathy need not have the goal of maximizing her welfare. In light of this conclusion, it is a mystery that Sen, in his later work, concedes sympathy to the clutches of orthodox rational choice theory, of which Sen identifies three aspects:

(α)  that human conduct is sufficiently regular that it may be interpreted as maximizing behaviour.
(β)  that the maximand may be interpreted as the individual's self-interest.
(γ)  that the individual's self-interest is 'narrowly self-centred', that is, 'unaffected by the interests of others'.

(2002a: 30–1)

Dropping the third aspect allows for sympathy, and Sen cites Gary Becker's (1996) work on rational choice theory as an extension of the theory which includes sympathy by 'accommodating within the concept of self-interest our many non-self-centred concerns' (Sen 2005a: 19). Sympathy, Sen clarifies, can be accommodated under the banner of self-interest but not under that of self-centredness (2002a: 31 note 48), for a self-centred person is one who is unaffected by the pleasures and pains of others. But whereas proponents of rational choice theory may be prepared to jettison the aspect enumerated under (γ) above, Sen wishes, in addition, to make (β) a non-necessary aspect of the theory of rational choice. He is, however, not willing to abandon (α), for although not sufficient, maximization is necessary, for rational choice (Sen 2002a: 40).[1] One need not, Sen argues, be conceived to maximize one's self-interest in each and every act of choice; one could maximize a host of other variables, for example 'aggregate social welfare, or some feature of equity or social justice' (Sen 2002a: 37). But maximization is a feature of rational choice on which Sen insists.

Now let us consider Sen's depiction of sympathy again. Actions based on sympathy, we argued in the previous section, do not have to be underlain by the goal of maximizing but merely increasing the actor's welfare. This, at least, has been the way in which Sen has presented sympathy both in and since 'Rational Fools'. But if, in the works cited in the previous paragraph, maximization is, for Sen, a necessary aspect of rationality, then we might have to conclude that actions based on sympathy are not rational, at least when the actor's goal is to increase but not maximize his welfare. And given that the goal of an actor who performs an action based on sympathy is, *ipso facto*, orientated to his own welfare, it is implausible to ascribe to the actor a goal which might involve the maximization of a variable other than his own welfare, and so we would be left with the conclusion that actions based on sympathy do not manifest the aspect of rational choice given under (α) on which Sen insists as an element of rational choice

The apparent inconsistency in Sen's work is not easily removed. One might speculate that the audience which Sen addressed in 'Rational Fools', which was published in a journal outside the discipline of Economics, is more philosophical than economic, and maximization was not a pressing matter in the presentation of sympathy for such an audience. In a reflection on the concepts of sympathy and commitment, Sen states that, in 'Rational Fools', he is chiefly concerned with matters of motivation and less so with the effects of actions (1987b: 28 note 12). Being less concerned about the effects of actions in 'Rational Fools' would explain why he is not at pains to distinguish actions based on sympathy on grounds of whether they maximize or merely increase the welfare of the person who performs such actions, for what is of import to him in 'Rational Fools' are the motivational implications of sympathy and commitment – the question of causation. One might, alternatively, state that Sen's later work, whence come his thoughts on the necessity of maximization for rationality, represents the apotheosis of his thought on rational choice, and this supersedes his earlier laxness *vis-à-vis* the notion of maximization and its relationship to the concept of sympathy. I will leave the matter open and mark it as an unresolved aspect of Sen's thought.

## Conclusion

This chapter has dedicated more attention to sympathy than is usual in discussions of Sen's work, though I hope to have shown that the concept responds well to being the subject of attention. The chapter has established the existence of two types of sympathy – contemplative and active. I have, furthermore, clarified two epistemological presuppositions of feeling sympathy, both of which indicate the importance of knowledge to sympathy. I have also observed that uncertainty, whilst it does not affect the conceptualization of contemplative sympathy, does require a reformulation of active sympathy. This was explained by the fact that contemplative sympathy is the primary type and that when Sen writes in general about sympathy, he is referring to its contemplative countenance which is indeed unaffected by uncertainty. Active sympathy is of greater complexity than its contemplative counterpart, for only active sympathy gives rise to questions about the actor's motivation for performing actions based on sympathy. These actions, we argued, are egoistic in the sense that the actor's goal in performing them is to derive welfare of a certain degree; without the prospect of this degree of welfare, the actor would not be motivated to perform the act in question, as Sen makes clear in his parenthetic remark. The egoism of actions based on sympathy does not, however, entail that the actor is motivated to act by the prospect of maximizing her welfare; if one performs an action with the goal of deriving but not maximizing one's welfare, this suffices to fulfil the conditions of actions based on sympathy.

Sen's understanding of actions based sympathy does not cast it in a terribly favourable light, for all actions based on sympathy, being egoistic, are simply vehicles through which the agent pursues his own welfare. This is not, however, the last word on the matter, for, in the following chapter, I resume the discussion of sympathy by asking whether it has a more edifying moment, as Philip Pettit implies in the passage quoted in Section I of this chapter. That discussion will involve a comparison of sympathy with commitment which explores the relationship in which each concept stands towards the concept of altruism.

**Note**

1 And in his later work, Sen makes it clear that he means *maximization* here which he distinguishes from the stricter notion of optimization (1997: 181–2; 2017a; 2017b: 454–6).

# 3 Commitment

## Introduction

Sen first introduced the concept of commitment by name in 'Rational Fools'. He has returned to it many times in his writings during which it has undergone much development since its inception in 1977. In this chapter, I refer sparingly to these subsequent developments. Later developments of the concept in Sen's *oeuvre* are treated at length in Chapters Seven and Eight, but in this chapter, such developments will be invoked only if they are necessary for clarifying the material in 'Rational Fools'.

Section I examines and compares the two definitions of commitment Sen offers in 'Rational Fools'. His initial definition divulges nothing about the agent's reason or goal for making a choice based on commitment, whilst his second, 'more inclusive', definition raises this aspect explicitly. This leads to discussion of the 'question of causation' which we met in the previous chapter. The question is: what motivates people to make choices based on commitment? Section II asks in which sense choices based on commitment are *counter-preferential*. The answer is found by looking at the reason an individual has for making her choice. By basing her choice on a reason which is independent of her preferences, the individual is able to choose counter-preferentially, and this is the basis of the non-preference-based aetiology of choice which Sen owed the world after his 1973 article (see Chapter One). The analysis reveals that the relationship between an agent making a choice based on commitment and the agent's expectations regarding the consequences of that choice for her own welfare is entirely open. That is, *a priori*, one can specify nothing about the expected welfare consequences to the agent of making choices based on commitment. This renders, I argue, Sen's initial definition of commitment otiose, for his more inclusive definition is the only one which addresses the issue of the reason for which a person makes a committed choice. Section III thematizes the nature of the reasons on which one must act if one's choice is to be based on commitment. The answer is that the reasons have something to do with agents' 'morals'. Sen gives this term a catholic extension but offers little substance to the content of morals. Section IV provides clarification on the question whether preferences, as Sen understands them, constitute a type of *reason* for choosing or whether preferences are to be classified as non-reason-based motivations for choice. The section also addresses the phenomenon of mixed motives, that is, being prompted to perform a certain action by two different sources of motivation. In Section V, I ask how the concept of altruism is best positioned in relation to sympathy and commitment. Each concept has affinities to altruism of its own, as Sen makes clear in an essay two decades after 'Rational Fools', and the discussion in Section V clarifies what each concept implies for the conceptualization of altruism. The section also scrutinizes an interpretation of sympathy offered by Philip Pettit, which opens up the issue addressed at the end of the previous chapter, namely, whether active sympathy is to be conceived solely as a vehicle for the pursuit of one's own welfare.

## I Commitment: two definitions

'One way of defining commitment is in terms of a person choosing an act that he believes will yield a lower level of personal welfare to him than an alternative that is also available to him' (Sen 1977a: 92). I shall call this Sen's *initial definition* of commitment and make a number of observations about it. First, according to the initial definition, commitment does not require that an individual be self-sacrificing in the sense that he become worse off as a result of making a choice based on commitment. Commitment includes such self-sacrifice, but, according to the initial definition, the conditions for commitment would be met when an individual's choice increases but does not maximize his personal welfare. The second observation is that the initial definition of commitment is cast in terms of the agent's expectation regarding the *consequences* which making a choice will have upon her own welfare. It would nevertheless be incorrect to say that Sen's initial definition makes commitment a purely consequential matter, for labelling it thus would neglect the importance of the word 'believes' in the definition. By including this word, Sen excludes from the set of choices which are based on commitment cases which involve miscalculation of the welfare consequences of a choice. That is, if one believes a given choice will maximize one's welfare but that belief transpires to be false due to one's 'failure to foresee consequences' (Sen 1977a: 92), the choice does not meet the condition for commitment laid down by the initial definition, even though the choice has non-welfare-maximizing consequences for the agent. Conversely, if one believes that one's choice will not maximize one's welfare and this belief turns out to be wrong, this does not vitiate the status of the action as one based on commitment. It is the agent's *beliefs* about the consequences, not the actual consequences, which determine whether a choice meets Sen's initial definition of commitment. As Sen writes, 'commitment relates choice to anticipated levels of welfare' (1977a: 92). My third observation is that, if a person believes that a particular choice will not maximize her welfare, she presumably has a reason for relinquishing an alternative option, the option which, she believes, will maximize her welfare. Sen does not explicitly attribute a reason to the person when he presents his initial definition of commitment, but it is reasonable to assume that he would agree with the attribution of a reason to the person, for although he once states that commitment 'does not presuppose reasoning' (1977a: 105), he immediately adds that commitment does not exclude it; and the overwhelming emphasis of Sen's discussion reinforces the view that commitment is to be defined in terms of the reasons the agent has for choosing. We must observe, though, that the initial definition is entirely silent about the nature of the reasons which underlie choices based on commitment. If, therefore, we had to infer the nature of the reasons compatible with commitment from the initial condition alone, we would say the following: any reason which prompts a person to make a choice on the belief that the choice will not maximize her welfare falls under the initial definition of commitment.

An agent's reason for choosing is related to the 'question of causation' which, as we noted in the previous chapter (Section III), concerns matters of motivation. In 'Rational Fools', these matters are discussed using the terminology of the agent's *reasons* for choosing. In Sen's later work, as we shall see, the 'reasons' terminology is superseded by the terminology of 'goals'. The two are closely related, and, in preparation for Chapters Seven and Eight, in which I discuss Sen's later work on choice theory and his discussion of goals, I will henceforth avail myself of the terms 'goals' as well as 'reasons' when examining the motivation of the agent. Hence, when I say, for example, that an agent's reason for choosing is to maximize her own welfare, this should be taken as synonymous with the statement that the agent's goal is to maximize her welfare. This is consistent with Sen's terminology. Sen's initial definition of commitment, as we established in the previous paragraph, divulges nothing which would allow us to determine the goal behind a committed choice, but it nevertheless excludes one goal, namely, that of maximizing one's welfare. To shed further light on the agent's goal or reason for making a committed choice, we must turn to the second definition of commitment which Sen offers and which properly illuminates the question of causation.

Following Sen, we shall call his second definition of commitment the 'more inclusive' definition. This definition addresses the possibility that a person's choice 'happens to coincide with the maximization of his anticipated personal welfare, but that is not the *reason* for his choice' (Sen 1977a: 92). The possibility addressed by the more inclusive definition concerns a choice made by an agent who believes her choice will maximize her welfare. The initial definition clearly excludes such a choice from the set of choices based on commitment because the choice foreseeably maximizes the agent's welfare. The more inclusive definition does not necessarily exclude such choices from the realm of commitment – hence its 'more inclusive' nature. The choices which Sen's more inclusive definition includes, but the initial definition excludes, from the set of choices based on commitment are those through which the agent expects to maximize her welfare. There is an ambiguity about such choices similar to one discussed by Immanuel Kant (1974/1786: 23) in the context of duty. Does an agent whose action is in accordance with duty (*pflichtgemäß*) actually act *from* duty (*aus Pflicht*)? The ambiguity arises because one's action can accord with duty without being undertaken from a motive of duty. The answer to the question just posed, Kant tells us, is difficult to ascertain when the acting subject has an inclination (preference) to perform an act which corresponds to the call of duty. Is she motivated to perform the act by a sense of duty or by the inclination to perform it? An act can have more than one motive underlying it, according to Kant. If the maxim of an act does not have solely moral content, it is a case of 'impurity' (*Unlauterkeit*) (Kant 1907/1793: 29–30). These impure motives will be discussed in the context of commitment in Section III below, but here I look at what Sen has to say about acting on duty, which he sees as a type of commitment. With the example to be discussed in the following paragraph, Sen illustrates the difference, as he understands it, between acting in accordance with and acting from duty, which, in turn, allows one to grasp the need of his more inclusive definition of commitment and the insufficiency of his initial definition.

Sen presents us with two different accounts of performing an action which accords with duty. In the first, 'the action is really chosen out of the sense of duty' (*aus Pflicht*, in Kant's parlance). In the second account, it is not; instead, the individual performs the act in order 'to avoid the illfare resulting from the remorse that would occur if one were to act otherwise' (Sen 1977a: 92). Avoiding this illfare in the second account gives the individual an inclination to perform the act. In the first case, by contrast, the individual's sense of duty is sufficient to motivate the agent to perform the act in question. Yet suppose the agent in the first case also correctly foresees that the dutiful act will maximize her welfare: so unpleasant will be the remorse at failing to do her duty, augmented by the disapproval of others who witness her act, that the action done from a sense of duty and the welfare-maximizing (remorse-minimizing) action coincide. This is the case for which Sen conceives his more inclusive definition of commitment. In such cases, to ascertain whether the choice is based on commitment, we must determine the individual's *reason* for choosing. This raises the 'question of causation'.

If an individual makes a choice which, she believes, will maximize her welfare, her choice cannot be based on commitment if her reason for choosing lies solely in the prospect of maximizing her personal welfare; such a choice might be in accordance with duty but it is not motivated by a sense of duty. In the terminology of goals, the agent's goal is to maximize her welfare, and this is incompatible with classifying the choice as committed according to the more inclusive definition. If, on the other hand, the individual believes that making a particular choice will maximize her welfare but this consideration is not what motivates her to act, her choice is based on commitment. We shall say henceforth that such choices are based on a *welfare-maximizing commitment*. Sen's more inclusive definition of commitment is intended to cover this special case in which the welfare-maximizing aspect of the agent's choice is incidental to her reason for acting. As a 'test' for distinguishing welfare-maximizing commitments from non-committed welfare-maximizing choices, Sen (1977a: 92) proposes the following 'counterfactual condition': a choice which the agent believes will maximize her welfare is based on commitment if the agent would have chosen the act had she anticipated that the act would *not* have maximized her personal welfare. The nature of this counterfactual condition lies in the fact that we imagine asking whether the agent would have chosen likewise under different, hypothetical, beliefs about the welfare consequences of the choice. To carry out this test, information beyond that acquired by observing behaviour might be required. Sen mentions 'introspection and discussion' as sources of evidence (1977a: 102).

The foregoing analysis reveals what appears to be a division of labour between Sen's initial and more inclusive definitions of commitment. The initial definition is apt to deal with the 'easy' cases in which the agent expects that her choice will not maximize her welfare. For such cases, the initial definition unambiguously classifies such choices as committed, and it provides a sufficient condition for choices being based on commitment. For the 'harder' cases, in which the agent believes her choice will maximize her welfare, the initial definition passes the baton to its more inclusive counterpart which alone can determine whether the choice is based on commitment. It can do this because the more inclusive definition does not limit the conditions on commitment to those pertaining to the agent's beliefs about the welfare consequences of her choices. If Sen's counterfactual condition is met, a choice which foreseeably maximizes the agent's welfare can be based on commitment. Sen's counterfactual condition is the sole and sufficient condition for a welfare-maximizing choice to be based on commitment.

## II Counter-preferential choice

Commitment, Sen writes, involves counter-preferential choice: it 'destroy[s] the crucial assumption that a chosen alternative must be better than (or at least as good as) the others for the person choosing it' (1977a: 93). He also describes commitment as something which 'drives a wedge between personal choice and personal welfare' (1977a: 94). In a further formulation of this idea, he states that the 'basic link between choice behaviour and welfare achievements in the traditional models is severed as soon as commitment is admitted as an ingredient of choice' (1977a: 94). Sen repeats this point in his official definition of commitment which states that commitment 'is concerned with breaking the tight link between individual welfare ... and the choice of action' (1982a: 8). This definition of commitment is 'official' for the same reason that his 'official' definition of sympathy, quoted in the previous chapter (Section II) was official, namely, that Sen quotes it numerous times in his subsequent characterizations of the commitment (1985b: 214; 2002a: 35; 2005a: 19; 2009a: 188–9). The ideas which Sen expresses here put commitment at odds with orthodox models of choice which make the assumption that a chosen option is also the one preferred in the sense that it maximizes the welfare of the chooser. The current section has two purposes, one of which is to examine what makes choices based on commitment counter-preferential. The second task consists in asking what Sen means with his terminology of 'destroying', 'severing', 'driving a wedge between' and 'breaking the link between' choice and welfare. In answering the second question, we will consider the possible welfare effects (or restrictions thereon) of choices based on commitment.

The 'identity' of choice and welfare on which 'much of traditional economic theory relies' is, Sen argues:

> sometimes obscured by the ambiguity of the term 'preference', since the normal use of the word permits the identification of preference with the concept of being better off, and at the same time it is not quite unnatural to define 'preferred' as 'chosen'.
>
> (1977a: 94)

If 'preference' is taken in Sen's 'normal use', then what is preferred makes one better off. In essence, this expresses the normative relationship as we called it in Chapter One, for it links one's preferences to one's personal welfare. Abrogating this relationship indeed severs the link between choice and welfare because one's preferences, though remaining the causal determinants of one's choice of behaviour, are no longer such that basing one's choices on one's preferences leads one to maximize one's welfare. One's preferences might, for example, be of the 'ultimate' sort, as Sen introduced them in his 'Behaviour' essay (see Chapter One, Section III). With such preferences, one 'ultimately' prefers whatever one chooses, but what one chooses is not necessarily preferred in the sense of making one personally better off. Ultimate preferences would, then, contradict Sen's 'normal use' of the term 'preference'. As a result of de-linking preference and welfare, ultimate preferences can produce a gap between choice and welfare but they do not thereby deliver the possibility of counter-preferential choice, for one's choices remain firmly based on, not contrary to, one's (ultimate) preferences. Let us therefore turn to the concept of preference in Sen's 'not quite unnatural' sense, whereby what is chosen is synonymous with what is preferred. By identifying what is chosen with what is preferred, one is expressing the aetiological relationship which states that all of one's choices are causally based on one's preferences whatever the content of those preferences might be. If this relationship is abrogated, choice and welfare become cloven because one's preferences do not form the causal basis of one's choices. One bases one's choices, not on one's preferences, but on some other basis, and hence there arises the *possibility* of choices which do not redound to one's personal welfare, though as we saw in the previous section, choices based on commitment only hold out the possibility of non-welfare maximization, but commitment is not incompatible with welfare maximization. Only choices of which the aetiological relationship does not hold are rightly characterized as *counter-preferential*.

At the close of Chapter One (Section II), we stated that choices of which the aetiological relationship does not hold were not fully elucidated in Sen's 'Behaviour' essay beyond the fact that such preferences have a non-preference-based aetiology. The material in 'Rational Fools', with its thematization of an individual's reason for choosing, offers us what the 'Behaviour' essay lacks, for a reason-based choice gives us a candidate for a choice which has non-preference-based aetiology of choice. And it would appear that choices based on a person's as-if ranking from the 'Behaviour' essay correspond to choices based on commitment in 'Rational Fools'; for the former choices are not based on one's (true) preferences but on an as-if ranking which deviates from one's preferences; they are non-preference-based choices. The reason for making a choice based on commitment overrides the individual's preferences and thus any choices based on such a reason have a non-preference-based aetiology; they are counter-preferential.

Although Sen is clear that commitment destroys the 'crucial assumption' that the option I choose must make me better off, there are different ways of conceiving this destruction. One *modum exitii* would be through a simple negation, whereby one would invert the term 'better than' and transform it into 'worse than' in the passage quoted in the first sentence of this section. This would yield the following statement: commitment involves the assumption that a chosen alternative must be *worse* than others for the person choosing it. This way of destroying the crucial assumption is suggested by Sen's initial definition of commitment, which implies that, to perform a choice based on commitment, the agent must expect the option chosen to make her worse off than at least one other option available. This, however, is not how Sen means the destruction of the crucial assumption, or so I shall argue, for only choices which fulfil the initial definition of commitment negate the crucial assumption in this way. Once we bring in Sen's more inclusive definition of commitment, we must allow for choices based on commitment which maximize the expected welfare of the chooser. And once we do so, we find that commitment leaves the relationship between the agent's choice and her expectations regarding its welfare consequences indeterminate. An agent who makes a choice based on commitment may, that is, believe that:

(i) her choice will maximize her welfare;
(ii) her choice will increase (but not maximize) her welfare;
(iii) her choice will leave her welfare unaltered;
(iv) her choice will decrease her welfare;
(v) her choice will minimize her welfare.

When Sen writes that commitment ruptures the connection between personal choice and personal welfare, he means that *nothing* about the actor's beliefs regarding the welfare consequences of making a choice is determined by the notion of commitment. The expected welfare consequences of making a choice based on commitment are open and a matter of empirical rather than conceptual determination. The foregoing alerts us to an important requirement when we characterize commitment: if making a choice based on commitment is compatible with any welfare consequence – (i) to (v) above – which the agent who makes the choice may anticipate, then the counter-preferential nature of choices based on commitment cannot be conceived in terms of a particular configuration of expected welfare consequences. This confirms something we established above, namely, that it is in the non-preference-based aetiology of a choice that one recognizes its committed nature. We cannot, for instance, say that, in making a choice based on commitment, the agent must expect the chosen option to be less good than an alternative available in terms of its welfare consequences for the agent, for this would only apply to choices captured by Sen's initial definition of commitment. As we have seen, some choices based on commitment do not fulfil the condition expressed in the initial definition, and this is why Sen needs his more inclusive definition. The latter definition allows a choice which the agent believes will maximize her welfare to be based on commitment. What makes such a choice a committed one is its non-preference-based aetiology, not anything about its anticipated welfare effects.

The foregoing analysis raises a question: we have established the possibility of welfare-maximizing commitments, but if a choice foreseeably maximizes my welfare, can it really be *counter*-preferential? For a welfare-maximizing choice surely accords and is not at odds with (counter to) my preferences, and had I based the choice on my preferences rather than on a reason derived from my commitment, I would have made the same choice as I did when basing it on a commitment. This does not sound obviously counter-preferential. The answer to the question posed is nevertheless 'yes, a welfare-maximizing commitment is counter-preferential'. But one only derives this answer if one does *not* conceive welfare-maximizing choices based on commitment according to their anticipated welfare consequences. If one considers such choices only according to their anticipated welfare consequences, as Sen's initial definition urges us to do, then it would seem that there is nothing to distinguish a straightforward welfare-maximizing choice from a welfare-maximizing choice based on commitment: in each case, the chooser anticipates that the choice will maximize his welfare. But if one shifts perspective and observes these two choices, not according to their anticipated consequences, but according to their respective aetiologies, one sees that the straightforward welfare-maximizing choice has a preference-based aetiology whereas the welfare-maximizing choice based on commitment has a reason-based aetiology. The latter makes welfare-maximizing choices based on commitment counter-preferential. Whether or not the agent expects the choice to maximize her welfare is irrelevant to its classification as committed, for a choice which has a non-preference-based aetiology is, as we ascertained above, compatible with any expected welfare consequence for the agent. In the terminology of goals, the two choices just contrasted are based on different goals, and though the committed choice maximizes the agent's welfare and does so foreseeably, this is a contingent characteristic of the choice when one looks at it from the perspective of the agent's motivation; for the agent makes the choice, not *in order* to maximize her welfare, but in order to pursue a commitment which she sees reason to value.

## III Commitment and morality

Having ascertained that the agent's reason for choosing is decisive in determining whether her choice is based on commitment, we can ask now which restrictions Sen lays on the content of the reasons which are compatible with commitment. The first and main task of this section is to answer this question. The second task is to add a layer of complexity into Sen's analysis which comes in the form of 'mixed motives', that is, when an agent is motivated to act partly by her commitment and partly by the goal of deriving welfare to herself.

If a choice is to be classified as committed, it must be based, we ascertained in the previous section, on a reason which is independent of a person's self-interested preferences, for unless this is the case, the choice would not have the requisite reason-based aetiology. Henceforth, I will call such a reason a welfare-independent reason, a term which corresponds to Peter and Schmid's apt characterization of commitment as 'motivationally unrelated to the agent's welfare, however, broadly conceived' (2007: 4). But beyond its unrelatedness to welfare, will 'any old' reason suffice to make a choice committed? Sen places a restriction on the content which such reasons must have if they are to form the basis of a committed choice. His restriction is, however, a weak one, and I will add a second which, though not explicitly stated by Sen, is congruent with his thinking on commitment. Sen hints at the nature of the sort of reasons one requires for a choice based on commitment in an example with which he first elucidates commitment, namely, torture: if 'you think it is wrong and you are ready to do something to stop it, it is a case of commitment' (1977a: 92). Your readiness to 'do something to stop it' is presumably related to the fact that 'you think it is wrong'. If so, one may say that thinking that something is right or wrong gives one the sort of reason one must have if one is to act on a commitment. Alternatively, Sen states that commitment is 'closely connected to one's morals' (1977a: 93). What does he mean by a person's 'morals'?

Sen conceives 'morals' broadly and stresses that they need not be understood in a universalistic sense typical of characterizations of morality in moral philosophy. Instead, he identifies a space 'between egoism and universalized moral systems' (1977a: 106) in which the moral reasons which motivate choices based on commitment are located:

> Groups intermediate between oneself and all, such as class and community, provide the focus for many actions involving commitment. The rejection of egoism as [a] description of motivation does not, therefore,

imply the acceptance of some universalized morality as the basis of actual behaviour. Nor does it make human beings excessively noble.
(1977a: 106; cf. Sen 1994: 389; 2001b: 59)

Whilst the rejection of egoism does not entail that that commitment be moral in a universalistic sense, this is in no way excluded, which is probably why Sen writes that 'ethics is somehow mixed up with the idea of commitment' (2005a: 22). But with the indented passage from Sen just cited, Sen is not putting forward a normative theory as to which reasons may be deemed sufficiently 'moral' to form the causal basis of choices based on commitment; rather he is proposing a positive theory about how people make certain choices independently of considerations which relate to their own welfare. One's morals can be highly particularistic, based on prejudice and even downright nasty. Whilst commitment 'may relate to the working of some universalized morality, it need not be ... so broad-based. Indeed, a sense of commitment to one's community, race, class, fellow-workers, fellow-oligopolists, etc.' can all suffice to motivate a choice based on commitment (Sen 1982a: 8); suicide bombers and members of the Ku Klux Klan can be paragons of commitment just as the John Browns and Harriet Tubmans of the world can be.

The foregoing discussion raises the following question: are all reasons which would suffice to motivate an individual to make a choice on the belief that doing so will not maximize her welfare to be classed as being 'closely connected to one's morals'? If so, then any choice which is causally motivated by such a reason is based on commitment. Sen could force the answer 'yes' by fiat, that is, by defining as moral all reasons which would motivate the individual to make a foreseeably non-maximizing choice. If he employed this definitional tactic, though, the moral nature of a reason would have no content independent of the fact that the reason makes a person willing to relinquish the welfare-maximizing option; if one's reason were able to motivate one thus, it would, by definition, be moral. That this is not a viable strategy can be seen by considering an example of a choice based on sympathy.

We ascertained, in Chapter Two, that choices based on sympathy are egoistic because the agent makes such choices with the goal of deriving welfare to herself. We distinguished two types of choice based on sympathy, one welfare-maximizing, the other welfare-increasing. With the latter, the agent increases the welfare of another person by choosing an option, $x$. The agent's goal thereby is sympathetically to derive a degree of welfare, $w$, which falls short of the welfare, $w_{MAX}$, associated with the agent's most preferred option. The prospect of deriving welfare $w$ by choosing $x$ is sufficient to motivate her choice; this is what makes it egoistic. Although she might be able to maximize her welfare by choosing a different option, she declines the maximizing option and chooses $x$. The agent's choice is clearly based on sympathy, but is it also based on commitment? If we take Sen's initial definition of commitment at its word, then it is, for the agent chooses an option which, she believes, will not maximize her welfare. This would lead us to conclude that one and the same choice can be simultaneously based on sympathy and on commitment. This creates dissonance in Sen's conceptual framework because Sen distinguishes sympathy and commitment on the grounds that actions based on sympathy are egoistic, whereas those based on commitment are non-egoistic (1977a: 92). Since an action cannot be simultaneously egoistic and non-egoistic, we have run into a problem. If Sen's initial definition of commitment leads to the incongruous conclusion that a choice can be simultaneously based on sympathy and commitment, can his more inclusive definition of commitment remove the dissonance by negating this conclusion? It cannot, for the more inclusive definition only addresses choices which maximize the actor's welfare; it does not address welfare-increasing but non-maximizing choices of the sort under consideration.

Are there grounds for divesting the non-welfare-maximizing choice based on sympathy depicted in the foregoing paragraph of its committed status, for if there are, the dissonance would disappear? There are, indeed, such grounds and they can be found in the conclusion to Section III above, which stated that the counter-preferential nature of choices based on commitment lies in their having a non-preference-based aetiology. To make a committed choice is to make a choice with a reason-based aetiology which means that the agent must have a reason for choosing the relevant option which is unrelated to her own welfare. If, as is the case with the choice based on sympathy described above, the agent's goal is to derive a certain degree of welfare, $w < w_{MAX}$, this does not answer to the description of 'being unrelated to her own welfare'. The agent's sole goal is to derive $w$ and being motivated to make the choice in light of this goal makes the choice egoistic. Choices based on commitment, on the other hand, must be underlain by a different, non-welfare-related, goal. Hence, non-welfare-maximizing choices based on sympathy, cannot be based on commitment because their aetiological provenance is not based on reason. The foregoing, then, leads to an additional restriction on the types of reason which are compatible with making choices based on commitment. Foreseeably non-welfare-maximizing choices based on sympathy are excluded from the set of choices based on commitment because the reasons behind the former choices fail to qualify as non-egoistic. Being egoistic, welfare-increasing choices based on sympathy are, by definition, underlain by a welfare-related goal, and this excludes them from being based on commitment.

Sen's initial definition of commitment is, as it were, eclipsed by its more inclusive counterpart, for, as we established above, the anticipated welfare effects of a choice have no bearing on whether that choice be committed. What is decisive for categorizing choices based on commitment is that they have a reason-based aetiology, and Sen's more inclusive definition of commitment suffices for such a categorization, thus rendering his initial definition of commitment otiose. What, then, in Section II of this chapter, was described as a division of labour between Sen's initial and more inclusive definitions of commitment is not that at all; for what I there called the 'easy' cases for which the agent anticipates that her welfare will not be maximized, can and should be captured by Sen's more inclusive definition of commitment, not by his initial definition. What is crucial to the committed status of a choice is not its welfare consequences for the agent who makes the choice but the fact that the choice is motivated by a particular type of non-welfare-related reason. The more inclusive definition encompasses all such cases as well as the 'harder' cases for which choices based on commitment happen to maximize the agent's welfare.

## IV Reasons, preferences and mixed motives

In the foregoing discussion, I have been contrasting choices which have a preference-based, from those which have a reason-based aetiology. Alternatively, I have separated choices motivated by welfare-related concerns or self-interest from choices motivated by reasons connected to a person's morals. It might be thought that I am implicitly excluding preferences from the sphere of reasons for making a choice. This exclusion could be challenged, as it is clear, for some at least, that having a preference for option $x$ gives one reason to choose $x$. A preference would therefore be a type of reason, a peculiar type indeed, but it is a reason nonetheless. Sen does not make a decisive pronouncement on whether he thinks reasons and preferences belong in separate motivational categories or whether preferences are a type of reason. His later work gives us some hints at his position. Sometimes he separates preferences from reasons, and he also adds 'values' as a separate category to the *mélange* (2002a: 5). This, however, comes as a passing comment in a discussion of freedom and should not, therefore, be taken to be a programmatic classification of motives. Elsewhere, Sen identifies the 'self-interested concerns (privileged by narrowly characterized "rational choice" ...)' as possible 'reasons for choice' and lists self-interested concerns alongside other, 'socially responsible and morally intelligible reasons' (2002a: 50). He also mentions 'desire' as a 'good reason for choosing in one's own personal sphere' (1983b: 398). And he remarks that there are 'many good reasons for thinking that one alternative rather than another is to be chosen, and the pursuit of self-interest is at best one such reason' (1986b: 344). There can therefore be little doubt that Sen holds preferences to be a type of reason for choice, though it is one which, when it motivates choices, excludes those choices from being based on commitment. And it is also clear that one of Sen's preoccupations is to resist 'arbitrarily narrowing permissible "reasons for choice"' to one motive only. 'Our motives', he writes, 'are for us to choose' (2002a: 5–6), and the freedom Sen accords to us in choosing our motives would be nullified were we prompted to choose only by the commands of self-interest.

There is a further possible misconception which arises from singling out preference-based choices from their reason-based counterparts and this is the view that a person who makes a choice must be motivated to do so either by her preferences or by her non-preference-based reasons, whereby being motivated by a mix of reasons – both welfare-related and non-welfare-related – is excluded. That this is not so was hinted at in Section I in which Kant's notion of impure motives was mentioned. Let us apply this idea to the concept of commitment, something which adds a little complexity to Sen's analysis.

The way in which Sen may be held to keep his analysis simple (and I have followed him in doing so heretofore) consists in his assuming that when a person's choice is based on commitment, her reason for choosing is sufficient to motivate her choice; she requires no further source of motivation to make the choice. Hence, when Sen discusses the example of acting on duty, he presents an either/or contrast: *either* the action is 'really chosen out of the sense of duty', *or* it is chosen 'to avoid the illfare resulting from the remorse that would occur if one were to act otherwise' (1977a: 92). If, as we have been assuming, a commitment, and it alone, motivates a person's choice without admixture of any self-interested motivation, we have what one may call a *pure commitment*. There are, however, cases of *impure commitment* which deserve attention, as they are likely to be empirically common. Such cases fall short of pure commitment and are exemplified by an agent who has a commitment too weak to give her sufficient reason to perform a particular act. The agent might be motivated to perform the relevant act if, in addition to her weak commitment, she anticipates that her action will increase her welfare and this, as it were, tops up her motivation to a degree which suffices to prompt her to perform the act in question. In such a case, the commitment together with the anticipation of increased welfare provide her with sufficient reason to perform the action, whereas neither the prospect of increased welfare nor the reason on which the commitment is based alone is sufficient to motivate the individual to act. Such an agent has mixed or impure motives, and the mixture which motivates her to act consists of both egoistic and non-egoistic parts. To the extent that the two motivating aspects of the action can be separated, we may say that an action is motivated by a lower degree of commitment the greater the self-interested 'top-up' required to give the agent sufficient reason to perform the action (cf. Schefczyk and Peacock 2010: §2).

## V Sympathy, commitment, egoism and altruism

Sen's concepts of sympathy and commitment raise the question as to where the concept of altruism is to be located in relation to them, a question explored, if briefly, by some of Sen's commentators (e.g. Anderson 2001: 22; Hausman 2005: 57–8; 2012: 58–9; Shiell and Rush 2003: 649–50). The answer, of course, depends on how one defines altruism. Rather than stipulate a definition of altruism and see whether it matches sympathy or commitment more closely, the following discussion is orientated to what Sen writes about altruism. This poses a problem, for he uses the term sparingly in his *oeuvre*, in which it is not a technical concept; when he does use it, it is usually to cite its use by other scholars (Sen 1975; 2002a: 30, 36). Nevertheless, he does give hints as to his understanding of altruism, and the discussion which follows clarifies Sen's position on sympathy and commitment, and the relationship between the two.

There are *prima facie* grounds for classifying actions based on sympathy as altruistic because the actor who performs such actions expects that she will thereby increase the welfare of another person. This, at least, appears to be a necessary condition for altruism. In a rather lapidary but nevertheless revealing discussion, Sen asks whether actions based on sympathy may be deemed altruistic. 'Altruism through sympathy', as he calls it, is 'self-interested benevolence' (1997: 760 note 33), 'benevolent', because it increases the welfare of another person, and 'self-interested' because it confers welfare on the agent whose goal is to derive welfare to herself by improving the welfare of others. Altruism through sympathy therefore fulfils the three conditions for actions based on sympathy we outlined in Chapter Two (Section III). There, we established that an action performed by person $A$ is based on sympathy if it (i) increases the welfare of another person, (ii) increases the welfare of $A$, and is (iii) performed by $A$ with the goal of increasing her own welfare. This is, however, a rather pallid notion of altruism, especially for proponents of 'psychological altruism' who insist that an altruistic act require that the actor have the 'ultimate goal' of benefiting another person (Batson 2011: 20–1). Though Sen's altruism through sympathy might involve an agent performing actions with the immediate aim of increasing another person's welfare, this is not the agent's *ultimate* goal, for she has at least one goal beyond increasing another person's welfare, namely, to increase her own; increasing the other person's welfare is a subordinate goal and a *means* to realizing this further goal.

Although Sen does not delve into the psychological literature on altruism, he is unconvinced that altruism through sympathy be the last word on the subject, and his further remarks on altruism reveal a nearness to the psychological approach. Altruism through sympathy, Sen writes, involves the actor maximizing a welfare function which '*incorporates* his altruism toward others' (1997: 760). This sort of sympathetic altruism, whilst not self-*centred* (because it presupposes that a person can derive welfare from increases in the welfare of others), is nevertheless self-*interested* because actors only 'take note of others' interests within their own utility' (Sen 2009a: 189; cf. 2002a: 31). Altruism through sympathy, that is, entails that an actor, $A$, register an increase of her own welfare as a result of an increase in the welfare of another person, $B$, whose welfare is increased by $A$'s actions; $A$ would not be concerned about $B$'s welfare and would not, therefore, be motivated to perform an action which increases $B$'s welfare unless $A$ registered the increase in $B$'s welfare in the manner just described.

Sen contrasts the above, self-interested, notion of altruism through sympathy with a non-self-interested type of altruism for which 'the other person's well-being remains a separate concern' (Sen 1997: 760). The term 'separate concern' implies that $B$'s welfare is of significance to $A$ in and of itself, that is, *beyond* rather than 'within' $A$'s own utility. Concern for others can therefore constitute a reason which motivates $A$ to act in favour of $B$ whether or not so acting is registered positively in $A$'s welfare function. Sen approaches the ground marked out by the psychological view of altruism here because, if $B$'s welfare is of significance to $A$ beyond the extent to which it influences $A$'s welfare, $A$'s interest in improving $B$'s welfare is not derived from $A$'s interest in raising her own welfare. However, this does not necessarily make $A$'s attempt to increase $B$'s welfare psychologically altruistic in the sense stated above, for $A$'s taking account of $B$'s welfare beyond $A$'s own utility need not entail that increasing $B$'s welfare be $A$'s *ultimate* goal; helping $B$ might, for instance, be $A$'s means of realizing a further goal, such as comporting herself in accord with the commandments of her religion. If $A$ does have some further goal beyond raising $B$'s welfare, $A$'s act is not psychologically altruistic but it is altruistic in Sen's non-self-interested sense of the term. So whilst compatible with psychological altruism – when $A$'s ultimate goal is to increase $B$'s welfare – Sen's non-self-interested type of altruism does not entail its psychologically defined counterpart.

Sen therefore entertains a concept of altruism which is distinct from self-interested benevolence. He thereby conceives a type of altruism freed from a motivational base in self-interest. Altruistic actions of this sort cannot be accommodated within the concept of active sympathy because they do not fulfil condition (iii) for actions based on sympathy which states that the prospect of attaining welfare is what motivates an action. Altruistic actions freed from a motivational base in self-interest fall instead under the heading of commitment because the actor must have a welfare-independent reason for performing acts which improve the welfare of others. This is what makes the other person's welfare a 'separate concern'. Although they do not fall under the heading of active sympathy, Sen's non-self-interested altruistic actions need not be independent of contemplative sympathy. To grasp why this is so, consider a person, $A$, who performs an action which increases another's welfare. Being not only the consequence but also $A$'s reason for performing this action, $A$'s choice to act thus is based on commitment. There is nothing, though, to stop $A$ deriving pleasure at his success in raising the other person's welfare, and if he does feel such pleasure, $A$ would be feeling contemplative sympathy. By basing her choice on a commitment to improve $B$'s welfare, $A$ would have performed the same action had she not expected to derive welfare from her success in raising $B$'s welfare. Our paradigm case of contemplative sympathy in Section II of the previous chapter was when $A$'s welfare rises as a result of $A$'s awareness that $B$'s welfare had risen, whereby $A$'s own action was *not* the cause of the increase in $B$'s welfare. But our discussion of altruism indicates that the latter clause is not a necessary one for contemplative sympathy; for, as we have just seen, $A$'s action might be the cause of $B$'s happiness, but as long as the prospect that $B$'s happiness would cause an increase in $A$'s welfare is not $A$'s reason for performing the action, we do not have a case of active sympathy. Instead it is a case of an action based on commitment in which $A$ derives sympathetic welfare as a result of her own committed action which increases $B$'s welfare.

Although Sen does not use the term egoistic in his discussion of altruism through sympathy, his description of the latter as *self-interested* benevolence suggests that he conceives altruism through sympathy to be egoistic. This is consistent with Sen's concept of action based on sympathy which is, as we ascertained in Chapter Two, a universally egoistic phenomenon. We closed Chapter Two by stating that the egoistic nature of actions based on sympathy did not cast a favourable light on such actions. One of Sen's interpreters, Philip Pettit, is dissatisfied with this conclusion and he puts forward an interpretation of altruism through sympathy which would shine a more favourable light on sympathy. Let us examine Pettit's interpretation in light of the foregoing discussion.

Pettit quotes Sen's characterization of altruism through sympathy as self-interested benevolence. He contends that altruism through sympathy:

> is not self-interested in the sense of being pursued with an instrumental eye to securing some personal benefit. It is self-interested in the sense that the person we favor is someone whose welfare matters to us, intuitively, in the same manner as our own; let them fare well and we feel good, let them fare badly and we feel bad.
>
> (Pettit 2005: 30)

To unravel this passage, let us first ascertain that, by calling altruism through sympathy self-interested, Pettit must be referring to active sympathy, that is, to sympathy as it manifests itself in and motivates action. Ascriptions of self-interest or egoism, it will be recalled, only apply to active sympathy which necessarily involves action; they do not apply to contemplative sympathy which consists solely in a feeling. Pettit makes this connection to action in the passage just cited with terms like 'we favour someone' and 'let them fare well', whereby it is presumably the sympathetic agent's own actions which do the favouring or ensure that the other fares well. Pettit claims that active sympathy is self-interested. In the following discussion, I refer to this as *sympathetic self-interest*. It is distinct, Pettit holds, from active sympathy of the sort which the sympathetic actor initiates 'with an instrumental eye to securing some personal benefit', or *instrumental-eye self-interest*, as I will call it. Can the distinction between sympathetic self-interest and instrumental-eye self-interest be ascribed to Sen's understanding of sympathy?

To answer this question, let us recall that a person performs actions based on sympathy with the goal of increasing her own welfare. Increasing your welfare is a means to achieve this goal; it is not an end in itself but an instrument for increasing my own welfare. Being my goal when I act sympathetically, increasing my welfare is not an unintended consequence of performing an act which increases my welfare but the very thing after which I strive when I perform the act, and if I expected to derive less welfare, I would refrain from acting thus. This is the point which Sen makes in his parenthetic remark on sympathy which we analysed in Chapter Two (Section III).

Because increasing the other person's welfare is an instrument for attaining my goal of increasing my own welfare, I may be said, when I perform actions based on sympathy, to be acting with an 'instrumental eye'. The distinction between sympathetic self-interest and instrumental-eye self-interest therefore eludes us. Pettit's instrumental-eye terminology might not be the most flattering way of stating that actions based on sympathy are underlain by the agent's goal of increasing his own welfare, and they do not make active sympathy a terribly noble undertaking. But in the sense that actions based on sympathy are a vehicle for pursuing one's self-interest through sympathy, the instrumental-eye terminology is an accurate depiction of the motivation of someone who acts on sympathy.

Sympathy does have a more noble countenance than what has been suggested above, and Pettit identifies this countenance when he writes that one is sympathetic when 'one's sentiments resonate in common with others' (2005: 31). He also writes that sympathy 'comes about via enlarging self-interest to the point where it encompasses others' (2005: 30). Many would see these psychological traits as commendable, and if we compare a person to whom these descriptions apply, she appears more humane than one to whom they do not apply. If, that is, my sentiments do not resonate with yours, whether you are experiencing pain or pleasure, my stolidity seems cold; and if my self-interest extends only to narrow concerns of my own but does not encompass other concerns, especially those of import to other people, then one might say that I am self-obsessed or egotistical, not merely self-interested. Sen identifies the noble countenance of sympathy when he writes that to be capable of sympathy, one must have 'concern for others' (Sen 1977a: 91). Sympathy is necessarily other-regarding and stands at odds with self-centredness. If one is self-centred, one is unable to feel the 'joys and pains from sympathy to others'. A sympathetic person, however, is able to share in others' joys and miseries and the 'derived joys and pains' which she feels are 'quintessentially [her] own' (Sen 2002a: 31). Being non-self-centred is therefore analytic to the concept of sympathy, but it has its roots in contemplative sympathy which consists solely in a feeling, and is independent of one's actions; contemplative sympathy cannot therefore be deemed self-interested (whether with or without an instrumental eye) because it does not in itself motivate action. Only active sympathy involves motivation to act. Any edification Pettit ascribes to sympathy, then, stems from its contemplative aspect. A person who is not self-centred and can therefore feel sympathy can choose to act on sympathy, but if he does so, his motivation is egoistic. And there is nothing terribly edifying about performing such actions the goal of which is solely to derive welfare to oneself. Furthermore, there is nothing about active sympathy which justifies Pettit's distinction between mere sympathetic self-interest and self-interest pursued with an instrumental eye.

To close this section, let us consider two implications of Sen's non-self-interested understanding of altruism which must be aligned with commitment rather than with sympathy. Altruistic acts, for which the well-being of others constitutes a 'separate concern', must be non-self-interestedly motivated; the goal of the altruist, as we argued above, is not to increase her own welfare by performing altruistic actions. Rather, the altruist's reason for choosing is based on her goal of increasing the well-being of another person. This is what makes these altruistic actions examples of commitment, for they are based on a reason which is unrelated to the actor's welfare. It is not, however, the case that committed choices are always altruistic, for, although many choices based on commitment are made with the goal of increasing the welfare of another person, there are commitments which are independent of this reason. If, for example, one's commitment consists in dedicating one's life to the worship certain gods, to the memory of a dead person or to saving an endangered type of cockroach from extinction, it is not orientated to improving the welfare of others, and hence one's commitment cannot be altruistic. Furthermore, one's commitment might involve harming others intentionally, for example, a commitment to burning infidels or planting incendiary devices in clinics which perform abortions. Those who perform such actions might sincerely claim that what they are doing is for a 'good' cause, and they might perform them independently of their beliefs about the consequences of these actions for their own welfare. But such actions are not altruistic because the goal of their actions is to harm others. These actions are, in Sen's sense, obviously committed, though, because they are based on the agent's 'morals'.

A final implication of aligning the concept of altruism with commitment is that it excludes self-sacrifice as a necessary condition for acting altruistically, a tenet shared by proponents of psychological altruism (cf. Batson 1991: 6–7). Sen's analysis in 'Rational Fools' allows choices based on commitment both to increase and to maximize the expected welfare of the agent, and hence commitment requires no self-sacrifice, although it is compatible with it. Sen's commitment-based notion of altruism tallies with psychological definitions because the actor's motivation or reason for acting rather than the consequences for the actor's welfare is the defining feature of altruism; and one's reason for acting, if one's action is to be altruistic, is to increase the welfare of another person. No self-sacrifice is required of altruistic actions.

Oddly, perhaps, in one of his writings, Sen narrows the scope of commitment compared to the scope he gives it in 'Rational Fools', and this narrowing would mean that acting on commitment as self-sacrificial. In his lectures on 'The Standard of Living', Sen writes: 'a case of "commitment" is observed when a person decides to do a thing (e.g., being helpful to another) despite its not being, in the net, beneficial to the agent himself' (1987b: 28). The definition suggests that not being 'in the net' beneficial to the agent be a necessary condition for actions choices on commitment. Not being in the net beneficial to the actor implies, contrary to Sen's analysis in 'Rational Fools', that the act must *decrease* the welfare of the actor; and this would make all choices based on commitment and, by implication, all commitment-based altruistic acts self-sacrificing. This narrowing of the scope of commitment is an anomaly which is nowhere else suggested in Sen's *oeuvre*. To be sure, Sen's focus in 'The Standard of Living' is different to that of 'Rational Fools'. In the former text, he writes, 'we are concerned primarily with effects rather than with motivations and thus the use of the distinction between "sympathy" and "commitment" is rather different here from its use in ["Rational Fools"]' (1987b: 28 note 12). But this shift of focus does not explain why Sen restricts the permissible welfare effects of choices based on commitment in 'The Standard of Living'. The definition of commitment in 'The Standard of Living' not only disregards the more inclusive definition of commitment from 'Rational Fools'; it also narrows the scope of the initial definition of commitment by excluding from the set of choices based on commitment those which, the agent believes, will increase but not maximize her welfare. And the definition conflicts with the conclusion for which I argued in Section II above, which was derived from Sen's pronouncements on commitment in 'Rational Fools'. The conclusion was that commitment was not to be defined in terms of any particular pattern of welfare which the agent expects to result from her choice but rather in terms of the nature of the reason on which the agent acts. We can do more than note the incongruity between Sen's writings here and make clear that, when analysing the expected welfare consequences of action in the context of commitment, Sen's unrestricted position in 'Rational Fools' is the one we will assume to be valid.

## Conclusion

This chapter has established that commitment is not to be defined in terms of the welfare consequences which the agent expects to redound to herself from acting on commitment. Instead, choices based on commitment are defined by their reason-based aetiology, that is, by their being motivated by a welfare-independent reason. This is what makes such choices counter-preferential. Sen associates the reasons which can motivate choices based on commitment with the agent's morals, though his understanding of morals is extremely broad. We have also determined the place of altruism in Sen's conceptual scheme. Although altruism can be defined to have affinities with either sympathy or commitment, Sen clearly demarcates a robust notion of altruism which has affinities to 'psychological' definitions of the term, though it is not identical with psychological altruism. As such, altruism is aligned with commitment rather than sympathy, and, as such, it is not egoistic in its motivation.

In presenting commitment in terms of reason-based choice in this chapter, I have said little about the strand of Sen's 1973 essay which called for a non-preference-based account of choice which is associated with acting on an as-if ranking. I merely stated, in Section II, that acting on an as-if ranking in Sen's 'Behaviour' essay resembles choices based on commitment as they are portrayed in 'Rational Fools' in that neither is characterized by a preference-based aetiology. Although parts of 'Rational Fools' discuss acting on as-if rankings, the concept of commitment can be elucidated, as I have done in the current chapter and as Sen does in much of 'Rational Fools', in abstraction from as-if rankings. Commitment, in the foregoing analysis, has been explained outside the context of strategic interaction, such as the prisoners' dilemma, which is the context in which Sen discusses as-if rankings in his 1973 essay. On the strength of this chapter, one would say that Sen does not conceive the reasons which ground commitments to be as-if reasons; if I pursue the eradication of torture through my actions, I am not acting as if I find torture abhorrent. But if commitment is related to acting on as-if rankings, and presumably it is, given that acting on as-if rankings involves making non-preference-based choices, we have still to explore how the two are related. This is the task of the following chapter which will draw closer thematic parallels between Sen's 'Behaviour' essay and 'Rational Fools'.

# 4 Commitment and meta-rankings

**Introduction**

Having commenced the analysis of 'Rational Fools' in the previous two chapters, I continue the task in this one by examining Sen's notion of meta-rankings. The latter part of 'Rational Fools' is occupied with meta-rankings, although Sen had already aired detailed thoughts on the theme in a conference presentation from 1972, subsequently published under the title 'Choice, Orderings and Morality' (Sen 1974a). One unifying thread which runs through both of these essays and is woven also in Sen's 'Behaviour' essay is acting on as-if rankings. Sen's understanding of acting on as-if rankings is further analysed in the current chapter in which the relationship between meta-ranking and commitment will be explored.

The chapter unfolds as follows. Section I lays out the idea behind meta-ranking and asks why Sen relates meta-ranking to morality. Sections II and III each look at a field of application of meta-ranking. The first is the prisoners' dilemma, the second weakness of will. As in his 1973 essay, in both his 1974a paper and in 'Rational Fools', Sen examines acting on as-if rankings as a way of achieving the social optimum, as Section II shows. In Section III, I examine how meta-rankings also allow Sen to conceive weakness of will, not as an all-or-nothing affair, according to which a choice either manifests weakness of will or it does not, but as a predicate which admits of gradations – one can be more or less weak (or strong) willed and therefore more or less moral in one's choices. Sen's analysis of weakness of will does not rely on the agent acting on as-if rankings but rather conceives her endeavour to be one of changing her preferences in a moral direction. This raises questions about the relationship between weakness of will and commitment. Section III also offers an account of the moral psychology of a person who makes and keeps commitments and of a person who makes but breaks commitments, and parallels between such people and the moral characters whom Aristotle depicts in his ethics are drawn. Section IV explores Sen's concept of personhood or identity and asks where personhood is to be located amidst the multiple rankings and meta-rankings which an agent is able to construct. The role of reason in the concept of personhood is brought to the fore here.

## I Meta-ranking

Imagine three alternatives, $x_1$, $x_2$, $x_3$, between which an individual can choose. The individual can rank these alternatives according to different criteria (Sen 1977a: 100–1). Ranking $A$ orders the alternatives according to the individual's 'personal welfare ordering' (which includes sympathy):

$$A: x_1 \geq x_2 \geq x_3.$$

Ranking $B$ abstracts from sympathy and orders the alternatives according to what Sen calls 'my "isolated" personal interests':

$$B: x_2 \geq x_1 \geq x_3.$$

Ranking $C$ is the ordering 'in terms of which actual choices are made by me' (Sen 1977a: 101). How one actually chooses might coincide with ranking $A$ or $B$, but it might be based on a 'compromise' between various criteria on which other rankings (like $A$ and $B$) are based. My actual choices might not be representable by a ranking at all, but let us assume that they can be represented by $C$, whereby:

$$C: x_1 \geq x_3 \geq x_2.$$

A further criterion according to which $x_1$, $x_2$ and $x_3$ can be ranked concerns their moral status. The 'most moral ranking', $M$, might or might not coincide with any of $A$, $B$ or $C$. There would, for example, be a coincidence between $M$ and $A$, if the individual held maximizing his personal welfare (including that derived via sympathy) to be the most moral basis on which to make choices. Whether $M$ coincides with a different ranking will depend on the individual's conception of morality. Once a person has ranked the options according to a variety of criteria and thus derived rankings ($A$, $B$, $C$, $M$ etc.), she can rank the rankings; this ranking of the rankings issues in a meta-ranking. If the rankings are morally meta-ranked, they will be ranked according to how moral they are, with $M$ being ranked first because, being a moral ranking of $x_1$, $x_2$ and $x_3$, it reflects the morality of the person making the ranking; $A$, $B$ and $C$, on the other hand, will be assigned places in the moral meta-ranking according to how they 'score' with regard to the person's morality. Moral meta-ranking therefore allows one to conceive of *degrees of morality* by ranking the rankings from the most to the least moral:

> Insofar as actual behaviour may be based on a compromise between claims of morality and the pursuit of various other objectives (including self-interest), one has to look at the relative moral standings of those action-rankings that are *not* 'most moral'.
> 
> (Sen 1977a: 100)

Sen (1977a: 101) proposes that $A$, $B$ and $C$ be morally meta-ranked as follows: $C \geq A \geq B$. If none of these three rankings corresponds to the individual's most moral ranking, $M$, we would have the meta-ranking: $M \geq C \geq A \geq B$.

Taken in itself, meta-ranking is a purely intellectual exercise. Options $x_1 \ldots x_n$ can be ranked according to infinitely many criteria, and these rankings can then be further ranked, again according to different criteria, thus issuing in as many meta-rankings as criteria. An agent could, for instance, arrange the available options into rankings *A, B, C ... N*, whereby these rankings might be constructed according to criteria such as their effects on the agent's consumption of sugar, the degree of racial prejudice they harbour or the likelihood that they will cause a world war. Once one has a series of these first-order rankings, each of which orders the options according to some criterion, these orderings can be meta-ranked. As Sen writes, 'meta-ranking is a general technique usable under alternative interpretations of the meta-ranking relation. It can be used to describe a particular ideology or a set of political priorities or a system of class interests' (Sen 1977a: 101). Meta-ranking, then, has no intrinsic connection to morality, but of all the imaginable meta-ranking relations, Sen is particularly interested in a moral meta-ranking. Why does he home in on moral meta-rankings?

Sen takes up the venerable question which concerns the relationship between rationality and morality (1974a: 74–5). He is interested in positing a theory of rational choice which has 'more structure' than that of orthodox economics. The 'traditional theory', he holds, has '*too little* structure' because it endows the rational agent with but '*one* preference ordering [which] is supposed to reflect his interests, represent his welfare, summarize his idea of what should be done, and describe his actual choices and behaviour' (1977a: 99). We can see, on reading this passage, why Sen is not more receptive to the idea of an ultimate preference ranking, as we discussed in Chapter One (Section III), for however encompassing such a preference ranking might be, it nevertheless equips the agent with one ranking for all occasions. The passage also explains why Sen does not warm to Daniel Hausman's notion of all-things-considered preferences about which Sen (2007: 352–4) makes some rather non-committal comments. Sen's ranking *C*, according to which an agent actually makes choices, seems to correspond with Hausman's idea of an all-things-considered ranking. It is the idea that people have '*one* all-purpose preference ordering' which renders them, Sen holds, somewhat moronic (1977a: 99), whence derives the titular fool of 'Rational Fools'.

As an antidote to the monotony of a person's preference ordering, Sen observes that there are theories of rational choice which offer more structure and do so by incorporating moral concerns. One such theory which Sen discusses is John Harsanyi's (Sen 1977a: 99–100). Harsanyi (1955) distinguishes two preference rankings an individual has – her 'ethical' and 'subjective' preferences. Harsanyi's ethical preferences express what an individual prefers 'on the basis of impersonal social considerations alone', and they are therefore 'impartial' (1955: 315). Subjective preferences, on the other hand, express what an individual 'actually prefers'. Harsanyi is concerned to make ethical preferences the basis of an individual's social welfare function, whereby an individual expresses her preference for social institutions under the assumptions that (i) she does not know how she would be placed in the society the institutions of which she is hypothetically choosing, and (ii) it is equiprobable that she will occupy any of the social positions in the society (Harsanyi 1955: 316). Harsanyi's distinction between these two types of preference resembles Arrow's conception of the individual as having a quotidian and an ideal ranking which was discussed in Chapter One (Section III). Whilst acknowledging that this attempt is a welcome antidote to 'too little structure', Sen demands yet more structure than Harsanyi offers because impartial considerations offer only one way in which a ranking of options can diverge from the agent's actual, or subjective, preferences. Choices based on commitment, as we saw in the previous chapter, involve counter-preferential choice and hence they do not issue from an agent's subjective preferences, in Harsanyi's sense. But committed choices are not necessarily impartial, for they can reflect highly partial attachments to one's family, class, community, profession and so on, all of which Sen captures under the heading of a person's 'morals' (Sen 1977a: 106; 1987a: 19–20). So Harsanyi's distinction between subjective and ethical preferences falls short of what Sen is seeking.[1] With the apparatus of moral meta-ranking, one can achieve a finer grained conception of morality, whereby morality can be conceived as a *graded* phenomenon, a matter of more or less, rather than all-or-nothing, as it is for Harsanyi. Sen applies the apparatus of moral meta-ranking to the possibility of overcoming the social inoptimality associated with the prisoners' dilemma (Sen 1974a: 78–9). This is the theme of the following section in which I resume the discussion of acting on an as-if ranking from Chapter One.

## II Morality, meta-ranking and the prisoners' dilemma

If each party to a prisoners' dilemma acts on what Sen calls her 'PD-preferences', she will select the dominant strategy, and the socially suboptimal outcome will ensue. PD-preferences are defined as representations of an agent's self-interest. If, instead, each player were to choose in accord with a different ranking of the available options, each could become better off (Sen 1974a: 78). For instance, if the players acted as if they had assurance-game (AG) preferences, whereby neither would choose to confess if she were assured that her counterpart would do likewise, a cooperative equilibrium would ensue, although a non-cooperative pairing, whereby each player 'defects' if she or he expects the other to do likewise, is also an equilibrium point of an assurance game. If players, on the other hand, acted as if they had other-regarding (OR) preferences, whereby each chose not to confess irrespective of his or her expectations about the other's behaviour, the cooperative result would be unique and each player would be better off compared to the equilibrium they would reach by acting on PD-preferences. 'Better off', here, means better off in terms of the player's true, PD-preferences (Sen 1974a: 79), just as it did in Sen (1973: 66). Sen, then, brings the apparatus of meta-ranking to bear on morality, not only because of his interest in the relationship between rationality and morality, but also because those attempts in the field of economic philosophy to address this relationship operate with a binary opposition between the two; although such an approach offers more structure than an approach which equips an agent with only one preference ranking, Sen finds two rankings too few. Meta-ranking holds out the prospect of adding further structure. Sen suggests that the meta-ranking of the three rankings mentioned above – PD, AG, OR – be one of ascending morality (1974a: 79). His reason for positing this order is that 'morality has got something to do with reaching social optimality'. By acting on AG- or OR-preferences, a player relinquishes the welfare-maximizing option: '[s]acrificing some individual gain – given the actions of others – for the sake of a rule of good behaviour by all which ultimately makes everyone better off is indeed one of the most talked-of aspects of morality' (Sen 1974a: 77–8).

'[T]he apparatus of *ranking of rankings* assists the reasoning which involves considering the merits of having different types of preferences (or of acting as if one had them)' (Sen 1977a: 103–4). Meta-ranking, then, is not merely a theoretical tool employed by economists who observe the behaviour of lay people; it is a practical tool which 'assists' people in their deliberation about which choices to make. The fillip which meta-ranking provides to people's reasoning comes from opening up two possibilities, both of which can overcome the social inoptimality of non-cooperative conduct. The possibilities are:

(i) Persuading the agent to act on orderings different to the PD-preferences which represent her actual preferences.
(ii) Persuading the agent to change her preferences so that considerations of self-interest no longer determine her motivation to act.

(Sen 1977a: 104)

These avenues of assistance are analogous to the two effects of socialist education on Chinese workers' degree of exertion in the production process which Sen discusses in his 1973 article (see Chapter One, Section IV). Let us direct our attention to the former case, for this is the one which requires that a person act on an as-if ranking. It is also the case which proves tricky for the view that, through her choices, an agent manifests her preferences in a straightforward way. Focusing on this case will also allow us to see what Sen's meta-ranking analysis has to do with commitment. The second possibility will be considered in the following section which is dedicated to the theme of weakness of will.

Under possibility (i), players' preferences are of the PD variety, so if they are to select the cooperative strategy, they must act as if they ranked the options in a different way. Sen imagines an individual who asks herself which preferences she would prefer her counterpart to have and then, 'on somewhat Kantian grounds', she acts as if she had the preference she wishes her counterpart to have (1977a: 103; cf. 1974a: 76; 1977b: 228). Sen continues: 'This line of reasoning requires [the player] to consider the modifications of the game that would be brought about by acting through commitment' (1977a: 103). And he describes the choices one makes when one follows this reasoning as counter-preferential (1977b: 228). The reason for making this identification is that, when one acts, not on one's preferences, but on an as-if ranking which derives from a moral norm, be it of a Kantian or other ilk, one's choices have a non-preference-based aetiology. The agent, that is, must have a reason for making choices based on an as-if ranking, and this reason overrides his preferences as causal determinants of his choices. Hence, we can conclude, on the basis of the analysis of the previous chapter, that acting on an as-if ranking means basing one's choices on commitment because all such cases are counter-preferential. This means that the reason on which one acts has something to do with morality.

Sen is not short of ideas as to the strategies open to players who wish to avoid the socially inoptimal outcome. A player might pursue a strategy of maximizing the other player's welfare (1973: 66); or perhaps each player selects a strategy which would achieve the social optimum on the assumption that her counterpart reciprocate this strategy (which is how Sen (1974a: 79) understands 'morality'). But these strategies do not reveal the player's reason for adopting them. And even, for instance, if we conceive maximizing my opposite number's welfare to be my goal, it is an as-if goal but not my real goal. It could be that my actual goal is based on my desire to increase my own welfare over and above what it would be if my counterpart and I both selected the dominant strategy (Sen 1973: 66; 1974a: 77, 83). Sen encourages this welfare-centred interpretation of acting on an as-if ranking in a reply to comments by J.W.N. Watkins (1974) in which Watkins reflects on Sen's 'Choice, Orderings and Morality'. After arguing that Watkins somewhat misses the point of his paper, Sen concludes his reply by stating that he had, in Sen (1974a), 'analysed the advantages of acting according to *as if* preferences–different from the real ones – precisely from the point of view of achievement of results' (1974b: 82). This raises the possibility that the goal of a person who acts on an as-if ranking is orientated to her own welfare. If this is so, there are grounds for denying the status of commitment to choices based on an as-if ranking. For let us recall from the previous chapter, that choices made by someone whose goal is orientated solely to increasing his own welfare – whether he is striving to maximize or increase his welfare – should be excluded from the realm of choices based on commitment because the latter are based on welfare-independent reasons. The word 'solely' here is important, for a different interpretation is possible: a party to a prisoners' dilemma who acts on an as-if ranking might state that her goal is to increase both her own and her counterpart's welfare in the name of achieving the *socially* optimal result. If so, her goal would not be exclusively *self*-welfare orientated, and this might allow an ascription of commitment to the choices she makes in pursuit of this goal. There is a lack of clarity here about the agent's goal which mirrors that in Sen's discussion of as-if rankings in his

'Behaviour' essay (see Chapter One, Section IV). Sen himself expresses misgivings about the explanation of cooperative conduct in a prisoners' dilemma on the basis of as-if preferences: '[w]hile there is considerable scope for getting such explanations in terms of moral reasoning involving metarankings and "as if" preferences, ... they are not quite adequate explanations of actual behavior' (1986b: 350). This matter is better addressed later in the monograph, after I have analysed Sen's understanding of what it is to act on social or moral norms (Chapter Five) and examined his post-'Rational Fools' work, in which the concept of goals comes more pronouncedly to the fore. The theme will reappear in Chapter Eight.

Sen's stance towards cooperative behaviour in his writings on as-if rankings from the 1970s carries the stamp of what he later calls prudential or advantage-based social morality (2009a: 202). This is the view he ascribes to the contractarian tradition in political philosophy which appeals to individuals' own benefit as a way of convincing them of the rationality of limiting their behavioural repertoire. If all other people do likewise, all will benefit *vis-à-vis* the status quo or 'natural condition' of humankind. The individual's goal is clearly related to his own advantage. The difference between Sen's approach and that of contractarians is that the latter focus on situations which are regulated by a formal, enforceable contract, whereas Sen's focus is upon 'social norms that may work voluntarily' (2009a: 203). Since the working of social norms is a topic of the chapters mentioned in the previous paragraph, I will close the current discussion of acting on as-if rankings here.

## III Weakness of will

We turn, in this section, to Sen's analyses of weakness of will which relate to the phenomenon to non-strategic choice situations. This provides a different context for the application of meta-rankings than social dilemma situations. At least this is what Sen's examples suggest. Sen also recommends meta-rankings as a tool for elucidating weakness of will because a person 'might wish to have a different preference ordering $R$ from the one he does have' (1974a: 80–1). In the context of weakness of will, then, meta-rankings can assist the agent to persuade himself to change his preferences and not merely to act as if he had different preferences. The phenomena of both weakness and strength of will give us insight into the moral psychology of the human agent, as Sen understands it.

Consider a meat-eating person who wishes to adhere to a strictly vegetarian diet because of his moral disapproval of killing animals for food. Should he fail to adhere to his desired diet, some observers would say that he manifests weakness of will. Sen (1974a: 81) asserts that this description 'might be a bit glib'. It would be glib, one may presume, because the only thing which is taken into account by such a characterization is whether the person succeeds in making the choice which he conceives to be the most moral; no credit would be given thereby to partial success, for example eating meat on only one day of the week or cutting factory-farmed meat out of his diet. Characterizing any failure to adhere exclusively to a vegetarian diet as weakness of will is to use a 'zero–one contrast' between one's actual choices and one's desired preferences, that is those which reflect one's moral values. A graded judgement, Sen submits, according to which one preference pattern may be deemed morally superior to another though not the most moral, would add nuance to the description of the agent's predicament (Sen 1974a: 80–1). Meta-rankings, Sen argues, offer the agent a 'sequence of preference orderings of outcomes ranked by this person in moral terms' (1974a: 80). The 'assistance' offered by these rankings lies in the identification of one ordering which the agent does not currently have but wishes to acquire. He meta-ranks this ordering higher than his extant one and can use it as an ideal toward which he can lure his actual preferences. Whilst a gap persists between his actual preferences and his most moral ranking, the agent can (i) act on his actual preferences, which, by his own admission, would be a case of weakness of will, for he would be choosing what he deems to be the wrong thing to do, (ii) approach his most moral ranking by basing his choices on an intermediate ranking which is nearer to though still short of his ideal, or (iii) act on his most moral ideal ranking. Strategy (ii) is something for which Sen wishes to commend the agent, though those who operate with a zero–one notion of weakness of will would spare no praise for this agent's accomplishment.

In the context of meta-rankings, one might characterize an agent who adopts either strategy (ii) or (iii) to be acting on an as-if ranking because he is substituting his actual, as yet unchanged, preferences with a different, more moral, ranking as a basis for making choices, rather like a party to the prisoners' dilemma does when she 'suspends' her rational calculus (Sen 1973: 64) and adopts a rule of good behaviour as a guide to choosing. One the other hand, one might relinquish the as-if framework for interpreting someone who adopts strategy (ii) or (iii) and instead characterize the non-preference-based choices through which he manifests strength of will in terms with which Sen first introduces commitment in 'Rational Fools'. According to this characterization, the agent would simply have a reason to resist the promptings of his self-interested preferences, whereby the causal force of this reason in motivating him to choose is stronger than that of his preferences. Nothing as-iffy is needed to explain these choices. The two characterizations of the agent's choices are contending explanations of the *explanandum* under consideration. Each explanation characterizes the agent's choices as manifestations of strength of will but do so in different ways. Let us now examine the moral psychology of this agent in the various stages of his preference reform and also ask how the agent's choices relate to commitment.

The agent obviously has a moral reason to adhere to a vegetarian diet, and if he acts on this reason, his choices must go against his carnivorous cravings. If his reason makes him willing to forgo his welfare-maximizing option of eating meat, his culinary choices are based on commitment. He resembles Aristotle's *enkratēs*, the continent person, who masters herself in the face of unruly passions. The continent person's appetites (preferences) conflict with reason, and although her preferences urge her to do what she knows to be wrong, she hearkens to reason and does the right thing (Aristotle 1985: 1151b32–1152a2), that is, that which accords with her moral reason. On those occasions of weakness on which the individual succumbs to the temptation of eating meat, he resembles Aristotle's *akratēs*, the incontinent person, whose passions get the better of her such that she knowingly chooses to do what she holds to be the wrong thing. In his analysis of weakness of will, Sen suggests that the individual not only wishes to make vegetarian choices but also to *acquire* vegetarian preferences (1974a: 80–1; 1977a: 101). The individual wishes to close the gap between reason and preference by altering the latter so that his preferences conform to reason. He therefore wishes to resemble those Chinese workers who, during the Great Leap Forward, underwent a 'reorientation of the[ir] individual welfare functions' such that they no longer had preference to shirk at the workplace (Sen 1973: 71). In the words with which Watkins (1974: 75) describes Sen's position, the individual wishes to 'lick his preferences into a good shape', though as Sen states, and as we noted in Chapter One (Section IV), Sen is not terribly excited about preference changes of the sort described because he is interested in the relationship between preferences as they actually are (before any change might occur) and the choices an individual makes (Sen 1974a: 82).

Let us not, however, be put off by Sen's relative disinterest in preference change in a moral direction. I will assume that our reluctant carnivore successfully transforms his preferences such that he truly has an aversion to meat eating. He no longer has to overcome his desire to eat meat because he now has the pukka article – real vegetarian preferences. Making vegetarian choices, then, means choosing in accordance with his (transformed) preferences. Does this mean that his vegetarian choices are no longer based on commitment? To answer this question, we must distinguish two types of choice, both of which maximize the individual's welfare:

(1) choices which have (i) a preference-based aetiology and which therefore maximize the agent's expected welfare, whereby (ii) they happen to coincide with the choices the agent believes to be morally right;
(2) choices which have (i) a reason-based aetiology, the reason being given by the agent's commitment to vegetarianism, whereby (ii) these choices coincide with the choices the agent believes will maximize his welfare.

In Chapter Three, we ascertained that what characterizes all choices based commitment is their non-preference-based aetiology, and therefore only type-(2) choices may be said to be based on commitment. If an individual's choice of vegetarian diet is motivated by the moral reason that it is wrong to kill animals, his choices are based on commitment. The fact that these choices maximize his reformed welfare function is neither here nor there for the purpose of this classification, for he would make the same choices if he expected them not to maximize his welfare. In other words, his reason for choosing vegetarianism motivates his choice, and so Sen's counterfactual condition applies to these welfare-maximizing choices. Having a reason-based aetiology, type-(2) choices must therefore be counter-preferential. Type-(1) choices, by contrast, are not based on commitment on account of their preference-based aetiology. Although these choices accord with a moral value which the agent holds, their relationship to that value is contingent because the choices are based, not on that value, but on his preferences. The distinction between acting on commitment and acting on one's preferences might not be apparent to a person who has aligned his preferences with his moral values; for in each case, the agent's choices will not give rise to an enkratic tension between reason and preference. Prior to the alignment of reason and preference, the tension between what one ought to do (given by one's commitment) and what one wants to do (given by one's preferences) is clear.

After his preferences become vegetarian, then, the individual's type-(2) choices are based on commitment. The individual's choices are like those of Aristotle's virtuous person insofar as he chooses $x$ because $x$ is choiceworthy (*hairetos*) in itself. The individual also derives pleasure from making these choices, which he did not prior to the alignment of his preferences with his moral values, when, that is, his choices were enkratic. The virtuous person feels no disharmony between his reason for choosing on the basis of a commitment and his preferences because he does not have to sacrifice his welfare in favour of acting on a commitment; he takes pleasure in doing what is right because his preferences have been sufficiently schooled that no gap exists between what he deems choiceworthy in itself and what he prefers. According to Aristotle, if one is truly virtuous, the pleasure one feels when one acts virtuously supervenes on one's knowledge that one is acting virtuously. Pleasures 'come second, after' (*deuterōs*) the actions undertaken; they therefore 'consummate' (*teleioi*) the action (Aristotle 1985: 1176a29; 1174b22–3, 32–3). Hence, to be virtuous, according to Aristotle, one must act having first acknowledged that the choice one is making is good. A person who acts on appetite might perform the same acts as a virtuous person, but her action, if it is based on appetite, has only a coincidental relationship to virtue. The choices one makes from this state correspond to type-(1) choices above; in such a case, one has, one might say, the luck of having a taste for virtuous actions, but this falls short of acting in the knowledge that virtuous actions are choiceworthy. Appetite-based actions have the wrong aetiology to be classed as virtuous, just as type-(1) choices have the wrong aetiology to be based on commitment. Aristotle's virtuous person, then, is akin to the person who makes type-(2) choices in the context of commitment. These choices, and they alone, have a reason-based aetiology and for that reason they are, in contrast to type-(1) choices, counter-preferential.

Although she bears a resemblance to someone who acts on commitment, Aristotle's virtuous person is of little interest to Sen because her choices do not give rise to enkratic tension between reason and preference. The virtuous person's choices resemble, as I have noted above, those of Chinese workers who, as a result of socialist education by the Party, have come to prefer cooperative conduct and hence do not shirk at the workplace. Preferences, here, respond to and follow education, and hence the enkratic tension disappears. Despite his relative disinterest in these choices, Sen's analysis allows us to make an important distinction when we conceptualize them, a distinction which those beholden to rational choice theory cannot make. Sen allows for a welfare-maximizing choice to be based on reason rather than on preference. He would characterize type-(2) choices above by saying that they are in accordance with the agent's preferences, although the agent does not base her choices on her preferences. This formulation is unavailable to a rational choice theorist who adheres to the aetiological relationship between preference and choice, and therefore holds all choices to be causally based on preference. Accordingly, a welfare-maximizing commitment is no different from a choice based on the goal of welfare maximization when viewed through the lens of orthodox rational choice theory.

## IV Preferences, meta-rankings and the concept of a person

Sen's analysis of meta-rankings gives rise to thoughts on his conception of identity, or personhood, as I shall call it henceforth. One matter to clarify here is the relationship between a person, her preferences and the reasons on which she bases her choices.

It might be thought that, for Sen, an agent's PD-preferences represent her true self. Sen might be held to encourage this suggestion when he describes these preferences as the agent's 'true', 'real' or 'actual' preferences (1973: 66; 1977a: 103). He stresses that, when an agent who finds herself in a prisoners' dilemma situation acts on an as-if ranking which prompts her to select the cooperative strategy, she can increase her welfare *in terms of her true (PD) preferences* if her counterpart also cooperates (1973: 66; 1974a: 78). Do such descriptions imply that there is something more authentic about the agent's PD-preferences compared to other rankings on which the agent might act, something, that is, which has a closer relationship with the concept of personhood than other, more moral, rankings? The answer is 'no', for one's PD-preferences are merely one representation of the options available, a representation according to the welfare one would derive from those options. There are, as the analysis of meta-ranking makes clear, countless other ways of representing the options, and Sen clearly abjures the idea that personhood is to be identified solely or even more closely with any *one* ranking of options (1977a: 99). A single ranking, whatever ordering criterion underlies it, is not sufficient to represent the variety of human interests and cannot therefore serve to unlock Sen's concept of a person. This explains his demand for 'more structure' in a theory of rational choice. It might appear that Sen makes a person's PD preferences more central to the concept of personhood when he refers to them as the person's true or actual preferences, but this reflects a methodological tactic in his critique of revealed preference theory; for in assuming that a person's preferences are self-interested and that acting on an as-if ranking does not involve a change of these preferences, the gap between preference and choice comes into view, and it is this gap which revealed preference theory denies. As to the point that acting on an as-if ranking can make one better off in terms of one's real (PD) preferences, Sen is not making PD preferences more central than others to the concept of personhood when he writes these words; rather his point here reflects an analytic truth about the concept of PD preferences, namely, that a person's preference ranking, and only this ranking, orders options in terms of their effects on a person's welfare. However 'major' a motive self-interest might be (and Sen (in Klamer 1989: 142) thinks that it is major), this does not signify anything special about self-interested preferences in relation to personhood. Consequently, if we are seeking Sen's concept of a person, we must not identify it with any particular ranking of options a person entertains. The concept of personhood must exist beyond any of the myriad rankings of options on which the agent can base her choices.

Let us therefore consider the agent's ranking of those rankings, her meta-rankings. Meta-rankings, Sen tells us, 'can provide the format for expressing what preferences one would prefer to have', for example 'I wish I liked vegetarian foods more' (1977a: 101; cf. 2002a: 617, 670). If a person does not have the preferences of which she approves, she can choose to base her choices on an as-if ranking which is more in line with, or corresponds to, the ranking she wishes to have. She can also take measures to change her preferences in the direction desired. The vegetarianism passage just cited indicates that, crucial to the concept of personhood, in Sen's eyes, is the ability to form preferences over one's preferences. If this were Sen's view, it would resemble that of Harry Frankfurt for whom the concept of a person is to be located in an agent's second-order desires which are the arbiter of which first-order desires one ought to have (Frankfurt 1971). Sen refers to philosophical literature on second-order desires (including Frankfurt's work) (e.g. Sen 1987a: 82–3 note 22; 2002a: 12), and Albert Hirschman (1982: 70) notes the 'very similar' nature of Frankfurt's and Sen's work on meta-preferences. If this were to be the best expression of Sen's view of personhood, he would, however, be open to a charge made against Frankfurt by Gary Watson (1975: 218), namely: if meta-preferences are simply preferences, albeit of a higher order than first-order preferences, their existence merely adds to the 'number of contenders' which vie to determine the agent's choices; but what gives a higher-order preference authority over those of a lower order? Frankfurt (1971: 16) avers that the agent 'identifies' with a particular first-order desire and this identification 'resounds' into the higher registers of one's desires where it is affirmed by higher-order desires. Other first-order desires to not reverberate in such a way, and therein one recognizes their relative unimportance to the person who has them. Frankfurt's metaphor is more striking than it is convincing, for it gives no indication as to how a person recognizes the sonority of lower-order desires or according to which criteria she makes her decisive identification, at a higher order of preference, with her first-order preferences. This is not, therefore, the view of a person we should ascribe to Sen if we can help it, and I shall argue below that Sen provides good grounds for rejecting this view of the person. We can find a more convincing notion of personhood in Sen's *opus*, and Frankfurt gives us our cue by introducing the concept of identity, about which Sen has had much to say.

In his later work, Sen emphasizes a person's many identities and abjures the view that a person may be reduced to one. One's identity can perfectly easily consist in being:

> an Asian, an Indian citizen, a Bengali with Bangladeshi ancestry, an American or British resident, an economist, a dabbler in philosophy, an author, a Sanskritist, a strong believer in secularism and democracy, a man, a feminist, a heterosexual, a defender of gay and lesbian rights, with a nonreligious lifestyle, from a Hindu background, a non-Brahmin, and a nonbeliever in an afterlife.
>
> (Sen 2006: 19)

Sometimes such identities can co-exist without tension. And which identity comes to the fore is often specific to context such that prioritizing one identity need not lead one to compromise or deny another (Sen 2006: 29). When, for instance, one is invited to a college reunion, one's identity as a member of the graduating class in Biochemistry at the University of Otago in 1985 comes to the fore; until, perhaps, one overhears a racist comment, at which point one's identity as a Maori is felt with most urgency without, however, negating or rendering unimportant one's *alma mater*, degree subject, year of graduation and so on as constitutive of one's identity. On other occasions, however, one's identities compete in the sense that they make demands which pull a person in different directions (Sen 2004: 13). Consider a person who proudly identifies himself with his professional status as a civil servant but also as a member of a minority ethnic group which has suffered discrimination at the hands of a majority ethnicity. If this person is called upon to recommend one of two hundred job applicants for a position in the civil service, the demands of his profession require him to make his recommendation on 'impartial', merit-based criteria alone. But he might find that doing so conflicts with his ethnic identity which, he feels, demands that he level a historically crooked playing field by favouring a candidate from his own ethic group (cf. Sen 2004: 15; 2006: 32). Both of the aforementioned identities give the person a commitment – they provide him with reasons for different courses of action, neither of which is chosen because the person expects them to redound to his self-interest. One may say, here, that each of a person's identities gives him an ordering criterion for ranking the options before him. Ordering the list of candidates according to the civil servant's professional identity will lead to a different ordering of the candidates when he judges them from the perspective of loyalty to his ethnicity. Or he might make some sort of compromise between the two rankings and choose in accord with a ranking which reflects this compromise. Seeing oneself as the bearer of only one identity, for example as a member of a particular ethnic group, and evaluating the options before oneself in terms of this one ordering criterion is akin, in the realm of personhood, to being a rational fool who has only one ranking criterion to express everything which is in some way important or of value to oneself. A person's identity, Sen holds, is not monotonous but plural. And personhood may be understood to be the ongoing work of doing justice to these multiple identities and ordering the demands which they make on a person.

If, then, different identities give a person a commitment, identities must be reason-giving in nature. Identities, that is, furnish a person with different, and sometimes competing, reasons to act. But identity does not tell us which reasons should be effective in determining the person's action. The person described in the previous paragraph feels the pull of his civil-service loyalties as well as of his ethnic loyalties, and he could adduce good reasons for making either a purely merit-based recommendation or for favouring a candidate from his own ethnic community. But he must choose with which identity he should side and therefore on which of the competing reasons he is to act. Identity alone cannot guide his practical reasoning. In making this choice, Sen holds, he must subject the competing reasons to scrutiny, *reasoned* scrutiny. This involves ascertaining which reasons can be reflectively sustained when critically examined (Sen 2009a: 180). Hence, one's reasons for acting must pass the court of reason if they are to be deemed, by the individual who holds those reasons, to be fully rational.

Sen therefore connects identity, or personhood as I have been calling it, which endows a person with loyalties to certain causes or groups, with the sorts of reason required to make choices based on commitment. Commitments do not always issue from such loyalties based on our feelings of identity (Sen 2006: 22–3) but I will focus here on those which do. These are the commitments which Sen already brought to light in 'Rational Fools', those which stem from a loyalty to a group 'intermediate to oneself and all' (1977a: 106), as discussed in Section III of the previous chapter. Such commitments, it will be recalled, are 'closely connected to one's morals' (Sen 1977a: 93), and hence, when one feels the reason-giving pull of such commitments, one is necessarily called upon to judge the efficacy of the moral values with which one identifies. Consequently, in subjecting one's reasons for action to scrutiny, one is necessarily subjecting one's moral values to scrutiny, and this implies a subordination of morality to reason (Sen 2000c: 274). Reason, one may say, is the meta-ranking arbiter through which reasons for action derived from identities must pass if one is to make a rational choice. It is in reason that one finds a concept of the person which exists beyond one's myriad identities and the rankings associated with them. The scrutiny of reason is located at the level of meta-rankings, above the myriad first-order rankings with which the person ranks the options between which she must choose (Sen 2002a: 616).

Without it, a person's freedom or autonomy would be compromised, for she would either be unable to escape the dictates of a single preference ranking if one preference ranking were all she had; or, if she is equipped with multiple first-order rankings, she would be unable to arbitrate rationally between them in any given instance of choice. Reason, and its power to scrutinize different first-order rankings, allows one to ascertain that one would value having different preferences (2002a: 669–71). In performing this exercise of critical scrutiny, '[t]he person herself is the ultimate authority in deciding what preferences make sense' (2002a: 671).

In conceiving Sen's concept of personhood thus, do we avoid the criticism which Watson levels at Frankfurt regarding the latter's second-order desires? For Sen might be thought to transpose the same problem from the level of desire to the level of reason: whereas Frankfurt adds higher-order desires to the fray of practical reason, Sen adds further doses of reason into the *mélange* and hopes that reasoned scrutiny will be able arbitrate between competing reasons for action. But why should reason of a higher order (that is, reasoned scrutiny) be able to do this any better than higher-order desires or preferences? Sen has a response to this, namely, that reason has a better claim than desire to adjudicate itself: 'in disputing the validity of reason we have to give reasons' (2000c: 288). This statement has a validity which it would not if we substituted the words 'reason' and 'reasons' with 'desire' and 'desires', or 'preference' and 'preferences' respectively. And whereas one can justify one's desires with reasons, doing the opposite – justifying one's reasons by appeal to one's desires – is questionable. Sen never quite states this explicitly but comes close to it when he outlines the relationship between *valuing* and desiring. He assents to the sense of the proposition: '*I value x, and so I desire it*', but not to the proposition: '*I desire x and so I value it*' (1999/1987: 21). Sen rejects the latter proposition because desiring in itself is not a valuation or a source of valuation whereas valuation is a source of desire. One has, that is, a good reason for desiring something if one values it, but desiring something does not in itself give one reason to value it (1985a: 196). Valuation, in contrast to desiring, is '*reflective* activity' (1999/1987: 19), by which I take Sen to mean that it is one which is subject to reasoned justification. What Sen calls 'valuation', here, corresponds to what he later terms reflection or reasoned scrutiny.

The 'reasoned scrutiny' formulation allows for the two possibilities we have explored in this chapter. If one's preferences do not withstand reasoned scrutiny, the agent can (i) act as if she had more reasonable preferences, or (ii) takes measures to change her preferences so that reason and preference become aligned with one another. Indeed, (i) can lead to (ii) if, following Aristotle, we give credence to the judgement that we become virtuous by performing virtuous actions (1985: 1103a1–2). That is, coaxing oneself into acting on a more moral ranking than that reflected by one's extant preferences can, over time, become habitual to the point that one actually comes to prefer acting in this more moral manner, at which point, any enkratic tension about one's choices disappears.

Reason has a more extensive role in Sen's estimation than that accorded to it by orthodox rational choice theory (Sen 2005a: 17). The role of reason in rational choice theory is limited to formal aspects of the preference function, for example, ordering preferences in a way which ensures that there is no intransitivity; but it is not conceived to play a substantive role of helping the individual decide what is of value or on which preference ordering the individual should act. For Sen, reason gives us the freedom to pursue things other than our self-interest, and hence it can liberate a person from her preferences.

## Conclusion

The modestly described 'general technique' (Sen 1977a: 101) of meta-rankings transpires to be of great import to Sen's work. The idea first appeared in Sen (1973) and reaches fruition in 'Choice, Orderings and Morality' and 'Rational Fools'. The fecundity of this general technique is shown in the use to which Sen puts it in analysing weakness of will and cooperative conduct in prisoners' dilemmas. But it also helps to unlock Sen's conception of personhood and the reach of reason in rational choice. The analysis of prisoners' dilemmas in light of meta-rankings once again raised the question about the moral status of the person who acts on an as-if moral ranking which holds out the prospect of improving on the non-cooperative equilibrium of the prisoners' dilemma. On the one hand, we can ascertain that the as-if moral actor does not maximize her welfare by basing her choices on such an ordering. And by acting on such an ordering, the actor's choices mirror those which morality commands. But how to characterize the moral status of such choices is not easily ascertained without information about the actor's goal for making such choices. It was argued in Section IV that Sen's analysis of cooperative behaviour was underlain by a prudential morality which, *ipso facto*, means that individuals have self-interested reasons for behaving morally if they believe that their conduct will be reciprocated by others. Sen, however, is not explicit about this, and we will seek further enlightenment on this topic in Chapter Eight when we investigate his later work.

The analysis of the current chapter has also exposed but not resolved an opposition between two accounts of a person who is susceptible to weakness of will. A presupposition of this susceptibility is a gap between reason and preference, which, when choices are determined by reason, makes those choices enkratic. In Section III above, I presented two possible accounts of an enkratic chooser. According to the first, the agent, because she has preferences which conflict with reason, acts as if she had different preferences when she manifests strength of will. In the second account, the agent recognizes the weight of reason *vis-à-vis* preference and acts on the former whilst resisting the latter. The agent in this latter account does not act as if his reason outweighs his preference but really has better grounds for acting on reason rather than on preference. Both accounts portray the enkratic choices to have a reason-based aetiology and so the choices are based on commitment. But which one better describes the choices and which captures better what Sen means by commitment is not easy to ascertain, and this is a further matter which will receive elucidation in Chapter Eight.

## Note

1 Sen (1977a: 85, 99) also criticises Francis Ysidro Edgeworth for limiting his analysis of the possible wellsprings of human action to egoism and non-egoism, the latter of which takes the form of classical utilitarianism which is impartial in a way which Sen's understanding of a person's 'morals' does not have to be. Dismissing the applicability of classical utilitarianism to economics ('trade'), Edgeworth holds that only egoistic motivation is of relevance to economic action.

# 5 Norms and commitment

**Introduction**

A theme which accompanies Sen's analyses of acting on as-if rankings is, as we have seen in foregoing chapters, that of acting on moral rules of behaviour or social norms. I turn to Sen's understanding of norm-following conduct in this chapter. I start by examining Sen's apples example from 'Rational Fools' with which he elucidates the distinction between sympathy and commitment. Sen's interpretation of the example has been challenged by Geoffrey Brennan whose criticism of Sen is used to clarify Sen's understanding of sympathy and commitment, his conceptualization of norm following and the relationship of agent relativity to both sympathy and commitment.

The chapter is structured in the following manner. Section I scrutinizes the apples example itself and it deals with issues of interpreting an example which is presented with such brevity. Following Brennan, I adopt a norm-following account of the main protagonist of Sen's example, and, in Section II, I explain Brennan's scepticism that the example demonstrates, as Sen claims it does, the nature of commitment. I then compare Brennan's and Sen's respective understanding of norm-following behaviour whereby I argue that Brennan's view of the phenomenon is at odds with Sen's. Section III goes on to contrast different models of norm following and highlights the centrality of counter-preferential choice in Sen's understanding thereof. This understanding is, I argue, something which makes Sen a heterodox economist. In Section IV, I draw on remarks from Brennan's commentary on Sen to argue that there is a connection between commitment and agent relativity. Sen has contributed to philosophical debates on agent relativity but never has he made its relationship to commitment explicit.

**I Apples**

Brennan (2007) offers an examination of Sen's apples example, to my knowledge, the first sustained and therefore overdue scrutiny to which the example has been exposed. Brennan (2007: 118) adverts to the 'risk of weighing down a striking example with an excess of analysis', and I fear that I will burden it yet further in a way which could sully the beauty of an example which, one might hold, is better left to speak for itself. What necessitates this analysis is the lack of detail, context and commentary which Sen gives the reader (the entire paragraph which contains the example occupies fewer than a dozen lines of printed page). If left to speak for itself, the example would do so polyvocally, and how one interprets it will vary according to the way in which one fills in the gaps that Sen leaves in his vignette.

First the example – 'of two boys who find two apples, one large and one small' – and then Sen's remarks thereon:

> Boy *A* tells boy *B*, 'You choose'. *B* immediately picks the larger apple. *A* is upset and permits himself the remark that this was grossly unfair. 'Why?' asks *B*. 'Which one would *you* have chosen, if you were to choose rather than me?' 'The smaller one, of course', *A* replies. *B* is now triumphant: 'Then what are you complaining about? That's the one you've got!' *B* certainly wins this round of the argument, but in fact *A* would have lost nothing from *B*'s choice had his own hypothetical choice of the smaller apple been based on sympathy as opposed to commitment. *A*'s anger indicates that this was probably not the case.
>
> (Sen 1977a: 93)[1]

How is the apples example supposed to illustrate the distinction between sympathy and commitment? Let us begin with the hypothetical choice with which Sen ends his example, namely, if *A* had chosen first. In this scenario, *A*, by his own declaration, would have chosen the smaller apple, and had he done so out of sympathy, Sen holds, *A* would have 'lost nothing'. Underlying this claim is presumably the following thought: if *A* had acted sympathetically, he would have derived personal benefit from beholding *B*'s satisfaction at getting the bigger apple (the apple which, *A* presumes, *B* would prefer). Note that Sen is dealing with a case in which *A*'s hypothetical choice is *based on sympathy*, as defined in Chapter Two. If *B* had played no part in the example, *A* would have been faced with a simple choice between two apples and he would presumably have chosen the larger one. However, with *B* on hand, the sacrifice of welfare which the sympathetic *A* would have felt when he relinquished the larger apple would have been outweighed by *A*'s sympathetic pleasure with *B* who gets the larger apple. By making a choice based on sympathy, then, *A* would have enjoyed a net increase in his personal welfare had he been in the position of first chooser and had chosen the smaller apple. So much for the hypothetical case in which *A* chooses first and is imagined to have been sympathetic towards *B*'s welfare. In the actual example, neither of these is the case, at least if we understand the example as Sen understands it.

In the example as it is actually depicted, *B* is prompted to choose first and chooses the larger apple. *B* might have done so simply because he thought that *A* would prefer the smaller one, though *B* is quickly disabused of this thought when *A* tells him that he, *B*, has been 'grossly unfair'. *B*'s apparent innocence with regard to the fact that *A* might be peeved by *B*'s choice of the larger apple might be based on the thought that *B* believes that *A* has sympathetic feelings towards him. *A*'s sympathy with *B* should not, *B* believes, be conditional on which of the boys chooses first, for the best outcome for both boys would be the same in each case – *B* getting the larger apple, and *A* deriving sympathetic welfare from his knowledge that *B* gets the apple from which he, *B*, maximizes his welfare. So if *B* believes that *A* would have chosen the smaller apple had *A* chosen first, that would appear to endow *B* with *carte blanche* to take the larger apple with impunity. And so it might have been, if the boys had both conceived the outcome narrowly, that is, in terms of what Sen (1997: 159) calls 'culmination outcomes'. Had they done so, the boys would have been concerned only with who gets which apple. Boy *A*, however, is obviously concerned with 'comprehensive outcomes', that is, with the manner in which the culmination outcome arises. According to comprehensive reckoning, *A* getting the smaller apple when *A* chooses first is a different outcome to *A* getting the smaller apple when *B* chooses first.[2] *B* obviously errs in forming his expectations about *A*'s reaction to *B*'s choice of the larger apple, and Sen concludes that *A*'s umbrage indicates that his behaviour is based on commitment, not sympathy. How does *A*'s disgruntlement indicate this? Let us turn to Brennan's interpretation.

Brennan (2007: 118) suggests that *A* adheres to a norm of politeness. Not only that: *A* obviously expects *B* to adhere to this norm as well, and *B*'s transgression of the norm is the source of *A*'s vexation. This interpretation is not only plausible but brings us to the topic of norms which I analyse in the coming section. Before we do so, however, I wish to draw attention to the skeletal nature of Sen's apples example, which allows one to interpret it variously according to how one fills in the many gaps which Sen leaves open. To finish this section, then, I offer an alternative account of the apples example – congruent with Sen's depiction – to show how flexibly the interaction between the two boys can be interpreted.

The alternative account makes *A* look less innocent than Sen suggests. The imperative 'You choose', with which *A* kicks off the interaction, may be seen as a strategic attempt by *A* to get the larger apple, the one which will maximize *A*'s welfare. Expecting, or at least hoping, that *B* will feel the weight of the norm of politeness which hangs over the situation, *A* deliberately places *B* into the position of the first chooser with the following thought in mind: '*B* surely wouldn't have the *chutzpah* to take the larger apple if I manoeuvre him into the position of first chooser because *B*, selfish though he can be, will feel a sense of reverence toward norms of politeness, and hence he will feel forced to take the smaller apple if he chooses first'. We may add that *B* would not even have to revere the norms of politeness for *A*'s scheme to succeed; if *B* only cared about his reputation for decorum, this might suffice to make him choose the smaller apple, lest *A* divulge news of *B*'s boorish behaviour to other people after *B* has taken the larger apple. As it happens, *B* is content to be boorish and he takes the bigger apple. Or perhaps *B* senses *A*'s attempt to manipulate him and decides that it is more important to teach *A* a lesson by taking the larger apple (which also conveniently maximizes *B*'s welfare) than it is to show respect to the rules of politeness. Either way, *A*'s scheme fails, and the only solace he can take is in chiding *B* for being so impolite as to take the bigger apple. *A*'s castigation of *B* is a continuation of the shenanigans which *A* has been up to all along, for *A* thereby feigns innocence of his attempt to manipulate *B*; *B*, and anyone else who might have observed *A*'s conduct will, *A* hopes, believe that his 'You choose' offer was a genuine gesture of politeness which, compared to *B*'s 'greedy' reaction, allows *A* to leave the situation as the wounded hero. If this account of the apples example were depicted in extensive form, the 'game' would have started, not with *B*'s choice of the larger apple but with *A* suggesting that *B* choose first.

One could go on with variations in the interpretation of Sen's apples example, though the ambiguity of interpretation would not be dispelled thereby. Sen might disagree that the example is ambiguous, and this would explain why he is not at pains to elucidate it. He even returns to the example in his later work in which he suggests that the conclusion to draw from it is: '*[r]easons* for choice do make a difference – not just the *fact* of choice' (2002a: 50). This pithy conclusion is also one which suggests that, in Sen's eye at least, the example is self-explanatory. It is time now to turn to the substantive disagreement between Brennan and Sen with regard to the way in which each depicts the choice situation in the apples example. The pivotal point is the way in which they conceive of norm-following behaviour.

## II Norms and preferences

Let us again place *A* before his hypothetical choice as first chooser and review how Brennan conceives *A*'s choice. Had he chosen first, Brennan argues, *A* would have faced a simple trade-off between two 'objects of desire' (2007: 119), namely, being polite and getting the larger apple. If *A* had chosen the smaller apple, it would have shown that *A* values being polite more than getting the larger apple. *B* suffers less compunction about being impolite; politeness, from *B*'s point of view, may be traded off in favour of getting his hands on a larger apple. Interpreted thus, the example poses no challenge to the orthodox notion of rational choice (Brennan 2007: 118–19; cf. Elster 1989; Goldfarb and Griffith 1991: 66): there are two objects of desire regarding which *A* and *B* have different preferences; *A* prefers to sacrifice the larger apple in favour of polite behaviour, and *B* prefers the opposite. The whole conceptual baggage – in particular, the conceptualization of *A*'s behaviour in terms of commitment and counter-preferential choice – with which Sen explains the situation is, according to Brennan, unnecessary.

According to Brennan's interpretation of norm following, then, if *A* had been in the position of first chooser, he would have looked for a way to suspend these tiresome norms of politeness, for they get in the way of his welfare-maximizing choice of taking the larger apple. But norms cannot be simply wished away, and so upon considering the negative after-effects of taking the larger apple (e.g., acquiring the reputation for being uncouth, or being subject to the reproaches of others), *A* would have adhered to the norms of politeness and chosen the smaller apple. Given the existence of these norms, *A* would have maximized his welfare by choosing the smaller apple, for he would thereby have avoided the reproofs of others. Brennan writes: 'it is perfectly proper to treat agents as having preferences for norm-fulfilment' (2007: 122). Indeed, from Brennan's perspective, it is as proper that an agent have preferences for norm-fulfilment as it is for the agent to have preferences over apples of different size. What makes the one analogous to the other and both perfectly proper is that, *qua* objects of choice, norm-following and bigger apples both 'connect to *preference*' in the same way (Brennan 2007: 120). There is consequently no need to invoke the idea of counter-preferential choice to explain *A*'s hypothetical choice if Brennan is right: if boy *A* happens to prefer the combination of being-polite-and-getting-the-smaller-apple to getting his hands on (and teeth into) the larger apple whilst breaking the canons of decorum, then this is an expression of his preference over two objects of choice. On the other hand, *B* prefers getting the larger apple to the combination of being-polite-and-ending-up-with-the-smaller-apple. There is nothing counter-preferential about the boys' conduct in Brennan's view of norm following, and hence neither acts on a commitment. Sen offers an alternative depiction of norm-following conduct. It is offered as an underlying presupposition of the apples example, though it is made more explicit in Sen's work after the 1970s. Sen does not deny the validity of the preference-based view of norm following as an explanation of behaviour in certain situations, but he encourages us to entertain an alternative view.

According to Sen, *A*'s conduct suggests that he acts on commitment. Sen does not divulge what *A* is committed to, but let us suppose, following Brennan, that *A* has a commitment to following the norms of politeness. If this is the case, according to Sen's conception of norm following, transgressing the norm (because he anticipates personal gain from doing so), is no longer an object of choice for *A*. The norm passes out of the world of choice and into that of self-imposed constraints where it disallows certain types of conduct, for example, using one's position as first chooser to one's own advantage *vis-à-vis* somebody else who is to choose subsequently. Following the norm, though it detaches him from his welfare-maximizing choice, is not something *A* is prepared to trade off against the advantages of breaching the norm. By virtue of being committed to following the norm, *A* places norm breaking out of reach of his preferences, and hence the option of breaking the norm becomes off limits to *A*'s rational calculation.

If he had had first choice of apple, *A*, according to Brennan, would have been free to choose between the larger apple and being polite. For Sen, by contrast, *A*, having committed himself to adhering to the norms of politeness, is no longer faced with two objects of desire, for *A* would have denuded himself of the freedom which Brennan ascribes to him, namely, the freedom to break the norm of politeness and choose the bigger apple. If *A* is genuinely committed to the norms of politeness, then adhering to these norms ceases to be an option which *A* may choose or discard as considerations of welfare maximization dictate; instead, adhering to norms becomes something by which *A* binds himself. This view of self-imposed constraints goes back to Sen's 1973 essay in which he writes: 'some of the traditional rules of good behaviour take the form of demanding suspension of calculations geared to individual rationality' (1973: 64; cf. 1997/1973: 98–9). By committing oneself to the norms of politeness, one divests oneself of the freedom to choose whether to be polite. *Pace* Brennan (2007: 120), norm breaking does not 'connect to *preference*'; it is disconnected therefrom, whence follows, according to Sen, that, had *A* chosen first and chosen the smaller apple, his choice would have been counter-preferential. There are presumably good reasons for choosing the smaller apple which *A* could adduce in support of his choice, reasons that form the basis of a commitment. Sen does not divulge why boy *A* has this commitment, but the reason on which it is based must be independent of *A*'s preferences.

This discussion has led us to the theme of self-imposed constraints, for it is in terms of such constraints that Sen conceives commitment. Self-imposed constraints, and particularly the psychology they entail, are a topic for the following chapter, and I leave further discussion of the phenomenon until then. In the following section, I compare Sen's view of norm following with two other, more orthodox, accounts in order to bring the peculiarity of Sen's view into relief.

## III Self-imposed constraints: orthodoxy and heterodoxy

In his work after the 1970s, Sen writes increasingly in terms of norm-following behaviour which he conceives in the manner in which he conceives of acting on as-if rankings. By introducing the possibility that people act on as-if rankings, or in accordance with norms, Sen's work may be deemed unorthodox in two ways. The first way is marked by the contention that human choices are not motivated by self-interest alone, and the second by the contention that an individual's choices are not necessarily based on his preferences. Many an enlightened economist would walk shoulder to shoulder with Sen on the first point. Behavioural economists, armed with the findings of experimental economics, are cases in point, for the results of experiments often show that subjects are not maximizers of monetary reward (whereby maximizing monetary reward is taken as an indication of selfish behaviour). Behavioural economists have made significant theoretical modifications to the rational-actor model which accommodate such findings. These modifications often consist in positing that individuals who do not maximize their monetary pay-off must have preferences for other, non-monetary, items which are traditionally excluded from the utility function. Thus behavioural economic models portray individuals to have preferences for following social norms, inequity aversion, reciprocity, altruism, fairness of procedures or behaving virtuously (Fehr and Schmidt 1999; Fehr and Fischbacher 2002; 2003; Gintis and Khurana 2008: 318; Jolls et al. 1998). Such tastes, which go under the name 'social preferences', give rise to behaviour which does not correspond to what people ordinarily understand by 'self-interested'.

From the term 'social preferences', one can descry the way in which behavioural approaches differ from Sen's: behavioural economists explain behaviour which looks suspiciously non-self-regarding by imputing the existence of a preference which the individual must have for such behaviour or for certain aspects of that behaviour; Sen, by contrast, abandons preferences as the causal basis for some of these types of behaviour. For behavioural economists, non-selfish behaviour is rational precisely because it is grounded in a person's preferences (Fehr et al. 2005: 346). The disagreement between orthodox economists and their behavioural counterparts lies in their respective conceptions of the content of people's welfare functions, with behavioural economists positing that individuals derive utility from non-self-regarding acts, such as following norms. There is no contradiction here between acting non-selfishly, acting on one's preferences and maximizing one's welfare, for a person's welfare is not simply a function of the monetary payoffs which are sacrificed in experiments. Sen does not impugn the rationality of non-selfish behaviour either (2009a: 191). But he does not make acting on preferences a condition for the rationality of choice. Committed choices which are causally based on reasons, which can make an individual choose contrary to his self-interested preferences, are also rational. This marks the second, and much further-reaching, way in which Sen's work may be deemed unorthodox; it concerns the possibility of a non-preference-based aetiology of choice.

Sen does not deny that people's preference functions might contain items which, from the perspective of material gain or narrow self-interest, appear to be anomalous. He is not willing, however, to adhere unceasingly to the view that all human behaviour is causally based on preferences, that is, to the aetiological relationship between preference and choice discussed in Chapter One. If one holds that human choices are not universally caused by a person's preferences, one necessarily supports the possibility of counter-preferential choice. Defenders of the more orthodox economic conception of human beings maintain the aetiological relationship between preference and choice. Maintaining this relationship requires that they fill the preference function with items for which people may be held to have a preference; once a person is ascribed a preference for some type of behaviour, however bizarre, absurd or selfless it might appear to be, the person's behaviour is explained by her having and acting on a preference for that type of behaviour or for some aspect thereof. Some scholars see the danger of ad hocness in this explanatory strategy – stuffing the utility function full with preferences for anything which can explain behaviour which is not narrowly self-interested (Bicchieri 2006: 113). Werner Güth (2002: 21) refers to this strategy as the 'neoclassical repair workshop', whereby economists' response to observations which, *prima facie*, are incompatible with the orthodox model of rational choice is to augment individuals' utility functions such that they acquire a taste for the behaviours they manifest in experimental situations or elsewhere. Sen offers his own version of Güth's criticism when he adverts to economists who purvey the art of 'skillfully "elongating" the self-interest model to deal with these challenges' (2002a: 23–4). Sen does not doubt that 'extending the reach of self-interest maximization' be of interest, and neither does he claim that such explanations be false. What prompts him, rather, to put forward an alternative explanation is his view that to posit self-interest maximization as an explanation of 'all apparently non-selfish behavior' stretches the self-interest model too far and excludes the exploration of other possibilities which do not rest on the maximization of self-interest.

In this context, let us recall from Chapter One, Sen's possible explanations of the individual's choice to return his empty bottles after use for recycling. The first three explanations all portray the individual's choices to be based on his preferences – for returning bottles as such (explanation 1), for escaping deleterious externalities he might impose on other people (explanation 2) or for avoiding the disapproval of others if he is caught disposing of his bottles in an environmentally unfriendly way (explanation 3) (Sen 1973: 68–9). What is peculiar to Sen's work is his fourth explanation which does not appeal to the individual's preferences as *explananda* of his choices. The individual, that is, would prefer to dispose of his bottles in the rubbish without having to return them to the store whence he bought them; this would be his welfare-maximizing option. But he convinces himself to override his preferences and to act instead in accord with the demands of 'social responsibility'. He does not have a preference for acting in a socially responsible manner but nevertheless has a reason to choose in a way which is contrary to his preferences. To maintain the preference-based nature of this choice, other economists might posit that he obtains utility from some aspect of his behaviour. Sen's fourth explanation does not exclude the possibility that there is utility to be had from returning bottles, but the derivation of utility does not constitute the bottle-returner's reason for returning his bottles.

What Sen offers us, then, is a particular way of conceiving norm-following behaviour which differs from other construals of norm following offered by economists. To bring the peculiarity of Sen's view into relief, I outline two other conceptions of norm following to which Sen's fourth explanation of the bottle-returner's behaviour does not conform. For the sake of illustration, I denote, in what follows, the person who follows the norm as *P*, and the norm in question as *n*.

One conception of norm following may be called the *cost-avoidance model*. According to this model, *P* follows *n* because doing so allows her to avoid the costs of transgressing *n*. Following *n* is a source of disutility for *P*, and, in an ideal world, at least from *P*'s point of view, *n* would not exist (or it might exist but would not apply to cases which involve *P* losing utility by having to follow it). As an example, one may imagine a familial norm amongst the

Capulets which forbids $P$, a scion of the family, from marrying a member of the Montague clan. In a world in which $n$ did not exist, performing an act, $\alpha$, would maximize $P$'s welfare by yielding her utility $U(\alpha)$. But in a world in which $n$ exists, to conform with $n$, $P$ has to choose the norm-abiding action, $\beta$, whereby the utility to $P$ from performing action $\beta$, denoted by $U(\beta)$, is less than $U(\alpha)$. In the non-ideal world in which $P$ lives, the full welfare consequences for $P$ of choosing $\alpha$ must include the disutility of transgressing $n$. If observed to transgress $n$, for instance, $P$ would run the risk of being sanctioned by others. She would be cast out of the family in the Capulets' case, perhaps becoming the object of an 'honour killing' by one of her brothers. If we denote transgressing $n$ as '$\sim n$', then the reduction in $P$'s welfare of transgressing $n$ is $U(\sim n)$. Consequently, $P$'s total utility from performing the norm-transgressing act $\alpha$ is given by: $U(\alpha) - U(\sim n)$. $P$ will choose the norm-abiding action $\beta$ when: $U(\beta) > U(\alpha) - U(\sim n)$. If this inequality holds, $\beta$ will be preferred to $\alpha$ because the agent will avoid the costs of transgressing $n$. Norm following becomes the welfare-maximizing, choice. Sen's third suggestion for explaining the bottle-returner's behaviour is akin to this conception of norm following.

Sen's fourth explanation of returning bottles also contrasts with a further conception of norm following, according to which $P$ has internalized the norm, $n$, to such an extent, that she derives welfare from adhering to it. I will call this the *internalization view* of norm following (cf. Coleman 1990: 293). According to this view, there is *intrinsic* value to $P$ of adhering to $n$, and hence following $n$ is not costly, as it is in the cost-avoidance model. Furthermore, the welfare $P$ derives from following $n$ is not outweighed by any advantage $P$ might reap by transgressing $n$. Here, one would say that $P$ has acquired a preference for following $n$. Full internalization of the norm might mean that following $n$ becomes second nature to $P$, whereby she habitually adheres to $n$ and does not even deliberate about whether to transgress $n$ (cf. Baker 2009: 10–12). If I am sitting in a bus and a stranger sits in front of me, then even though I could remove his wallet from his open rucksack without being noticed, I do not conceive this as an option about which I have to deliberate; rather, my internalization of the norm 'do not steal', prevents me from conceiving the act of stealing as one which is open to me. I have developed a preference for honesty. This explanation of norm following is akin to Sen's first explanation of returning bottles. My behaviour in this example may be likened to that of Aristotle's virtuous person discussed in the previous chapter.

These cost-avoidance and internalization views of norm following have something in common: they both conceive norm following to be the preferred option for the person concerned. They do so for different reasons. In the cost-avoidance view, pained though she is that the norm forbids a choice she would like to make, $P$ abides by $n$ in order to avoid the costs of transgressing it which weigh more heavily on her than the pain she experiences from abiding by the norm. In the internalization account, by contrast, a norm follower values the norm intrinsically and does so sufficiently to make her abide by it. Both accounts, despite their differences, give us a preference-based view of norm following. Neither view captures the enkratic moment which Sen's fourth explanation of the bottle-returner brings to the fore. The bottle-returner's welfare would be maximized by his choosing act α (dumping his bottles on the sly), and his decision to perform act β (returning his bottle for re-use) is based, not on considerations of his own welfare, but on considerations of social responsibility. Neither has the bottle-returner internalized the environmentally friendly norm of returning bottles. Returning his bottles, rather, requires that he overcome the urgings of his preferences.

## IV Commitment and agent relativity

To finish this chapter, I address a further issue raised by Brennan's critique of Sen, one which presupposes a brief analysis of agency, as Sen understands it. After outlining what Sen means by agency, I proceed to discuss the relationship between commitment and agent relativity.

The agency aspect of a person refers to 'his or her aims, objectives, allegiances, obligations, and – in a broad sense – the person's conception of the good' (Sen 1985a: 203). Sen distinguishes a person's 'agency achievements' from her well-being achievements. The latter is a type of agency achievement which is orientated to the pursuit of one's own well-being. Other agency achievements are not necessarily undertaken for the pursuit of one's well-being. Such achievements include the fulfilment of commitments. One may ask why Sen insists on a conceptual separation between agency achievement and well-being achievement if the latter category is subsumed under the general heading of 'agency'. An example helps to explain this:

> if one fights hard for the independence of one's country, and when that independence is achieved, one happens also to feel happier, the main achievement is that of independence, of which the happiness at that achievement is only one consequence. It is not unnatural to be happy at that achievement, but the achievement does not consist only of that happiness.
>
> (1987a: 43–4)

This passage is premised on the assumption that the actions of the person herself who fights for the independence of her country are a contributing factor to that independence; national independence is not something which simply happens independently of the person's efforts but is a goal to which she contributes as part of a collective effort. What would the situation be like if the country gained independence but the person made no contribution to achieving that goal? The person might still feel happy at the achievement of others, perhaps admiration and reverence towards the heroism of her compatriots; but the country's independence would not have been an achievement to

86  *Norms and commitment*

which her actions were directed as a goal. This would change the relationship between the person's agency and the achievement of the country's independence. However much she supported the cause of independence, one would not say that she had a commitment to this cause unless she undertook action to the end of bringing about what, to her, was a valuable state of affairs. The pursuit and/or realization of a commitment might or might not be the source of well-being for the agent, but when it is, the commitment is not pursued with the goal of deriving well-being (Sen 1985a: 203–4, 207; 1987a: 41; 1987b: 28). The importance of the person's agency in bringing about a state of affairs becomes visible when it is conceived in abstraction from any well-being achievement which that state of affairs might involve. Indeed, the formulation of the previous sentence might mislead because, following Sen, part of what constitutes that state of affairs from the viewpoint of the agent involved is the agent's actions (or absence thereof) in bringing about that state of affairs. From the perspective of agency, Sen writes, 'a person is seen as a doer and a judge', but from the viewpoint of well-being, the person is to be seen as a beneficiary (1985a: 208). The example gives us a glimpse into the relationship between agency and commitment which I now explore at greater length.

In his discussions of agency, Sen addresses the theme of agent relativity (Sen 1982b; 1983a; 1985a; 1993b), and it is this aspect of agency on which I focus in the section. Sen does not, however, relate agent relativity to commitment, though a relation there is, as I will now argue. To introduce this discussion, I return to Brennan's remarks on Sen, and, in particular, to his questioning of the view that Sen's distinction between sympathy and commitment corresponds to the distinction between preferential and counter-preferential choice. I consider an example presented by Brennan (2007: 120) who suggests the following contrast:

> Suppose C has a commitment to looking after D and makes transfers to D in amount T. Suppose C* has sympathy for D* to an extent that is behaviourally indistinguishable: the transfer T is the same in both cases. Now consider the responses of C and C* to an increase of some amount in D['s] (and D*[']s) well-being. One might conclude that in the sympathy case, C* will be made better off by the increase in D*'s well-being; whereas in the commitment case, C will not be affected one way or the other. Because C has not brought about the increase in D's well-being, the increase simply does not bear on C's commitments.

With this example, Brennan puts his finger on an important facet of Sen's notion of commitment. To explore this facet, let us pursue an embellished form of Brennan's examples. Let us begin with Brennan's C* and D* case, the case of a benefactor who feels sympathy with a beneficiary to whom the benefactor, however, has no commitment. We will call this case *variation one* of the example.

Penelope decides to make in-kind donations to Ferdinand, an aged widower and neighbour on whom she takes pity. Never having learned to cook, Ferdinand looked decidedly wizened after the death of his wife, who cooked for Ferdinand every day. Feeling sorry for Ferdinand, Penelope brings him a portion of her family's evening meal each day. She acts from sympathy, for what motivates her munificence is the desire to avoid the pangs of conscience which she would feel if she did not attend to Ferdinand's dietary needs. Her choice is made with the goal of increasing her own welfare, being based on sympathy.

Months after this arrangement has been established, Ferdinand's son, Roger, takes it upon himself to arrange a meals-on-wheels delivery every evening to his father. Not being shy about his philanthropic feats, Roger announces this to Penelope when he sees her on one of his visits to his father. Penelope sees Roger's initiative as a reason to cease her daily offerings to Ferdinand, for there is no point in the latter being presented with two evening meals simultaneously. To Penelope, whose goal in making her daily gift of food to Ferdinand was to derive welfare to herself, what is important is that Ferdinand be well nourished; if Roger meets Ferdinand's needs, she can relieve herself of the effort of delivering a daily meal to Ferdinand and also be rid of the feelings of guilt that Ferdinand is not being properly fed. Penelope derives the same level of welfare from knowing that Ferdinand is well nourished via Roger's meals-on-wheels service as she did when she provided his meal herself; and she now gets this feeling of comfort without bearing the costs herself. In the language of Chapter Two, Penelope's was a case of active sympathy before Roger commenced with the home delivery service, for it was Penelope's acts from which Penelope herself derived the sympathetic increase in her welfare. After Roger takes over, Penelope's sympathy becomes purely contemplative, for her welfare increases *vis-à-vis* what it would be if nobody saw to Ferdinand's dietary needs as a result of the actions of a third party. From a moral point of view, one may say that Penelope's decision to stop providing meals to Ferdinand is, given the circumstances, blameless. Prior to Roger's assumption of responsibility for feeding his father, Penelope's actions may be deemed supererogatory.

Let us now construct a second variation of this example which corresponds to Brennan's case with C, who has a commitment toward his beneficiary, D. After the death of his mother, Roger realizes that his father cannot live alone at home if he does not receive help. Since it is Ferdinand's ardent wish to live and, when his time comes, to die within his own four walls, Roger decides to provide a meals-on-wheels service to deliver his father's meals. When Roger informs Ferdinand about this plan, the latter reveals that Penelope, a neighbour, has been bringing Ferdinand a home-cooked meal every evening, and Ferdinand tells his son to cancel the service. Should Roger take his father's advice and free-ride on Penelope's generosity? In answering this question, I will address two further questions:

88  *Norms and commitment*

(1) is it generally the case that a person, *A*, who derives welfare sympathetically as a result of an increase in the welfare of a second person, *B*, should be indifferent to whether *A* herself or a third party bring about the increase in the *B*'s welfare?
(2) And is it the case that, to a person, *C*, who has a commitment to increasing the welfare of a second person, *D*, it should not be a matter of indifference whether *C*'s actions or those of a third party be the cause the *D*'s heightened welfare?

Brennan's (2007: 120) argument implies that, in variation two of our example, Roger 'will not be affected one way or the other' if Penelope provides Ferdinand's evening meal. I interpret Brennan's phrase here to mean that Roger will not have an incentive to change his actions as a result of Penelope's offer. There are two reasons for Roger remaining unaffected in this way, the first of which Brennan regards as 'a side issue' (2007: 120), namely, whether Roger derives welfare from upholding his commitments. This is indeed a side issue, for whether Roger derives welfare from providing his father's meals and how much welfare he derives is irrelevant for his motivation to carry out his commitment. The derivation of welfare, as we have said previously, is incidental to the goal of someone who makes choices based on commitment, for such choices are made for a non-welfare-related reason. So if Roger does happen to derive welfare from carrying out his commitments, his persistence in providing Ferdinand's meals even after Penelope has been doing so for some months is not because Roger does not wish to be deprived of any welfare he happens to derive from carrying out this commitment. The second reason that Penelope's offer of support for Ferdinand does not bear on Roger's commitment in variation two is that, if Penelope supplied Ferdinand's meals, it would be *her* actions, not Roger's, which would be the cause of the increase in Ferdinand's welfare. This apparently makes a difference to Roger. In variation one of the example, by contrast, Penelope, whose welfare varies sympathetically with Ferdinand's, changes her behaviour after Roger provides meals for Ferdinand. Brennan (2007: 120) captures this by saying that a person in Penelope's position 'might be predicted to respond to the change in [Ferdinand's] circumstances', though he does not tell us how someone in Penelope's position will respond. It is plausible, though, to posit that Penelope will call it a day with her offerings to Ferdinand, precisely what Roger, Brennan informs us, will not do in variation two when he hears from his father that Penelope has offered to cater for Ferdinand.

Brennan's intuition about the two variations is sound, but spelling out why this is so requires some explanation. To start with, let us consider variation two and assume that Ferdinand's welfare is increased by the same amount regardless of who – Roger or Penelope – provides his evening repast. The outcome, one is tempted to say, is the same in each case, so why should Roger care whether he or Penelope provides the food if his father's welfare will be the same in each case? But Roger might care because the outcomes, from his perspective, are not the same. Here, we must recall Sen's criticism of defining 'outcomes' (or 'states of affairs' or 'consequences') too narrowly. As we established in Section I of this chapter, an outcome, for Sen, may be conceived 'comprehensively', that is, in a manner which incorporates information about who is the author of the actions from which those outcomes ensue. This contrasts with conceiving them as 'culmination' outcomes, that is, as the 'aftermath' (Sen, 2009a: 216) which is left when all the acting is done and the dust has supposedly settled, leaving the outcome to present itself rather like an archaeological find, after the doers of the actions which brought about the outcome are long gone and unknown to posterity. Conceiving outcomes comprehensively allows us to distinguish:

*Outcome I*: an increase in Ferdinand's welfare brought about by Roger who has a commitment to looking after Ferdinand.
*Outcome II*: an increase in Ferdinand's welfare brought about, not by Roger who has a commitment to looking after Ferdinand, but by a third party.

These outcomes may culminate in the same state of affairs when an observer judges them according to Ferdinand's welfare. Comprehensively considered, however, they are not the same. What makes Outcome I morally superior, in Roger's judgement, is that his agency increases Ferdinand's welfare. This is of significance to Roger because he and Ferdinand stand in a particular relationship of father and son. This 'tie', as Sen (1982b: 27) calls it, grounds the view that an elderly person's children, rather than a well-wishing neighbour, should look after that person in her or his dotage; the familial bond grounds Roger's commitment to looking after his father. Looked at comprehensively, Outcome I includes the fulfilment of a duty that Roger has toward his father, whereas Outcome II includes a dereliction of duty on the part of Roger. This is morally important information in the assessment of the two outcomes. This interpretation goes beyond what Sen says about either commitment or agent relativity, so let us investigate whether he would concur with the above conclusion by examining some of his pronouncements on commitment.

In Chapter Three, I cited what I termed Sen's official definition of commitment (Section II). The definition contains a parenthetic example: 'acting to help remove some misery even though one personally does not suffer from it' (Sen 1982a: 8). The active aspect is necessary to the notion of commitment and, in 'Rational Fools', it is exemplified through the example of torture and one's readiness 'to do something to stop it' (1977a: 92; cf. 1987b: 28). Sen's official definition of commitment refers explicitly to the action of the person who has the commitment: commitment, he writes, 'is concerned with breaking the tight link between individual welfare ... and the *choice of action*' (1982a: 8 emphasis added). The agency aspect of the person who has the commitment comes to the fore. Sympathy, by contrast, is defined in terms of the welfare, not of the actions, of the person who is able to feel sympathy, as one would expect from a well-being-orientated concept. The distinction between contemplative and active sympathy which we identified in Chapter Two would make no sense in the context of commitment, for commitment implies an imperative to act on the part of the agent who has the commitment; there can be no 'contemplative commitment' but at best a feeling of contemplative sympathy in response to the committed actions of others or, indeed, of oneself, whereby the reason for one's performing the committed action oneself is not to derive this sympathetic welfare. If $B$ performs an action which fulfils a commitment of $A$, it is not, from $A$'s point of view, that same as $A$ fulfilling the commitment through her own actions. Though $A$'s welfare might increase when $B$ brings about the state of affairs related to the fulfilment of $A$'s commitment, this increase in $A$'s welfare affects only the well-being aspect of $A$'s agency but not other aspects of $A$'s agency achievement (Sen 1987a: 43–5).

Let us now return to the question posed earlier: in variation one, does Penelope, who has sympathy with, but no commitment towards, Ferdinand, have reason to evaluate the outcome differently, according to whether she or Roger provides Ferdinand's meals? If Penelope's actions towards Ferdinand are based solely on sympathy, the only difference between Outcome I and Outcome II is that, in Outcome II, she spares herself the expense of bringing Ferdinand food. But this is not a moral difference between the outcomes but merely one of convenience from Penelope's point of view. That is, the contemplative sympathy (and corresponding increase in welfare) which Penelope feels when Roger provides Ferdinand's meals is every bit as good as the active sympathy (and the corresponding increase in welfare) she feels when she provides Ferdinand's meals herself. This point is echoed in Sen's official definition of sympathy which, as we have ascertained, prioritizes contemplative sympathy because it makes no reference to the sympathetic agent's actions. Instead, the agent is conspicuously passive. In a case of contemplative sympathy, one's awareness of an increase in one person's welfare causes an increase in one's own welfare (Sen 1977a: 92). Sen makes no suggestion that the sympathetic agent's evaluation of an increase in the welfare of another person should differ according to whether the sympathetic agent herself or someone/something else brings about this change in the welfare of the other person. The moral evaluation of this outcome is not influenced by taking a comprehensive rather than a culminatory perspective, and hence the sympathetic agent's judgement is not agent relative. There are numerous variations one could make to this example which would make Penelope's verdict towards outcomes I and II more sensitive to comprehensive features. For example, when she considers Outcome II comprehensively, Penelope might be aghast at Roger's dereliction of duty towards his father, and this might reduce Penelope's welfare because she deems this neglect to be morally bad. The gap between Outcome I and Outcome II would, then, in Penelope's eyes, be wider than it would be were she indifferent to whether Roger fulfilled or neglected his filial duty, that is, if she were concerned only with Ferdinand's welfare and not with Roger's obligations. The important point to note in wrapping up this discussion is that, regardless of Penelope's assessment, Roger has reason to ensure that his father is well fed as a result of Roger's own agency, and any outcome in which Ferdinand is well fed thanks to the agency of somebody other than Roger is, from his perspective, inferior.

## Conclusion

The material of this chapter derives from Sen's apples example, with which he elucidates the distinction between sympathy and commitment, and from Brennan's commentary thereon. The food for thought which this example has given us might seem remarkable in light of the pithiness of the vignette, yet it has led us, via Brennan's remarks, to the themes of norm following and agent relativity. We have established a gulf which exists between Sen's account of norm following and other accounts of this type of behaviour. Sen is unique in entertaining an explanation of norm following which not only makes no reference to the norm follower's preferences, but conceives the norm follower to be acting counter-preferentially. Therein lies the difference between Sen's and Brennan's accounts of the apples example, and therein lies the difference between Sen's account and the two more orthodox accounts of norm following which I have outlined in Section III. It is hard to overestimate the importance of Sen's account of norm following to understand Sen's conception of human action and the peculiarly heterodox nature of his thought, and his view of norm following will be further discussed in Chapter Eight. Yet his account also raises questions about its plausibility, two of which we address in the following chapter. The first concerns the way in which commitments to norm following are best conceived, and the second pertains to the source and strength of the binding nature of such commitments.

## Notes

1 Sen's apples example might have been inspired by Ragnar Frisch's choosing-between-two-cakes example. Sen (1997) quotes the English translation of Frisch's article, but he had already referred to an unpublished translation of the article in 'Rational Fools' (Sen, 1977a: 97 note 31). Frisch's example, as quoted by Sen (1997: 177) is as follows:
   Assume that my wife and I have had dinner alone. ... For dessert two cakes have been purchased. They are very different, but both are very fine cakes and expensive – according to our standard. My wife hands me the tray and suggests that I help myself. What shall I do? By looking up my own total utility function, I find that I would very much like to devour one particular one of the two cakes. I will propound that this introspective observation is *completely irrelevant* for the choice problem. The really relevant problem is: which one of the two cakes does my wife prefer? If I knew that the case would be easy. I would say 'yes please' and take the *other* cake, the one that is her second priority.
   Obviously, Frisch, as he narrates himself, has a better sense of decorum than boy *B* in Sen's apples example, and the similarity of the two examples is, I hope, clear.
2 Sen addresses the notion of an 'outcome' and of the distinction between 'comprehensive' and 'culmination' outcomes numerous times (1982b: 29; 1983a: 118, 128; 1985a: 212–16; 1997: 159; 1999: 27–8; 2000: 487–92; 2009a: 215–17; 2017b: 433–4).

# 6 Binding oneself
## Self-imposed constraints

**Introduction**

In this chapter, I further pursue the theme of norm following by way of a discussion of binding oneself. One type of commitment involves the imposition of restrictions on one's own conduct in accord with a norm. Daniel Hausman has questioned Sen's conceptualization of this type of commitment, as I detail in Section I. He rightly attributes to Sen a *constraint view* of norm following, whereby one's commitment represents a constraint which one imposes on oneself. How firmly, though, can and should commitments constrain the actions of their authors? And what prevents a person from breaching a norm of behaviour to which she has committed herself? Around these questions, Hausman poses an important challenge to Sen. I defend the latter in developing a notion of constraint which is neither too determining, nor too easily broken. I do so, in Section II, by constructing an analogy between commitments and Sen's understanding of rights.

**I Binding oneself**

Sen characterizes commitments as self-imposed constraints, a depiction which Hausman challenges. Hausman writes that, according to Sen, 'commitments can constrain choices in the same way that physical facts do' (Hausman 2012: 60); how else, asks Hausman, could an individual's choice be counter-preferential? Hausman's analogy with physical facts can be interpreted variously. A plausible way in which to characterize the position he ascribes to Sen is to imagine commitments to be like the constraint which Odysseus imposes on himself, which allows him to hear, but not to be seduced by, the song of the Sirens. Bound to the mast, Odysseus faces a constraint which is, indeed, physical, and no act of strength or appeal to his ear-plugged crew will suffice to free him. Odysseus' bonds physically constrain him from going back on his commitment to avoid landing his ship on the isle of the Sirens (Homer, *Odyssey*: book XVII, lines 39–54, 165–200). If this is the view of commitment to which Sen subscribes, it is relatively easy to undermine, for not all self-imposed constraints are like physical facts; they are rather – and this is the objection to the physical-fact view – 'purely psychological' (Hausman 2012: 61). They are not, as Hausman (2012: 3–4) writes in the context of moral obligation, 'something external to the self – like a ball and chain preventing people from doing what they really want to do'. Hausman's view of self-imposed constraints reminds us of something important about commitment: it is possible to turn some commitments into physical facts by establishing a 'causal process in the external world' which will 'add force to your inner resolution' (Elster 1979: 43, 37) – this is what Odysseus manages to do. But in and of itself, making a commitment consists in an internal mental act, one which, as Hausman states, is purely psychological.

The psychological nature of commitments raises the following question: let us suppose that I commit myself to exclude certain options or types of action from the set of objects of choice before me; what stops me changing my mind and choosing one of these excluded options when the time comes to make a choice, and I find that a 'forbidden' option is the one I most prefer? Thomas Hobbes (1968/1651, Chapter XXVI: 313 [138]) raises just this doubt about self-imposed constraints: it is not, he holds, 'possible for any person to be bound to himselfe; because he that can bind can release; and therefore he that is bound to himselfe onely, is not bound'. We are all familiar with commitments which, despite trying to bind ourselves to them, we have failed to keep. However much I try to commit myself not to cheat in the exam which I am to sit tomorrow morning, on the day itself I can plainly go back on my commitment and enter the exam with a list of dates, formulæ or irregular verb conjugations written on the inside of my arm. On the other hand, we are probably equally familiar with cases of success in adhering to commitments which we have imposed on ourselves, and have done so solely through the mental act of forcing ourselves to adhere to the commitment despite the temptations to break it. Both occurrences – adhering to as well as breaking commitments – are sufficiently common that any account of binding oneself to one's commitments must accommodate them. Commitments must be conceived to have two empirical facets: they must have some degree of binding force but they must also be flexible enough to be broken.

If commitments lacked all binding force to constrain the future choices of an individual, our success in keeping commitments would be at the mercy of our occurrent reasons or preferences at the time of acting, against which our commitment is supposed to form a bulwark. In such a case, we would not speak of a person having a commitment at all but rather as her having an *intention* (cf. Hobbes 1994/1650, Part XII: Chapter 9). When I have an intention, it is, like a commitment, directed to my future choices. But commitments constrain in ways that intentions do not: I can intend to go shopping tomorrow morning but not get around to doing so, postpone it until the day after or simply forget; but if I commit myself to something, the commitment connects itself with greater force to my motivation to act in accord with it; one requires a better reason for neglecting a commitment than one does for going back on an intention because a commitment is connected to a person's moral and not merely to her prudential plans. Commitments have special normative status in the reckoning of the agent who holds them, and this marks them off from our 'run-of-the-mill endeavours' (Goodin 1980: 135).

Whilst they require a certain binding power, commitments do not determine future choices rigidly, and therein lies the ever-present possibility to break them. Sometimes, as in the case of Odysseus, commitments appear to limit a person's options to one. But it is not the commitment itself, *qua* psychological act, which does this but 'a causal process in the external world', as Elster puts it, which buttresses the commitment, perhaps physically. If commitments were to bind future choices deterministically, they would be made far less frequently, for unforeseen contingencies can arise which make adhering to the commitment disadvantageous; making a commitment which one cannot break involves considerable risk and might be irrational (Bratman 1987: 5). Odysseus might be deemed rational in making his commitment firm because of the disastrous consequences, divulged to him by the sorceress Circe, of wavering from the commitment to steer clear of the Sirens. But in situations in which breaking a commitment does not carry potentially calamitous consequences, people 'would like to be *loosely bound* to the mast – with ties strong enough to keep them from acting against their own interests, but not so strong as to prevent them from intervening in an emergency' (Elster 1992: 42; cf. Bratman 1996: 303–4).

Hausman's physical-fact analogy does not shine the best light on commitments, as Sen conceives them. Indeed, Sen abjures the analogy when he writes that constraints based on Smithian or Kantian thinking – that is, constraints which one imposes on the types of action available to oneself – 'differ from constraints given from outside' (1994: 387), or 'external' constraints, as Sen also calls them (2007: 353–4). External constraints may be conceived in analogy to physical facts, but the psychological nature of self-imposed commitments does not sit well with the physical-fact view. Hausman is correct to reject the physical-fact view, but in doing so, he is not rejecting Sen's view. Although Sen does not explain the difference between self-imposed and external constraints in detail, we may return to his two-boys-and-two-apples example, which was discussed in the previous chapter, to elucidate self-imposed constraints. Boy $A$ in the apple example faces a self-imposed constraint. He is committed to the norms of politeness and would, had he been the first chooser, have chosen the smaller apple for this reason. Boy $A$ could have breached the constraint he imposed on himself in a way in which Odysseus cannot breach his constraint, for the latter, unlike boy $A$, makes his constraint physically unbreakable. Odysseus and boy $A$ have in common that they have imposed upon themselves a constraint through the mental act of commitment, but only Odysseus makes his commitment adamantine. Had he not made it so, Odysseus' constraint would have been merely psychological and, in light of the seductive nature of the Sirens' voices, he is led to believe that he would not have been able to resist. Boy $A$'s temptation to break his constraint, had he chosen first, is more easily resisted than the Sirens' song, but he, too, would have been able to break his commitment by choosing the larger apple, though in Sen's rendition of his interaction with boy *B*, boy *A* would have adhered to his commitment despite his preference for the larger apple.

In light of this, we may return to something we wrote in the previous chapter (Section II) about self-imposed constraints when we compared Brennan's and Sen's understanding of norms. There we suggested that, by committing oneself to following a norm, one divests oneself of the freedom to transgress the norm; breaking the norm is no longer an object of preference once one has committed oneself to adhering to it, it was suggested. But in light of what we have just said, this is too extreme a position on the binding force of commitment: boy *A* could have broken his commitment and chosen the larger apple had he chosen first; his commitment to the norms of politeness represents an *attempt* to denude himself of the freedom to neglect these norms in situations like the apples example, but he might not succeed in this attempt. This encapsulates the distinction between a commitment *qua* self-imposed constraint, which can be broken, thus giving the individual a choice, and a physical-fact-like constraint, which, like Odysseus' bonds, rule out a choice to break one's commitment. The ability to break one's self-imposed constraints speaks in favour of conceiving norm adherence as Brennan does, that is, as an object of choice rather than as something which one somehow places beyond the grasp of one's preference-based choice, as Sen holds. But if we conceived self-imposed constraints like this, we would be open to the Hausman–Hobbes observation that a self-imposed constraint is no constraint at all. And if we can choose to keep or break our commitment willy nilly, there seems to be no difference between choices based on commitment and those based on our occurrent preferences: if we keep our commitment, it is because doing so sits atop our preference ranking; if, on the other hand, we break it, some other option must have found its way to the pinnacle of our preference ranking between the time at which we make the commitment and the time at which we execute the corresponding choice. Adhering to or breaking a commitment would be an object of choice, and making a commitment would not constrain us in the way that Sen suggests it does; choices based on commitment would simply be a species of preference-based choice.

If we are to follow Sen's understanding of norm following, we must ask whether self-imposed constraints can be described to have some binding force but without being determining. If they are not binding, self-imposed constraints seem to be little more than preferences for avoiding certain types of action; but if such constraints are too rigid, they would have to have a physical-fact-like constitution which is incompatible with their origin in acts of the will. In the following section, I explore how commitments, *qua* self-imposed constraints, are best conceived. I propose a different analogy to that of physical facts. My proposal draws on a seemingly distant aspect of Sen's *opus*, and it suggests an analogy which Sen himself does not suggest. The analogy will unfold in two stages.

## II Commitments and rights

Stage one of the analogy concerns Sen's depiction of the libertarian approach to rights. Taking Robert Nozick as a representative of this approach, rights, we may say, are 'side constraints' – the 'rights of others determine the constraints upon your actions' (Nozick 1974: 29) and they are non-negotiable. Nozick (1974: 30 footnote) gestures at one caveat to the non-negotiability of rights when he asks whether they 'may be violated in order to avoid catastrophic moral horror'. However, Nozick remains, throughout his book, true to his 'hope' that he will avoid addressing such matters. Sen draws attention to a passage from Nozick (1974) in which the latter describes the status of rights: '[r]ights do not determine a social ordering but instead set the constraints within which a social choice is to be made, by excluding certain alternatives, fixing others, and so on' (Nozick 1974: 166, quoted in Sen 1982b: 5). In other words, rights *operate upon* a social ordering to constrain the choice it can yield' (Nozick 1974: 166). Sen's construal of Nozick's point is that 'right violations and realizations do not enter the valuation of states of affairs' (Sen 1982b: 12; cf. 2002a: 628); upholding rights, in Sen's depiction of the libertarian position, is 'simply "above" (with unconditional priority over) other considerations that influence the valuation of states of affairs', and hence there is no question, for Nozick, of allowing rights to be violated if such violation can be traded off against some benefit which outweighs the violation (Sen 2002a: 630). One is not, for example, permitted to ask: if we abrogate the property rights of a certain group of people, will the benefits to other groups justify the abrogation? Being absolute constraints, rights are not to be treated in this manner; they are not objects of choice in a social welfare function.[1]

If commitments, in the form of self-imposed constraints on action, were analogous to rights, as Nozick conceives them, they would constitute absolute values or principles through which an individual regulates her conduct. They would not admit of exception, and hence an agent would bar herself from deliberating in the following way: if, at time $t_2$, I break a commitment which I imposed upon myself at $t_1$, would it be the right thing to do? Some commitments are made with this absolute nature in mind, as Sen suggests when he mentions 'Mahatma Gandhi's deontological insistence on nonviolence irrespective of the consequences' (Sen 2000b: 560). When Gandhi explained his idea of *Satyagraha*, in the context of Indian independence, he stated that it was an 'absolutely non-violent weapon' (1996/1927: 316–17). He not only made his commitment to non-violence *expressis verbis* absolute, but did not waiver therefrom even under the most extreme circumstances. For instance, during the salt marches in 1930, Gandhi and his followers are reported to have refrained from defending themselves against the violence of the British, lest they themselves commit acts of violence in self-defence. As they approached a cordon beyond which the British would not allow them to pass, an observer wrote that police officers subjected Gandhi and his entourage:

to a hail of blows to the head delivered from steel-covered Lathis (truncheons) [but] [n]one of the protestors raised so much as an arm to protect themselves against the barrage of blows. They fell to the ground like pins in a bowling alley. From where I was standing I could hear the nauseating sound of truncheons impacting against unprotected skulls.

(Webb Miller, cited in Milligan 2013: 88)

There are apparently, then, such firm commitments to non-violence, that those who hold them manage to adhere to them even on occasions when breaking them would seem highly propitious. The use of violence, for such a person, is not an object of choice, even though he or she would have preferred, on grounds of self-interest (or self-preservation), to have escaped the agonizing pummelling meted out to them by British troops. But not all of us are Gandhis, and not all commitments are like this. If they were, there would be no such thing as weakness of will; nor would commitments have the flexibility which Elster identifies as a *desideratum* which allows one to intervene in an emergency by breaking one's commitment in response to unforeseen circumstances. Hence, I conclude this part of the argument by stating that commitments are not best conceived in analogy with Nozick's conception of rights. Nozick's exclusion of rights violations from a social ordering matches Sen's constraint view of commitment *qua* norm following, for both represent attempts to exclude certain options from being objects of choice. But the rigidity with which Nozick excludes any rights violations is not paralleled in Sen's understanding of norm following. I therefore return to Sen's analysis of rights to prepare the second stage of the analogy between rights and commitments.

To introduce the second stage of the analogy, let us recall that Hausman (2012: 61–2) wonders how a purely psychological commitment can exclude an agent from choosing an option which is part of a class of actions, for example breaking a promise, from which she has committed herself not to choose. In the context of rights, Sen addresses an analogous issue. The conferral of a right imposes constraints on future actions, not on those of the right-holder, but on those of others who are required to respect the rights of the right-holder. If I have a right to do $x$, then nobody may try to prevent me from doing $x$. If it is conceived in libertarian fashion, my right to do $x$ may, under no circumstances, be violated. Sen disagrees. One not only may but is obliged to ask, he holds, whether one right may be violated for the sake of upholding another, more important, right, or for the sake of realizing a different, non-rights-based value (Sen 2000a: 499). Rights may therefore enter in principle into a moral calculus in which realizing or abrogating them become objects of choice, to be decided in accordance with the consequences of realizing or abrogating them. Rights thereby lose the absolute status which Nozick ascribes to them. Some rights will withstand the moral calculus and trump other concerns with which they are compared; such rights may not be violated, although, in contrast to the libertarian view, this conclusion is derived *a posteriori*, after an investigation of the consequences of violating the rights in question and comparing these consequences with those which would ensue when the rights are upheld. Before we enquire into the circumstances in which rights may be violated, let us explore the status of rights in Sen's view, and second, the novel manner in which he conceives consequences or states of affairs, the latter point being one Sen discusses many times (1995b: 278–81; 2000a: 487–92; 2000b: 559–61).

Sen (1987a: 74) holds that the violation of rights is something bad in itself, independent of the possibly salutary consequences of rights violations on social welfare or on some other value. Conversely, upholding rights is good. Hence rights, in contrast to the utilitarian view of them, are not to be valued only derivatively or instrumentally – in terms of the consequences of violating or realizing them for aggregate utility (Sen 1982b: 4). This marks the special normative status which Sen accords to rights. But in Sen's view, and in contrast to Nozick's position, the securing or violation of rights does not stand beyond the valuation of states of affairs. As Sen writes:

> the remark that the period of Emergency Rule in India was a bad one because so many rights of so many people were violated ... is a statement about a state of affairs, and it does include the violation of rights directly in the evaluation of the state.
>
> (Sen 1982b: 13)

Thus, *pace* Nozick, whether rights are upheld or nullified is, according to Sen, a matter which (co-)determines a social ordering: '[t]here is a clear need to bring the violation of rights and freedoms into the evaluation of states of affairs, going well beyond exclusive reliance on utility information only' (Sen 2002a: 635). This point gives us an insight into Sen's defence of consequential reasoning. He stresses, on the one hand, the intrinsic importance of upholding rights; upholding and abrogating rights both consitute consequences in themselves, the one good, the other bad. Realizations and violations of rights, on the other hand, also have consequences which must be taken into account when we judge social states of affairs. This, latter, *instrumental*, significance of rights is to be distinguished from the intrinsic value of upholding them (Sen 1987a: 75), though both the instrumental and the intrinsic value are to be viewed as part of the state of affairs which ensues.

Let us, then, consider the sort of circumstances which compel us to ask, in Sen's opinion, whether it might be justified to violate rights. Sen offers an example in which an individual is faced with a choice whether to respect or violate the right of another. In the example, Donna must decide whether to break into Charles' apartment in order to acquire information located there on the whereabouts of a certain Ali, a shopkeeper of East African origin who lives in London (1982b: 7–12). Donna wishes to warn Ali that he is going to be subject to a physical attack by the 'bashers', a gang of local racists, who do not take kindly to 'foreigners' residing in 'their' neighbourhood. Being unable to secure Charles' consent to her entering his apartment, should Donna violate Charles' right to privacy in the name of upholding Ali's right to bodily integrity? With the example, Sen wishes to convince us that holding rights to be inviolable under all circumstances is rather restrictive, and it prevents us from deliberating about courses of action which, though they might involve an abrogation of someone's rights, could be morally permissible, perhaps obligatory, with regard to their consequences.

A second example comes from Sen's analysis of famines and concerns a governmental decision whether to violate or uphold rights. Mass death from starvation, Sen observes 'can reflect legality with a vengeance' (1981: 166). Malnutrition and death, that is, can occur as a result of entitlement failure without a transgression of anyone's rights (Sen 1999: 66; cf. Peacock 2010). Sen discusses various measures to prevent starvation, one of which is the abrogation of property rights (1988: 62; cf. 1985a: 217). This measure is not, however, amongst those which he and Jean Drèze discuss from historical famine situations. In discussions of these cases, they mention public employment which was implemented to great effect in Maharashtra in the early 1970s (Drèze and Sen 1989: 88, 125–33; Sen 1991: 329–32). Public employment had the effect of redistributing purchasing power to those whose entitlement to food had collapsed. Though it sounds less drastic than an abrogation of property rights, to libertarian ears, public employment would be unacceptable if it were funded through compulsory taxation, which, according to the libertarian, is akin to expropriation. This applies also to many of Sen's proposals for famine prevention which are likely to involve expenditures financed by taxation, for example state-funded provision of basic medical care and education (1991: 327–8). Such would be rejected by libertarians of a Nozickian ilk on the ground that they violate rights. Sen, by contrast, finds it perfectly legitimate to ask whether upholding a right be justified in light of what could be achieved by abrogating it.

A final example involves government declarations of a state of emergency in which certain rights, for example the right to freedom of movement (through the imposition of curfews), freedom of the press, *habeas corpus* and so on are suspended (Sen 1982b: 13). With regard to Indira Gandhi's declaration of a state of emergency in June 1975, Sen is obviously sceptical about the justification for abrogating rights (Sen 1982b: 16 note 24; 2005b: 117, 194, 358 note 14). This shows how vulnerable rights can be, and also that some violations of rights are, in Sen's estimation, unjustified. Other violations, though, may be justified; in contrast to what he says about Indira Gandhi's emergency measures, Sen appears to share his imaginary Donna's intuition that she should contravene Charles' right to privacy by breaking into his room in order to save Ali from a worse fate; and his analysis of famines suggests that Sen envisages quite far-reaching violations of rights, even if they are temporary, if malnutrition and starvation can by avoided thereby. Sen's examples, though, demonstrate that only exceptional circumstances permit one to relax prohibitions on the violation of rights; rights are not to be entered willy-nilly into the moral calculus of ascertaining how to bring about the best state of affairs. Some rights will transpire to be 'unrelaxable' under all circumstances which arise, and hence Sen's broad consequential approach would not, in such cases, differ from the conclusions of a deontological approach which bars trading off rights against other values (Sen 1982b: 39). Other rights, though, 'include more "give," without "giving in" every time to what the over-all values of the consequent state recommend' (Sen 1983a: 130). This conception of rights marks the middle ground between utilitarianism and the constraint-based deontology of Nozick. We are now ready to propose the analogy between Sen's conception of rights and his conception of commitments *qua* self-imposed constraints.

Commitments in the form of self-imposed constraints are, like rights, devices for excluding certain items as options which may be chosen. If I commit myself not to do $x$, the purpose of the constraint I impose upon myself is to place $x$ beyond the bounds of my preference function so that $x$ is not an object of my choice. As we have seen, however, commitments are not physical facts; committing myself not to do $x$ does not, in itself, make it impossible for me to do $x$. Neither, I argued above, would we always wish our commitments to make it impossible that I choose $x$, not even for some apparently deep-seated commitments (cf. Sen 2000a: 490–1).[2] Circumstances unforeseen at the time of making a commitment can arise which make a breach of the commitment the best course of action, just as circumstances can arise which justify a violation of certain rights. But the 'best course of action', here, does not mean that course which I most prefer for reasons of self-interest. If this were the meaning of 'best course of action', breaking one's commitment would be a case of weakness of will. The best course of action, rather, means that which is morally best, as judged from the perspective after unforeseen circumstances have arisen which, as an exception, make keeping one's commitment the morally unacceptable course of action.

Does this account of self-imposed constraints, however, make commitments too flexible, that is, too easy to break? Hausman's objection has not been banished, for although Sen can make a good case against the view that self-imposed constraints are like physical facts, does he go too far in the direction of conceiving commitments to be too flimsy? Here, we can descry a difference between rights and commitments, for rights, at least those of a constitutional nature, can usually be suspended only under particular circumstances and if special parliamentary or other political procedures for their suspension are followed (Elster 2000). These procedures are part of the causal machinery which governments have imposed on themselves as a means of making the suspension of rights difficult. Commitments, on the other hand, especially those buttressed by a rickety causal process in the external world or by none at all, do approximate to Hausman's description of being 'purely psychological'. What would be the point in having them if they were really so easy to break? And are we deceiving ourselves if we view our commitments to be anything other than preferences over future courses of action?

One argument in favour of distinguishing between items toward which we have a commitment and items toward which we have a preference is that, only with this distinction does the normative significance of commitments come to the fore. Sen's understanding of commitment is in this sense analogous to his understanding of rights. Consider a person, *Q*, who is committed to veganism but who finds himself stranded on an island on which his only means of sustaining himself is to eat the meat of crustaceans which can be caught on the beach. If *Q* deems his survival to be of higher moral value than his prohibition on consuming the flesh of dead animals, his consequence-sensitive evaluation will justify breaking his commitment and thus killing the creatures. Although *Q* holds that sustaining himself on crabs is undoubtedly the right thing to do under his shipwrecked circumstances, he will look upon killing his fellow creatures as something bad in itself which he would not, under normal circumstances, allow himself to do simply in order to increase his welfare. *Q*'s breaking of his commitment must weigh negatively in his assessment of the state of affairs, and he would not account for its weight merely in psychic terms of reducing his utility. Just as realizations and violations of rights are not to be valued solely in terms of their effects on utilities, so keeping and breaking commitments have an intrinsic significance which cannot be captured through consideration of their welfare effects alone. Donna, from Sen's 'bashers' example, can be construed similarly: knowing what a private fellow Charles is, Donna, let us assume, had, prior to discovering the bashers' intentions, committed herself never to pry into those parts of his life which Charles does not willingly reveal to her; but with the bashing of Ali imminent and with Donna uniquely placed to prevent it, Donna feels justified in breaking her commitment to maintaining Charles' privacy because thwarting the bashers' plan is a goal worth striving for at the expense of Charles' right to privacy. On the other hand, if, on a different occasion, Donna were tempted secretly to enter Charles' domicile purely because she cannot contain her nosiness, this would be a goal which is unworthy to pursue given that doing so comes at the expense of one of Charles' rights.

In this sense, commitments are like rights, and asking what is the point in making commitments which can be broken would be like asking: what is the point in having rights if they are not inviolable? Sen's answer to the latter question would be that, whilst rights may, under certain circumstances, be violated, their violation is normatively not equivalent to other actions which do not violate rights, and the significance of a particular rights violations cannot be captured in terms of its perhaps positive effect on social welfare. Similarly, upholding or violating a commitment in a given situation, whilst it might have a positive effect on the welfare of the individual concerned, is not of significance in terms of its welfare effects alone, for the breach is also of normative significance.

A further argument which favours distinguishing commitments from preferences concerns the special place in our lives which commitments have and which returns us to the theme of personhood or identity which occupied the discussion of Chapter Four. A person might commit herself to vegetarianism, not crossing union picket lines and buying fairtrade coffee but not to things like changing her socks every day or spending two weeks in Cuba over New Year. It is not that the latter two items are too trivial to constitute commitments, but for most of us, basic hygiene and taking holidays do not require the psychological effort of a commitment because one can rely on one's (self-interested) preferences to do the job of motivating one to undertake these practices. Keeping commitments, by contrast, requires that special effort which we associated in Chapter Four with Aristotle's continent person, abstracting here from the special case of welfare-maximizing commitments and from the case of Aristotle's virtuous person whose preferences and reason stand in harmony to one another. As we have observed before, Sen is interested especially in enkratic commitment. We seem to require, therefore, from a purely linguistic point of view, a distinction between acting on commitment and acting on preferences to mark the different ways in which our choices are caused. By their very meaning, commitments should not be broken willy-nilly but only under particular circumstances. In this sense, they are like rights, as Sen conceives them.

As to the ease with which commitments can be broken, this is a matter of the moral psychology of the individual who makes commitments. Some individuals will be more morally disciplined in keeping their commitments than others. Depending on the nature and import of the commitment, a given individual might find it relatively easy to keep one commitment but near impossible to do so with another. As John Broome (2013: 1–2) writes, some people have 'the enkratic disposition more strongly than others, and some may not have it at all; some are strongly disposed to intend to do what they believe they ought to do, and others are not'. Broome focuses on one explanation for keeping or breaking commitments which involves strength or weakness of will. This must be distinguished from another which involves moral weighing, whereby one breaks a commitment for the exceptional reason that the moral consequences of keeping the commitment would be unacceptable. Both cases presuppose that commitments are not like physical facts, but they are no less commitments because of this.

**Conclusion**

This chapter has been occupied with the best way of conceptualizing commitments *qua* self-imposed constraints on action. I have developed an analogy between Sen's understanding of rights and his notion of commitment in order to defend him against two charges, (i) that he unrealistically depicts commitments as if they were physical constraints and (ii) that making commitments is pointless in light of the fact that they can be broken. In contrast to Nozick's conception of rights as inviolable, Sen develops a notion of rights which allows their realization and violation to be incorporated into an expanded notion of social consequences which are to form the basis of judgements about what the best course of action is. Sen thereby acknowledges the intrinsic importance of upholding rights and his view therefore contrasts with the utilitarian view of rights. But the intrinsic importance of not contravening rights does not place them outside the bounds of a social ordering, as Nozick holds they should. According to Sen, if one incorporates realizations and infringements of rights into the concept of consequences which are to be considered when one judges a state of affairs, one can take account of the intrinsic importance of rights but nevertheless allow for rights violations if they are required to avert states of affairs which would be deemed worse than that in which certain rights were violated. Commitments, *qua* self-imposed constraints on action, are aptly conceived to have a similar status in Sen's work. They have intrinsic importance to the agent but lack absolute inviolability. Breaking a commitment may therefore be conceived as something bad in itself but nevertheless permissible if the consequences of doing so (in which consequences are included any breaches of commitment) justify a breach. Cases of weakness of will, for which breaking a commitment is not deemed by the agent herself to be the right thing, are to be distinguished from cases in which the agent deems a breach of commitment to be justified.

This brings our analysis of Sen and norm following to a close. Absent from the discussion was an answer to the question: how is acting within self-imposed constraints psychologically possible? The question is of interest for those constraints which have not been reinforced by a 'causal process in the external world' which makes the constraint unbreakable (Elster 1979: 43). If, that is, one's constraint is purely psychological, one's ability to break it in face of one's occurrent preferences makes the constraint vulnerable. Sen does not doubt this, as his discussion of weakness of will shows. But he does not address the question just posed, presumably for the reason that he sees the human ability to act counter-preferentially as a relatively unproblematic phenomenon, the existence of which is not terribly controversial.

## Notes

1 In elucidating his concept of side constraints, Nozick (1974: 30–3) forcefully defends the principle that '[i]ndividuals are inviolable' which, if accepted, makes it impermissible to treat people in certain ways. Other libertarian scholars are more permissive about the absolute standing of these constraints (see, e.g., Narveson 2001: 53–6). Sen acknowledges this point about post-Nozickian procedural theories of justice (2017b: 345).
2 See Edgerton (1985) on instructive exceptions to some very deep-seated rules.

# 7 Goals

**Introduction**

In this chapter, I examine the developments in Sen's thought on rational choice presented in his essay, 'Goals, Commitment, and Identity' (1985b) and on which he has expatiated since first making these developments (2005a; 2007; 2009a). In the aforementioned essay, Sen outlines three characteristics of the 'privateness' of the 'rational economic man' who is depicted in orthodox economic theory (1985b: 213). Elsewhere Sen refers to these characteristics as 'three components of self-love' (Sen in Klamer 1989: 143) or as 'three different aspects of the "self" that are all invoked ... in the standard characterization of self-interest' (Sen 2002a: 33). Sen calls the three characteristics self-centred welfare, self-welfare goal and self-goal choice. Not only can each characteristic can be violated, Sen claims, but each can be realized or violated independently of the realization and violation of the other two characteristics. They can, that is, be put together in any combination. I call this claim Sen's *independence claim*, and the main task of this chapter is to test whether it be true. This task seems to be a simple one, but to test Sen's claim requires clarity about what constitutes an adequate test, and the nature of the test depends on how one interprets realizations and violations of the three characteristics of privateness.

In Section I, I suggest an interpretation of realizations and violations of these characteristics at the level of capabilities. The violation of each characteristic, according to this capability-theoretic interpretation, means endowing a person with a particular capability; in the case of self-centred welfare, the capability to feel sympathy, in the case of self-welfare goal, the capability to make commitments, and in the case of self-goal choice, the capability to make non-teleological choices. The realization of each characteristic, conversely, denies a person the corresponding capability. The test itself is conducted in Section II and consists in ascertaining whether a person can possess or not possess the capability associated with each characteristic independently of whether she possesses the capabilities associated with each of the other two. It transpires that Sen's independence claim passes muster when the characteristics of privateness are interpreted this way. Whilst this is certainly something to write home about, the test is not terribly stringent when the three characteristics are interpreted at the level of capabilities. This leads me, in Section III, to propose a second, more exacting, test. My motivation for doing so lies not solely in wishing to make life more awkward for Sen than it might otherwise be; it is because Sen encourages a different interpretation of his characteristics of privateness for which their respective realization and violation are interpreted, not at the level of capabilities, but at the level of the concrete choices which a person makes. Wherein realizations and violations of the characteristics according to this choice-theoretic interpretation consist is laid out in Section III. The second test of Sen's independence claim commences in Section IV in which the question becomes: can each characteristic be realized or violated independently of the realization or violation of the others at the level of choice? Can we, that is, conceptualize a choice for each of the eight possible combinations of realizations and violations of the characteristics? This proves to be a stricter test than that carried out in Section II. Sen's independence claim passes this more demanding test for cases which do not involve violations of self-goal choice. I demonstrate this in Section IV by providing examples for the cases which do not involve this violation. Cases which involve the latter violation are treated in the following chapter in which I examine the meaning of a violation of self-goal choice as Sen conceives it.

## I Characteristics of privateness: the capability-theoretic interpretation

Sen's characteristics of privateness are as follows:

> *Self-centered welfare*: A person's welfare depends only on his or her own consumption, which rules out sympathy or antipathy toward others, as well as the effects of processes and relational concerns on one's own welfare.
> *Self-welfare goal*: A person's only goal is to maximize his or her own welfare, which rules out incorporating within one's own objectives other considerations (such as the welfare of others), *except to the extent that it influences the person's own welfare.*
> *Self-goal choice*: A person's choices must be based on the pursuit of his or her own goals, which rules out being restrained by the recognition of other people's goals, *except to the extent that these goals shape the person's own goals.*

(2005a: 18)

These definitions from Sen (2005a) are slightly refined versions of their originals (1985b: 213–4). They are nevertheless very close to their original formulations, and I work with the 2005 versions because they are less ambiguous than their earlier counterparts, particularly through the addition of the italicized phrases in the definitions of self-welfare goal and self-goal choice.

The traditional theory of rational choice upholds all three characteristics of privateness. As we saw in Chapter Two (Section IV), Sen notes that recent developments of the theory have allowed for deviations from self-centred welfare (Sen 2002a: 30–1; 2007: 19–20), and he discusses Gary Becker's work as an example which incorporates sympathy into the theory of rational choice (Becker 1996). The other two characteristics – self-welfare goal and self-goal choice – remain firmly upheld in the orthodox theory of rational choice. Sen holds that each characteristic can be relaxed or violated; indeed, they 'can be used – or not used – in any combination' (2002a: 31, 34; cf. 1986a: 7; 1987a: 80; Sen in Klamer 1989: 143). *Pace* proponents of orthodox rational choice, Sen argues that there is no logical necessity in assuming that all, or indeed that any, of the characteristics be realized. Before we analyse this claim in the following section, let us examine the realization and violation of the three characteristics. What follows will henceforth be called the *capability-theoretic interpretation* of these realizations and violations.

*Self-centred welfare*

I will, for the sake of simplicity, ignore the passage 'as well as the effects of processes and relational concerns on one's own welfare' with which Sen ends his 2005a definition, quoted above. My reason for doing so is first, that Sen does not include the passage in his 1985b definition of self-centred welfare; second, and more importantly, it is sufficient, for present purposes to define self-centred welfare in terms of its relation to sympathy alone, and attending to the processes-and-relational-concerns passage would complicate the analysis without adding anything of substance thereto.

The realization of self-centred welfare implies that a person cannot feel sympathy. Its violation, by contrast, means that a person is able to feel sympathy, and hence sympathy suffices to violate self-centred welfare (Sen 1985b: 214; 2002a: 35; 2007: 19). Two matters are of note about sympathy and the violation of self-centred welfare. First, it is the mere feeling of sympathy, that is, sympathy in its contemplative form, which violates self-centred welfare. Sen makes this point clear by citing his own official definition of sympathy when he establishes that sympathy violates self-centred welfare; as we saw in Chapter Two (Section II), this official definition refers only to contemplative, not active, sympathy. It is also clear in the definition of self-centred welfare cited above, a definition which includes no reference to the actions of a person who realizes self-centred welfare and so is independent of active sympathy. The second matter of note is that the violation of self-centred welfare endows a person with a capability – the capability to feel sympathy. The definition of self-centred welfare, however, makes no reference to the choices a person makes, and so it does not reveal how often, if at all, a person will activate this capability in her choices. The definition of self-centred welfare in the capability-theoretic interpretation, then, is independent of choice.

## Self-welfare goal

The realization of self-welfare goal means that an agent knows of no goal other than to maximize her own welfare. The violation of self-welfare goal, by contrast, means that the agent is capable of entertaining different goals, including, but not limited to, the maximization of her own welfare. The realization of self-welfare goal means that an agent is unable to make commitments, for if one only ever has one goal, namely, to maximize one's welfare (as the realization of self-welfare goal states), then one obviously cannot have commitments, for commitment presupposes an ability to act on non-welfare-related reasons or goals. One might conclude, conversely, that violating self-welfare goal implies that a person can have commitments. Strictly speaking this would not be true, not, at least, according to the analysis of Chapter Three (Section III). For in that chapter, we established that not only choices made with the goal of maximizing, but also those made with the goal of increasing one's welfare were incompatible with commitment if one's reason for making the choice were exclusively welfare-orientated. Consequently, a choice made with a welfare-increasing (but not maximizing) goal is not to be classified based on commitment. But welfare-increasing choices do violate self-welfare goal as Sen formulates it because having any goal other than the maximization of one's welfare violates this characteristic. In his work on the characteristics of privateness, Sen explicitly associates commitment and only commitment (or, as we shall see, one type of commitment) with the violation of self-welfare goal. He writes that commitment 'can take the form of modifying the person's *goals*, which can include effects on others beyond the extent to which these effects influence her own welfare (thereby violating self-welfare goal)' (2002a: 35; cf. 2007: 350). Since Sen makes the relationship between commitment and the violation of self-welfare goal so explicit, I will, in what follows, associate a violation of self-welfare goal with the capability to make commitments. I thereby ignore the capability to have the goal of increasing but not maximizing one's welfare, for although this capability strictly violates self-welfare goal, it does not constitute a commitment because one's goal is directed to one's own welfare. The violation of self-welfare goal, then, will be understood in what follows to endow a person with a capability – the capability to make commitments. But since the definition of self-welfare goal refers only to a person's goals and not to her choices, the capability to make commitments given by the violation of self-welfare goal tells us nothing about the frequency with which the person will make choices based on commitments. The definition of self-welfare goal, like that of self-centred welfare, is independent of choice in the capability-theoretic interpretation.

## Self-goal choice

The realization of self-goal choice means that one's choices are made exclusively in the pursuit of one's own goals, whatever those goals might be. Its violation presumably means that one's choices are *not* based on one's own goals, at least not exclusively. But what does this mean? The realization of self-goal choice, quoted above, states that a person is not 'restrained by the recognition of other people's goals, *except to the extent that these goals shape the person's own goals*' (2005a: 18). This implies that realizing self-goal choice includes cases in which a person takes other people's goals into consideration and reformulates her own goal in light of these others' goals. An example is as follows: in the autumn of a given year, it might not be a goal of mine to spend a holiday during the summer of the following year in Japan; but once my spouse informs me that she or he has this goal, I come to adopt this goal myself. I make my spouse's goal my own and, having 'acquired' this goal myself, it becomes my goal. This example is of what Philip Pettit calls a 'goal-modifying commitment', whereby 'I recognize the goals of others … and alter my own goals as a result' (2005: 31–3). A goal-modifying commitment does not violate self-goal choice because, after modifying my goal on the urgings of my spouse, I pursue this modified goal which is now my own goal. By making this my own goal and pursuing it through my choices, I would violate self-centred welfare (if, for instance, my goal were to derive sympathetic welfare by increasing that of my spouse); or it would violate self-welfare goal (if I were acting on a commitment, perhaps a commitment to furthering my spouse's well-being for a non-welfare-related reason), but it does not violate self-goal choice, for although one may say that my goals have changed in response to my spouse's expression of her or his goal, once this goal becomes my own, pursuing it is the same as pursuing any other goal which is my own, and therein lies the realization of self-goal choice. If one is to violate self-goal choice, something else is obviously implied: that one be able to restrain one's choices through a recognition of the goals of other people *without* thereby reformulating one's own goals and without making the goals of other people one's own. This is rather cryptic, and in Section II, I examine this matter in greater detail. For the moment, one may say that a violation of self-goal choice implies that a person has the capability to refrain from pursuing her goals. I will call this the capability to make *non-teleological choices*. Once again, how often, if at all, a person who is endowed with this capability makes non-teleological choices cannot be ascertained from the definition of self-goal choice on the capability-theoretic interpretation.

The interpretation of the three characteristics of privateness discussed above can be summarized in tabulated form. Table 7.1 (on the following page) presents the interpretation.

Despite some lack of clarity surrounding violations of self-goal choice, the foregoing discussion allows us to move on, for, having introduced and analysed each of Sen's characteristics of privateness, we can make a start on the task of ascertaining whether the realization and violation of a given characteristic are indeed independent of realizations and violations of the other two. Only if this is the case is Sen's independence claim vindicated.

*Table 7.1* Violations of characteristics of privateness and their implications for an agent's capabilities

| Characteristic violated | Capability associated with violation of the characteristic |
|---|---|
| Self-centred welfare | Feeling sympathy |
| Self-welfare goal | Making commitments |
| Self-goal choice | Making non-teleological choices |

## II Testing Sen's independence claim, part 1

Let us start with self-centred welfare and self-welfare goal and ask whether the realization and violation of the one are independent of the realization and violation of the other. If they are, there would be four possible combinations:

(1) *Realizing self-centred welfare but violating self-welfare goal.* With this combination, an agent would be incapable of feeling sympathy (thus realizing self-centred welfare); she would, however, be capable of having goals other than the maximization of her own welfare, and hence she would be able to make commitments (thus violating self-welfare goal).
(2) *Realizing self-welfare goal but violating self-centred welfare.* With this combination, the agent would have only one goal, namely, the maximization of her own welfare (thus realizing self-welfare goal) but she would be able to feel sympathy (thus violating self-centred welfare).
(3) *Realizing both.* This combination would apply to an agent who is incapable both of feeling sympathy (and hence realizing self-centred welfare) and of having goals other than the maximization of her own welfare (wherein consists the realization of self-welfare goal).
(4) *Violating both.* This combination would mean that the agent is capable of feeling sympathy (constituting a violation of self-centred welfare), and she would have goals other than the maximization of her welfare, which means that she can make commitments (thus violating self-welfare goal).

Are these four combinations feasible? They are. What allows one to pair realizations and violations of self-centred welfare and self-welfare goal in any combination can be seen from the fact that neither characteristic impinges on the jurisdiction of the other. Self-centred welfare tells us only about the sources from which a person can derive welfare – whether through his own consumption alone or also via sympathy. Self-centred welfare, therefore, imparts no information whatsoever about a person's goals and hence poses no restrictions on the goals a person may have. Hence, whether self-centred welfare be realized or violated has no impact on the realization or violation of self-welfare goal. Self-welfare goal, meanwhile, because it is concerned solely with the goals a person is capable of forming, imparts no information about

110  *Goals*

the sources – whether sympathetic or purely self-centred – from which a person is capable of deriving welfare. The two characteristics – whether they are realized or violated – are logically independent. Consequently, Sen's independence claim is upheld when we consider self-centred welfare and self-welfare goal.

Let us move on to combinations of self-centred welfare and self-goal choice. Here again there are four to consider, all of which must be feasible if Sen's independence claim is to be vindicated:

(1) *Realizing self-centred welfare but violating self-goal choice.* Here, the agent is incapable of feeling sympathy and can make choices in which she forbears from pursuing her own goals.
(2) *Violating self-centred welfare but realizing self-goal choice.* In this case the agent can feel sympathy but is able only to make choices through which she pursues a goal of her own.
(3) *Realizing both.* The agent here is able neither to feel sympathy nor to make choices through which she does not pursue her own goals.
(4) *Violating both.* With this combination, the agent is able to feel sympathy and able to make choices which are not in the pursuit of her own goals.

We noted, when investigating the compatibility of self-centred welfare and self-welfare goal, that the former makes no reference to the nature of a person's goals, because self-centred welfare makes claims only about the sources from which a person can or cannot derive welfare. We may add that self-centred welfare contains no information which pertains to whether a person pursues his own goals with the choices he makes or whether he be able to restrain his choices through a recognition of others' goals without thereby making those others' goals his own. Consequently, one's ability or inability to make non-teleological choices (upon which depends whether one violates self-goal choice) is left open by assumptions made about the sources from which one derives welfare (upon which depends whether one can feel sympathy and hence whether one realizes or violates self-centred welfare). Once again, the jurisdictions to which each applies have no overlap, and hence they can vary independently.

Being incapable of feeling sympathy (thus realizing self-centred welfare) is compatible with an ability to make non-teleological choices (thus violating self-goal choice), and hence the conditions of combination (1) can be fulfilled. Similarly, I can be capable of feeling sympathy (thus violating self-centred welfare) and capable of pursuing only my own goals when I make choices (thus realizing self-goal of choice). This fulfils the conditions of combination (2). Furthermore, being incapable of feeling sympathy (and so realizing self-centred welfare) is compatible with being incapable of making choices through which I do not pursue my own goals (hence realizing self-goal choice), and combination (3) is therefore also feasible. And finally, my ability to feel sympathy is equally compatible with an ability *not* to pursue my own goals exclusively, and with that, combination (4) is feasible. Consequently, Sen's independence claim is upheld when we consider self-centred welfare and self-goal choice in the capability-theoretic interpretation of Sen's characteristics of privateness.

We now turn to self-welfare goal and self-goal choice. Let us begin by assuming that the latter is realized, and so a person only pursues her own goals through the choices she makes. To vindicate Sen's independence claim we must establish that both (i) the realization of self-welfare goal is compatible with the realization of self-goal choice, and (ii) the violation of self-welfare goal is compatible with the realization of self-goal choice. Starting with (i), if self-welfare goal is realized, then the person's only goal is to maximize her own welfare. This is undoubtedly her own goal, and hence realizing self-welfare goal is compatible with the realization of self-goal choice. Combination (i) is therefore feasible. What about (ii)? If self-welfare goal is violated, we ascertained above that the person is capable of making commitments. Having this capability is compatible with the realization of self-goal choice because whether my commitment consists in my fighting for my country's independence or in campaigning to rid the world of state-sponsored torture, being committed to these causes implies having the corresponding goals, namely, furthering the causes just mentioned. These goals, though they have nothing to do with maximizing my own welfare (which is what makes these goals commitments), are decidedly my own. This suffices for the realization of self-goal choice. Consequently, self-welfare goal can be violated whilst self-goal choice is realized. And so we have established that combination (ii) is also feasible.

We are left, then, with violations of self-goal choice. Can one (iii) realize self-welfare goal and (iv) violate self-welfare goal when one violates self-goal choice? One can. Considering (iii), the realization of self-welfare goal makes one incapable of having any goal other than the maximization of one's own welfare. The violation of self-goal choice, on the other hand, endows me with the capability to make choices through which I do not pursue a goal of my own. Having this capability for non-teleological choice still allows me to realize self-welfare goal because the capability of non-teleological choice does not mean that I supplant my one and only goal of welfare maximization with another goal. If it did require that I supplant this maximizing goal with another and hence be able to pursue non-welfare-maximizing goals, I would no longer realize self-welfare goal, for the latter realization makes me incapable of having any goal but that of welfare-maximization. But violating self-goal choice simply means that I can make choices which do not pursue this welfare-maximizing goal without usurping it with another goal. And so welfare-maximization remains my only goal, though I be able to make choices in which I refrain from acting on this goal or on any other. Consequently, the violation of self-goal choice is compatible with the realization of self-welfare goal.

The same logic applies, *mutatis mutandis*, to combination (iv). A violation of self-welfare goal, we argued above, means that I am able to make commitments. Having these commitments implies having the goals associated with them and these goals are, without doubt, my own goals. Once again, a violation self-goal choice entails that I am able to make choices through which I do not pursue a goal which I call my own. Having this capability for non-teleological choice implied by the violation of self-goal choice does not therefore impinge on the goals which I do have – be they derived from my commitments or not. The capability for non-teleological choice leaves all of my goals untouched and only enables me to make choices which do not pursue these goals. At the level of capability, the capability to have commitments (wherein consists the violation of self-welfare goal) and the capability to make non-teleological choices (wherein lies the violation of self-goal choice) are logically distinct from one another. Hence the violation of self-welfare goal imposes no restriction on the violation of self-goal choice and *vice versa*. And so the two violations are mutually compatible.

We have, therewith, vindicated Sen's independence claim, and it has been a relatively simple matter on account of interpreting the characteristics of privateness on the basis of capabilities. Interpreted in a capability-theoretic way, Sen's characteristics of privateness reign over non-overlapping jurisdictions, and hence each can be realized or violated independently of the others. Some might think that the examination carried out in this section is adequate and that no further testing of Sen's independence claim be necessary. There is, however, a suspicion that we have made life a little too easy for Sen by interpreting his characteristics at the level of capabilities, and it could be that the capability-theoretic interpretation of the characteristics of privateness is not a sufficient basis for testing Sen's independence claim. But how else can one interpret these characteristics if not in a capability-theoretic manner? Sen's own discussions of one of these characteristics provides a hint, for his example of a violation of self-goal choice, which we will meet in Chapter Eight, does not endow a person with a particular capability but is instantiated in a choice which the person makes. In the example in question, the capability is not merely possessed by the person but is activated in her choice. This encourages the view that violations and realizations of the characteristics of privateness are to be interpreted, not at the level of capability, but at the level of choice. With regard to the other characteristics, Sen does not provide such a detailed example in the case of self-centred welfare and self-welfare goal, but the terminology with which he describes these characteristics does not rule out a choice-theoretic interpretation. For instance, he writes: 'a person whose welfare *is* affected by the misery of others certainly does violate self-centred welfare' (1985b: 214). Is this person simply capable of being affected by others' misery or is she affected in the here and now of her concrete act of choice? And of a violation of self-welfare goal he writes: 'a person's goals may include objectives other than maximization of her own welfare, for example, pursuit of her concept of social justice' (2005: 18). This, too, may be

Goals 113

interpreted capability-theoretically, as in the previous section, but it could be that the person has goals like social justice which she pursues in the act of choice. The choice-theoretic interpretation of Sen's characteristics of privateness, then, is at least a permissible interpretation. If we understand the characteristics in this way, the question for Sen's independence claim becomes: can one conceive of a choice which manifests every combination of realizations and violations of the characteristics of privateness? This question will form the basis of a further, more stringent, test of Sen's independence claim in the following section.

## III Characteristics of privateness: the choice-theoretic interpretation

To undertake this second test of Sen's independence claim, it is necessary to ascertain what realizations and violations of the characteristics of privateness mean in their choice-theoretic interpretation. Once this task is accomplished, the test of Sen's independence claim will consist in constructing an example for each possible combination of realizations or violations of the three characteristics.

### *Self-centred welfare*

With the realization of self-centred welfare, we must consider a person whose choices confer welfare on her solely on account of their relation to her own consumption. The choices concerned yield no sympathetic welfare to the person because the realization of this characteristic renders her welfare unaffected by the welfare of others. Two remarks about this realization of self-centred welfare are in order:

(a) The realization of self-centred welfare does not entail that the person who makes a choice does so with the goal of maximizing her welfare. For the goal of maximizing one's welfare makes one's choice self-interested, whilst the realization of self-centred welfare makes a person self-centred (Sen 2009a: 189). A choice which realizes self-centred welfare can therefore have a non-welfare-maximizing goal; the only restriction which the realization of self-centred welfare imposes is that, if the person derives any welfare from making the choice, that welfare may not be derived sympathetically but must derive from her own consumption.

(b) Lest the reader think that one's own consumption alone be too narrow a basis for conceiving the sources from which a self-centred person can derive welfare, in one of his formulations of self-centred welfare, Sen writes that a 'person's welfare depends only on her own consumption *and other features of the richness of her life*' (2002a: 33 emphasis added). The italicized phrase is a sensible addition because one can be self-centred but derive welfare from more than one's own consumption. Deriving welfare from one's own accomplishments rather than from one's own consumption would be one such feature of the richness of one's life from which one may derive welfare. Being able to derive welfare from this source is compatible with the realization of self-centred welfare. The point will be of relevance to combination three below. In a different formulation, Sen expresses the realization of self-centred welfare in terms of there being 'no externalities in the individual welfare function' (Sen in Klamer 1989: 143). This, too, widens the sources of welfare which one may derive beyond what one consumes directly.

When it comes to the violation of self-centred welfare, we are dealing with a person who can feel sympathy. What does this violation mean for the agent's choices? A choice which instantiates this violation is one through which the agent actually derives sympathetic welfare. Once again, nothing is implied about either welfare maximization or the goal underlying the choice. What, in Chapter Two (Section III), we discussed under the name of actions based on sympathy would be an example of a choice which violated self-centred welfare. These choices are made, it will be recalled, in pursuit of a welfare-orientated goal. But a choice which violates self-centred welfare is not necessarily one made with the goal of pursuing one's welfare; for, as we saw when we analysed Sen's more inclusive definition of commitment in Chapter Three, there are choices based on commitment from which a person derives, indeed maximizes, her welfare; these choices are made in the pursuit of a non-welfare-related goal but they confer welfare on the person as an unintended consequence. The derivation of this welfare is therefore unrelated to the goal which one pursues, and if such a choice is to violate self-centred welfare, the welfare may be derived sympathetically, though the choice must not involve an action based on sympathy in Sen's technical sense of this term because the goal which underlies actions based on sympathy is, *per definitionem*, the furtherance of one's own welfare. But making a choice based on commitment, through which one by definition pursues a non-welfare-related goal, can violate self-centred welfare as long as any welfare one derives from the choice comes to the agent through the channel of sympathy. We will meet an example of one such choice when we discuss combination four below.

### *Self-welfare goal*

The realization of this characteristic implies that a person's *only* goal is to maximize her welfare (Sen 1985b: 213). How does this relate to the choices the agent makes? Since it prohibits the pursuit of any goal other than the maximization of personal welfare, the agent's choices must be underlain by the goal of maximizing her welfare. Conversely, the violation of self-welfare goal entails that a choice be made with a goal other than the maximization of personal welfare. As in the previous section, I will, following Sen, associate the violation of self-welfare goal with commitment. Consequently, a choice which manifests the violation of self-welfare goal will be understood to be a choice through which one pursues a commitment.

*Self-goal choice*

The realization of self-goal choice at the level of choice implies that the person's choices are based '*in each case* on the pursuit of her own goals' (Sen 2002a: 34 emphasis added). There can be no exception to this, for the 'person's choices must be based on the *exclusive* pursuit of his or her own goals' (2005a: 18 emphasis added). The violation of self-goal choice, by contrast, manifests itself in choices through which the agent does not pursue her own goals, that is, choices for which the agent activates her capability for non-teleological choice.

Having clarified the meaning of the realizations and violations of Sen's characteristics of privateness when they are predicated on choices, our task is to find an example of each combination of realizations and violations. There are eight combinations in all, as given in Table 7.2. As stated in the introduction to this chapter, the first four combinations in the table will be treated in the remains of this chapter, whilst those involving violations of self-goal choice will be handled in the next chapter.

*Table 7.2* Combinations of the characteristics of privateness (or their relaxation)

| Combination | Characteristic(s) realized | Characteristic(s) violated |
| --- | --- | --- |
| One | SCW, SWG, SGC | None |
| Two | SWG, SGC | SCW |
| Three | SCW, SGC | SWG |
| Four | SGC | SCW, SWG |
| Five | SCW, SWG | SGC |
| Six | SCW | SWG, SGC |
| Seven | SWG | SCW, SGC |
| Eight | None | SCW, SWG, SGC |

Notes:
SCW = Self-Centred Welfare
SWG = Self-Welfare Goal
SGC = Self-Goal Choice

## IV Testing Sen's independence claim, part 2

*Combination one (realization of all three characteristics)*

To fulfil the conditions of combination one, we must construe a choice which confers welfare on the individual through non-sympathetic means, thus realizing self-centred welfare. Furthermore, the agent is incapable of acting on any goal other than the maximization of her welfare, and so self-welfare goal pertains. Her choice, then, must be made in the pursuit of welfare-maximization. The agent is also incapable of acting on goals which are not her own, and this realizes self-goal choice. Her choice must be based on the pursuit of her own goal. In fact, the realization of self-goal choice is implied by the realization of self-welfare goal, for the latter realization entails that the agent act only on the goal of maximizing her welfare, and since this goal is her own, self-goal choice, by virtue of the agent pursuing her own goal, must also be realized. As an example, consider a shopper who is unaffected by the plight of a homeless man who begs for money at the entrance to her local supermarket. Only the items she chooses to place into her basket have an impact on her welfare. This is a manifestation of self-centred welfare. The shopper, furthermore, has but one goal, namely, to maximize her welfare. She has no commitments which will distract her from this goal, and hence her choice realizes self-welfare goal. The realization of self-goal choice follows from the realization of self-welfare goal, for if the shopper unwaveringly strives to maximize her own welfare without exception, she invariably acts on this, her own, goal. The conditions for combination one are therefore realized.

*Combination two (realization of SWG, SGC; violation of SCW)*

In case two, the individual's welfare is affected by other people's welfare, for she is capable of feeling sympathy, a consequence of the violation of self-centred welfare. Our shopper from case one provides an example. Equipped with the capability to feel sympathy, she now feels pangs of conscience when she sees the homeless man because her welfare is not determined only by self-centred concerns. Furthermore, she is moved by her feelings of sympathy to make a choice based on sympathy, namely, to buy food for the man, for, by relieving his hardship, she increases her own welfare, just as Thomas Hobbes' pain was allegedly eased when he gave alms to an old beggar.[1] This choice, which is based on sympathy, violates self-centred welfare. It also ensures the realization of self-welfare goal if we assume that the shopper's sympathy-based choice is a welfare-maximizing one. And as with combination one, the realization of self-goal choice falls together with the realization of self-welfare goal: the shopper's goal in making this choice is to maximize her welfare (now augmented by sympathy), and since this is obviously her own goal, self-goal choice is also realized. Hence the all conditions for combination two are met.

*Combination three (realization of SCW, SGC; violation of SWG)*

Let us adopt an example from Sen to illustrate case three. A doctor has decided to work in 'some poor and miserable country' (1992: 61–2). Doing so involves leaving a lucrative job in the doctor's less miserable home country, and she expects that the switch will not maximize her welfare. We will assume, furthermore, that the doctor's choice is based on a commitment to combating injustices in global healthcare. The committed nature of her choice works a double shift in this example. First, a choice based on commitment violates self-welfare goal. Second, her commitment entails the fulfilment of self-goal choice, for her commitment to eliminating injustice involves the pursuit of her own goal, namely, reducing inequity in global health. Let us now consider how we can fit the realization of self-centred welfare into this example. To do so requires that we rule out the derivation of welfare via sympathy on the doctor's part.

Let us suppose that the doctor successfully pursues her commitment and improves the health of people in the 'poor and miserable country' in which she has elected to work. The doctor's efforts will thereby increase the welfare of the people whose health she improves. What might happen to the doctor's welfare as a result? It is plausible to posit that her own welfare will increase, but this would not allow for a realization of self-centred welfare, as required in combination three. The rise in the doctor's welfare, if such there be, must derive from a source other than sympathy, that is, it must be wholly unrelated to the increase in the welfare of those whose health the doctor improves. If this is not the case, the attempt to realize self-centred welfare would be thwarted.

Can we imagine the doctor deriving welfare from a different, non-sympathetic, source? We can if we conceive her in the way Kant conceives his philanthropically disposed character who is befallen by an obsession with his own sorrow which extinguishes all fellow-feeling for others. Though he has no inclination to help others in need and finds no joy in ameliorating their lot, the person whom Kant portrays nevertheless tears himself out of his 'deadly insensibility' and strives to improve the condition of those who suffer (Kant 1974/1786: 24). Kant presents this character to exemplify humans' ability to act on duty, and Sen's doctor can be portrayed similarly. Indeed, Sen presents this as a possibility when he discusses the simultaneous violation of self-welfare goal (given by her commitment to social justice) and realization of self-centred welfare: '[a] person may not feel any better off ... by her pursuit of social justice, and yet may be determined to pursue social justice because it is "the right thing to do"' (2002a: 34). Not becoming better off as a result of pursuing one's commitment is akin to the deadly stolidity of Kant's reluctant philanthropist. But Sen immediately calls this a 'rather extreme case', presumably because it is implausible to posit that the agent obtain no welfare as a result of the successful pursuit of a commitment. Sen insists that there is 'no contradiction' in the psychology of such an agent but suggests a 'more realistic' alternative, which does not exclude an increase in the doctor's welfare: the doctor derives welfare from pursuing her commitment, but she pursues this commitment 'not *because* this make [sic] her happier, or otherwise better off, but *because* she is committed to that value [of social justice]' (Sen 2002a: 34). In the passage just quoted, Sen is presenting us with a version of his counterfactual condition for commitment from 'Rational Fools': the doctor's welfare is promoted by her decision to work abroad and her success in pursuing her commitment, but the prospect of attaining this welfare is not her reason for making that decision, for she would have decided to work abroad had her welfare not been thus promoted. Sen's words are carefully chosen, for he posits that the doctor derives welfare 'from being able to pursue social justice'. He does not suggest that she derives welfare from the improved welfare of those whose health she improves, for this latter possibility would mean that the doctor derive welfare sympathetically which, *ex hypothesi*, she cannot do if self-centred welfare is to be realized. By deriving welfare from her pursuit of social justice, the doctor derives intrinsic satisfaction from that pursuit (Sen, 2002a: 34–5). And we must believe that she derives this intrinsic satisfaction whether or not she improves the welfare of others, and if she does thus improve others' welfare, it makes no difference to her own welfare.

As depicted above, there is something fishy about the doctor's psychology, for we are asked to believe that she (i) take pleasure in the pursuit of justice in global health, whilst (ii) remaining indifferent to the welfare of those whose health is affected by this pursuit. What is odd is that increasing the welfare of those whose health she improves is an ineluctable consequence of the successful pursuit of her commitment; one might speak of a necessary relationship between the successful pursuit of the commitment and improvements in the welfare of others; the whole point of pursuing the commitment is to bring about beneficial health effects for others. Consequently, separating (i) and (ii), though not illogical (for it involves, as Sen writes, 'no contradiction'), is difficult to imagine in practice. If she succeeded in making this separation, the doctor would be rather like a master chef who has a commitment to culinary excellence but does not give a damn whether anybody enjoys eating the delicacies he prepares. But the psychology of the doctor, though odd, is not incoherent, for it is possible, even if implausible, that the doctor derives welfare from the pursuit of her commitment whilst remaining completely unmoved by the outcome of that pursuit for other people's welfare. By making the latter assumption we guarantee the realization of self-centred welfare. Hence we must grant that the conditions for combination three can be met. To summarize, then, self-welfare goal is violated by the doctor's choice which is based on commitment; self-goal choice is realized because the goal of her commitment is her own goal; and self-centred welfare is realized because she derives no sympathetic welfare from beholding that her pursuits relieve the suffering of others, though she may derive welfare from other, non-sympathetic, sources.

### *Combination four (fulfilment of SGC; violation of SCW, SWG)*

A modification of Sen's doctor from case three forms the basis of our example for case four. The doctor is now capable of feeling sympathy, for case four requires a violation of self-centred welfare. The violation of self-welfare goal will be met if the doctor's choice to work abroad is based on commitment, again, we will assume, on a commitment to fighting global health inequalities. Promoting this commitment is the goal of her choice and, because it is her own goal, the requisite realization of self-goal choice is achieved. Because of

*Goals* 119

her ability to feel sympathy, the doctor in combination four, unlike her *Doppelgänger* in combination three, may derive welfare from increasing the welfare of those whose health she betters. Deriving this welfare is not, however, the goal of her choice to work abroad, for were this so, she would realize rather than violate self-welfare goal. The doctor's choice, therefore, is not based on sympathy. Consequently, any welfare the doctor derives sympathetically comes to her contemplatively as an unintended consequence of pursuing her commitment. Indeed, the fact that her goal is non-welfare-related ensures not only that her choice is not based on sympathy but also that it her choice is based on commitment. So the doctor pursues her commitment with the goal of increasing others' welfare independent of the effects of doing so for her own welfare. It just so happens that success in this pursuit brings about a state of affairs of improved health for others from which the doctor derives welfare sympathetically. Therewith the conditions of this combination are met.

**Conclusion**

In this chapter, we have met Sen's three characteristics of privateness as well as his independence claim. The violation of self-welfare goal is Sen's way of reformulating what he means by commitment, though the manner in which the three characteristics relate to commitment will further discussed in the following chapter. Sen's independence stood up to the test to which it was subjected in Section II, in which the three characteristics of privateness were understood as endowing the agent with, or denying her, certain capabilities. The relative ease with which Sen's independence claim passes the test when the characteristics of privateness are interpreted in a capability-theoretic manner emboldened us to subject it to a more stringent test, one which required that we conceive of the eight combinations of the realizations and violations of the characteristics of privateness at the level of choice. Four such combinations have been investigated in Section IV, and again the independence claim withstood the test. None of those combinations, however, involved the most controversial aspect of Sen's work on choice, namely, a violation of self-goal choice. In the chapter which follows, the four remaining combinations, each of which involves a violation of self-goal choice, will be explored. Whilst exploring these four combinations, more detailed discussion about what this violation involves will be undertaken.

**Note**

1 The full anecdote, as bequeathed to us by John Aubrey, is as follows:

> One time, I remember, going into the Strand, a poor and infirm man craved his [Hobbes'] alms. He beholding him with eyes of pity and compassion, put his hands in his pockets, and gave him 6d. Said a divine (that is Dr Jasper Mayne) that stood by – 'Would you have done this, if it had not been Christ's command?' 'Yes,' said he. 'Why?' said the other. 'Because,' said he, 'I was in pain to

consider the miserable condition of the old man; and now my alms, giving him some relief, doth also ease me'.

(Aubrey 1975: 166)

Abraham Lincoln offers a similarly quotable example:

Mr Lincoln once remarked to a fellow-passenger on an old time mud-coach that all men were prompted by selfishness in doing good. His fellow passenger was antagonizing this position when they were passing over a corduroy bridge that spanned a slough. As they crossed this bridge they espied an old razor-backed sow on the bank making a terrible noise because her pigs had got into the slough and were in danger of drowning. As the old coach began to climb the hill, Mr. Lincoln called out, 'Driver can't you stop just a moment?' Then Mr. Lincoln jumped out, ran back and lifted the little pigs out of the mud and water and placed them on the bank. When he returned his companion remarked: 'Now Abe, where does selfishness come in on this little episode?' 'Why, bless your soul Ed, that was the very essence of selfishness. I should have had no peace of mind all day had I gone on and left that suffering old sow worrying over those pigs. I did it to get peace of mind, don't you see?'

(cited in Feinberg 1971: 492)

# 8 Self-goal choice

**Introduction**

Four combinations of the realization or violation of Sen's characteristics of privateness are discussed in what follows, and I will attempt to provide an example for each. This will complete the second test of Sen's independence claim commenced in the latter half of the previous chapter. Each of the four combinations requires a violation of self-goal choice and the example in combinations five, six and seven is drawn from an example with which Sen illustrates this violation. As with the four combinations from the preceding chapter (Section IV), the four combinations under consideration in this chapter involve realizing and violating each characteristic of privateness at the level of choice. This means that the examples involve choices in which the relevant capabilities or incapabilities discussed in Section I of the previous chapter are activated. It transpires that both the realization and violation of self-welfare goal conflict with a violation of self-goal choice. A remedy for this conflict is suggested. If the remedy is deemed allowable, it brings us closer to fulfilling the conditions of the four examples, but does not fulfil them completely.

The structure of the chapter is as follows. Section I further elucidates violations of self-goal choice and does so through a critique of Sen's interpreters and critics who have commented on the violation of self-goal choice. I argue that Sen's critics misrepresent Sen and that the best way of interpreting what the latter means by violations of self-goal choice is to conceive them in terms of goalless choices. In Section II, I continue and complete the test of Sen's independence claim using the choice-theoretic interpretation of the characteristics of privateness. In Section III, I offer remarks on the violation of self-goal choice in an attempt further to elucidate its meaning and offer an assessment of its plausibility.

## I Self-goal choice and Sen's critics

The violation of self-goal choice – its meaning and possibility – has proven to be the most controversial aspect of Sen's writing on choice. I therefore clarify what Sen means by this violation beyond the remarks on the matter which I made in Chapter Seven. A good approach to self-goal choice is to see how Sen's critics interpret its violation and what they find so vexatious about it.

Sen's interpreters assume two things about violations of self-goal choice:

(i) that self-goal choice is violated when an agent does not act on his own goal;
(ii) that an agent who does not act on his own goal must be acting on the goal(s) of others.

Ann Cudd writes that a violation of self-goal choice consists in 'a motivation that replaces ... the agent's goal with another's goal or the goal of a group' (2014: 43; 2017: 412; cf. Davis 2007: 313). And Christoph Hanisch follows suit when he describes this violation as a case in which 'we "replace" our goals with those of other individuals or with collective goals' (2013: 163–4, cf. 162). It is perfectly conceivable that an agent replaces her own goals with the goals of others and acts on the latter. The Japanese holiday example in the previous chapter (Section I) exemplifies this phenomenon. But this is not how Sen understands violations of self-goal choice, for he rejects the second element of his critics' interpretation of this violation. Sen, that is, insists that an agent whose choice violates self-goal choice does not make the goals of others her own; with a violation of self-goal choice, he writes, one's choice is altered 'through a recognition of other people's goals *beyond the extent to which other people's goal get incorporated into one's own goals*' (2002a: 35 emphasis added; cf. 2005: 19; 2007: 351). As Sen understands it, then, a violation of self-goal choice does not consist in one's adopting others' goals and making them the basis of one's action. What we are seeking rather is a choice for which the agent abnegates his own goals without replacing them with others'. Sen's position, then, is irremediably inconsistent with assumption (ii) made by Sen's interpreters (cf. Schmid, 2005: 217–18). Sen's critics' first assumption, however, that, when self-goal choice is violated, the agent does not act on her own goal, is correct.

To exemplify a violation of self-goal choice, Sen offers the following example:

> You are occupying a window seat in a plane journey, with the window shade up, when you are requested by the occupant of the aisle seat next to you to pull down the shade so that he can see his computer screen better to be able to devote himself fully to playing some computer game, which in your view is a 'plainly silly' game. ... You are frustrated that there is so much ignorance around, with so many people playing inane games rather than reading the news. ... You decide, nevertheless, to comply with the game-enthusiast's request to help him see the computer screen, and you oblige him by pulling down the shutter.
> 
> (2007: 348–9; 2009a: 192–3)

Since the example will occupy us for some time, let us name the two protagonists in the story, the game-playing, aisle-seat-occupying character being Paul, and the passenger who occupies the window seat Cyrilla.

If Cyrilla's choice is to constitute a violation of self-welfare goal, she cannot be acting on her own goal when she lowers the blind. But do her goals simply vanish in this example? They do not. Sen tells us that, prior to the exchange with Paul, Cyrilla is 'rather enjoying the sun' (2009a: 193). This, we may suppose, is her goal, one which, we will also assume, would maximize her welfare if she pursued it by keeping the blind open. Furthermore, it remains her goal throughout the interaction with Paul. Cyrilla therefore *has* a goal, but she does not pursue it when she lowers the blind. It is therefore her choice of action only, not her goal, which changes after she considers Paul's request. As Sen writes, 'even when the person sticks to his own goals, the question of behavioral response does remain' (1985b: 211). This applies to Cyrilla who does stick to her goal, although one would not be able to infer this directly from her behavioural response to Paul's request.

By shutting the blind, Cyrilla becomes, in Philip Pettit's words, the 'executor' of Paul's goal, whereby Paul's goal is to establish the optimal conditions for game-playing (2005: 32). It is easy, and some would think natural, to conclude from this that Cyrilla is pursuing Paul's goal when she lowers the blind. But nothing of the sort is happening, claims Sen, for although Cyrilla's choice certainly helps Paul to pursue his goal (this is explicit in Sen's depiction of the encounter with the statement '[y]ou decide, nevertheless, ... to help him'), this does not mean that Cyrilla's goal is to help Paul pursue his goal. To say that Cyrilla's choice helps Paul pursue his goal is a statement about the *consequences* of her choice, but it reveals nothing about Cyrilla's goal. If she were pursuing Paul's goal, then Paul's goal would become Cyrilla's own, and we would therefore have a goal-modifying commitment, as Pettit describes it (see Chapter Seven, Section I).

Sen explicitly rejects the idea that Cyrilla is pursuing Paul's goal. In answering the objection that one 'cannot pursue other people's goals without making them your own', he asks: '[b]y agreeing to pull the shade down, are you to be seen as acting according to the game-player's goal?' (Sen 2007: 352). His answer is that this is 'not at all a good description of what is actually happening. You are not actively pursuing another person's goals, but just letting that person pursue his'. Sen does not deny that we often make other people's goals our own and pursue their goals through our choices; many of our commitments are based on our choice to pursue what we perceive to be others' goals. But this is not what he has in mind when he speaks of violating self-goal choice, and he is decisive in rejecting this interpretation of this violation: 'considering the priorities of others can influence [one's] action *even without its being a part of one's self-understood goal*' (Sen 2007: 351 emphasis added). Alternatively, he stresses that not acting on one's own goal does not entail that a person acts on other people's goals or that one otherwise 'endorse[s] the goals of others' (Sen, 2007: 347, 348, cf. 351, 352; 2009a: 192).

Violations of self-goal choice, then, do not involve the agent acting on the goals of others.

We have therefore eliminated two possible candidates for the goal which Cyrilla might be pursuing when she lowers the blind: she neither pursues her own goal (continuing to enjoy the sun), nor does she pursue Paul's goal (establishing the optimal conditions for game-playing). Is there a different candidate for the goal which Cyrilla is pursuing? There is, and to reveal it, we must consider more closely the two depictions of the aeroplane episode which Sen offers. In the first, the occupant of the window seat follows 'a norm of good behaviour' which may be expressed as 'let others be' (2007: 349). In Sen's second depiction, Cyrilla considers it unfair to (ab)use her proximity to and control of the shutter by dictating its position (2009a: 193). Both correspond to a possibility which Sen outlined when he first introduced the idea of violating self-goal choice: one follows 'rules of conduct' which constitute 'self-imposed restrictions on the pursuit on one's own goals' (1985b: 214). And this brings us back to the topic of norm or rule following which was discussed in Chapter Five. These depictions give us a further possibility as to a goal which Cyrilla pursues when she lowers the blind: could her goal be to conform with a rule of conduct or a norm of good behaviour? This might be what Cudd is suggesting, when she writes that a person who violates self-goal choice 'replaces' her own goals with 'an impartial moral norm' (2014: 43).

Sen explicitly rejects the notion. I insert the Roman numerals in square brackets for ease of interpretation of the following passage:

> a person's choice behavior may be constrained or influenced [i] by the goals of others, or [ii] by rules of conduct, thereby violating self-goal choice (that is, the influences may affect the person's choice *without* their taking the form of goals that the person can be seen as pursuing himself).
>
> (1985b: 214 emphasis added)

This passage tells us that [i] the goals of others and [ii] rules of conduct (or what Cudd calls an impartial moral norm) can influence a person's choice; but they can alter a person's choice without thereby becoming goals of the person, as the parenthetic phrase, with which the passage ends, states ('*without* their taking the form of goals that the person can be seen as pursuing himself'). It might be the case that acting in accordance with a social norm will have the effect of 'selecting' that norm evolutionarily which, in turn, will improve the welfare of all members of the community in which one finds oneself because the continued existence of the norm is of benefit to all. This, however, is a consequence of adhering to a norm, and one cannot infer the agent's goal from the consequences of her act.

One question which Sen raises with regard to the effects of norm following on a community of people is whether the individual sees these norms to be of intrinsic or merely of instrumental significance (1987a: 83–6). If she deems them to be intrinsically important, does this imply that norm adherence is her goal? In one pronouncement on the matter, Sen suggests that it does not. When distinguishing between different ways of violating self-goal choice, he writes: '[t]here may be good ethical reasons for being non-consequentialist ... A person will let go of an opportunity to promote his or her goals because of some ethical values not well-reflected in the objective function' (Sen in Klamer 1989: 144). Imagine, for instance, that one is committed to promise keeping and that this commitment derives from one's belief that promise keeping is ethically good. Adhering to this commitment 'non-consequentially', as I interpret Sen, means that one does so as a matter of principle because one attaches intrinsic value to norm adherence; one does not decide on a case-by-case basis whether to adhere to the commitment on any given occasion with a view to the consequences which one expects promise keeping will bring about. If, as Sen writes, this represents a violation of self-goal choice, a person who adheres to her commitment relinquishes the opportunity to promote her own goals even when her goals are best pursued by breaking a promise she has made. This argument, if it represents Sen's view accurately, can be traced to remarks he makes in the closing section of 'Rational Fools'. There he states that commitment is non-consequentialist and it is so because, unlike the concept of rationality typically used in much of economic theory, commitment involves '*rule* evaluation' as opposed to relying exclusively on '*act* evaluation' as a basis on which the agent is held to decide how to choose rationally (1977a: 104). Commitment can involve 'the lack of personal gain in particular *acts*' by 'considering the values of *rules* of behaviour'. The individual, then, ties her conduct to '*rules* of behaviour', and the constraints which she imposes on herself go 'beyond the consequences' (1977a: 104; cf. Vanberg 2008). This allows Sen to see the case of adhering to ethical values which the agent deems to be of intrinsic import to be a case of violating self-goal choice (Sen in Klamer 1989: 144).

Elsewhere, however, Sen expresses what appears to be the opposite opinion about the relationship between adhering to rules of behaviour which one holds to be of intrinsic importance and goal-orientated conduct. He writes: '[i]f behavior is intrinsically important, then the patterns [of behaviour] can, of course, figure as part of our goals' (1985b: 212). What he calls 'the patterns', here, are rules of behaviour. But in the passage just quoted, Sen suggests the following of such rules, when doing so is of intrinsic import to the agent, to be the latter's goal. This view strikes me as more plausible, for if asked why I keep a promise when doing so on a given occasion be to my disadvantage, I would answer by saying 'I kept my promise in order to conform to the rule of promise keeping to which I have committed myself as a matter of principle regardless of the possibly negative consequences for my welfare of doing so'. The 'in order to' formulation in this answer is the way in which I express my goal – that after which I strive. If this interpretation is correct, no violation of self-goal choice is implied. Let us now move on to the case which is of greater interest to Sen in which following rules of conduct is deemed to be of instrumental, rather than of intrinsic, import.

With instrumentally important rules, we may imagine again that the individual would prefer, on grounds of welfare maximization, to perform a rule-breaking action, just as Cyrilla would prefer to keep the shutter open or a party to the prisoners' dilemma would rather elect not to cooperate. But this time, whatever rule one has committed oneself to follow, one does not consider it to be intrinsically good. If the individual refrains from performing her welfare-maximizing action, she does so because she acknowledges the instrumental importance of the rule she follows. 'Instrumental', here, means that she ascertains that universal adherence to the rule by the members of her interaction community would allow all such members better to realize their true goals (*ex hypothesi*, welfare maximization) without any of them necessarily seeing the rule to be of intrinsic value. In manifesting reciprocity toward the members of one's interaction community, Sen writes that, 'it is hard to argue that the person's "real goal" is to follow reciprocity rather than their respective actual goals' (1987a: 86). The individual acts on the norm which she accepts 'for the *general* pursuit of *individual* goals' (1987a: 85–6). In this particular case, she would prefer to break the rule for her own advantage but doing so, she reasons, would redound negatively to her endeavours to pursue her goals on future occasions when others thwart her attempts to do as she wishes because they break the norm on those occasions on which they interact with her. Through this type of reasoning, individuals come to see the benefits of following a rule as a general policy of action. By accepting the rule because it is mutually beneficial (and thus beneficial to oneself), one attaches only instrumental importance to it. This seems to be what 'instrumental importance' means in this context. There might be rules, for example, cooperating in prisoners' dilemmas if others will do likewise, adherence to which never redounds to one's immediate advantage on a given occasion, because the strategy of non-cooperation will always place one in a better position regardless of what others do. But here, too, because general acceptance of a rule of cooperative behaviour is beneficial to all (including oneself), one is willing, instrumentally, to curb the pursuit of one's goal (welfare maximization), thus allowing others to pursue theirs, without thereby making their goals one's own, let alone acting on their goals. This is how Sen eliminates the third possibility for a goal which someone in Cyrilla's position might be held to pursue: making one's conduct adhere to a norm when that norm is not of intrinsic importance on a given occasion (because one prefers to break it), is not the goal pursued by an agent whose conduct conforms to the norm; her choice therefore violates self-goal choice.

Does Sen offer a different candidate for the goal we may impute to Cyrilla when she closes the blind? He does not: at no point does he attribute the pursuit of any goal to the occupant of the window seat. Consequently, Sen holds that Cyrilla does not replace her original goal of continuing to enjoy the sun. She maintains this goal throughout the encounter with Paul, but she does not pursue it through her choice to lower the blind. In fact, she pursues no goal whatsoever when she lowers the blind, and therein lies her violation of self-goal choice. She makes what we may call a *goalless choice*.

Sen identifies this violation of self-goal choice with a type of commitment, a *goal-negating commitment*, as I will call it henceforth. Pettit (2005: 32) describes such commitments as 'goal-displacing'. I prefer the term 'goal-negating', for displacement might imply that these commitments displace the agent's goal with another goal, whereas the point on which one must insist is that they negate the agent's goal, without replacement. Just as Archimedes' body displaced water in the bathtub by occupying the position which the water occupied before he jumped in, 'displacing' comes too close to 'replacing' to be an adequate description of violations of self-goal choice.[1] In a passage which we have already quoted above, Sen states that a violation of self-goal choice consists in 'a recognition of other people's goals beyond the extent to which other people's goal get incorporated into one's own goals' (2002a: 35). The context of this passage is Sen's identification of two types of commitment, the first of which violates self-welfare goal, as we discussed before (Chapter Seven, Section I). This first type involves making choices which, though based on a goal, expand the agent's repertoire of goals beyond concerns for his self-interest. Of this type of commitment, Sen writes:

> It would be committed behavior all right if one acts entirely according to one's goals when those goals include consideration of the interests of others – over and above the extent to which one's own well-being or interest is directly influenced by the well-being or interest of others.
> (2007: 350)

The second type of commitment violates self-goal choice and is explained by Sen in the passage just quoted. This second type of commitment, then, may be conceived, in accord with my analysis of violations of self-goal choice, to consist in goalless choices. With the idea of goalless choices in our conceptual repertoire, we may now proceed to examine the remaining four combinations of the characteristics of privateness.

## II Testing Sen's independence claim, the third and final part

### Combination five (realization of SCW, SWG; violation of SGC)

This combination and the two which follow it use Sen's aeroplane example as a vehicle for testing his independence claim.

To realize self-centred welfare in combination five, Cyrilla must be incapable of feeling sympathy. She can therefore only derive welfare self-centredly. Applied to her choice to lower the blind, this means that Cyrilla's welfare is unaffected by her awareness of any increase in welfare which Paul might experience as a result of the blind being shut. With regard to the relaxation of self-goal choice, Cyrilla must be conceived to be making a goalless choice, as explained above, for she is *not* pursuing her own goal or any other goal when she lowers the blind. She does, to be sure, have a goal, which we identified as continuing to enjoy the sun, but she does not pursue this goal when closing the shutter. This violation of self-goal choice is compatible with the realization of self-centred welfare, for whatever choice she makes, whether goalless or goal-orientated, as long as Cyrilla derives no sympathetic welfare from it, her choice will realize self-centred welfare. Can Cyrilla's choice also be conceived to realize self-welfare goal, the third and final condition to be fulfilled in combination five? The realization of self-welfare goal means that the goal of Cyrilla's choice is to maximize her own welfare. This immediately causes a problem for the violation of self-goal choice: if a person's goal is to maximize her welfare and this goal is manifested in her choice, then this goal is surely her own goal. If it is, though, this would make it impossible to violate self-goal choice whilst realizing self-welfare goal, and so the conditions for combination five cannot be met. This is a problem which can be partially circumvented if we conceive violations of self-welfare goal in the manner which I put forward in the ensuing paragraph. It should be noted, though, that even if the reader accepts this reformulation, we would approach the conditions required in combination five more closely but not meet them fully, for the proposed reformulation does not entail a realization of self-welfare goal.

The reformulation of self-welfare goal is as follows:

> A choice which realizes self-welfare goal entails that a person's goal is to maximize her own welfare. Hence, when she pursues a goal through her choices, she pursues this goal and no other. When a person's choice is goalless, however, as it must be if she is to violate self-goal choice, her choice does not violate self-welfare goal because self-welfare goal is violated only by choices for which the individual pursues a goal derived from a commitment. A person whose choice is goalless pursues no such goal, and so self-welfare goal is not violated. But neither does she pursue the goal of welfare maximization if she violates self-goal choice, and so her choice does not realize self-welfare goal either.

The conditions of combination five require that the individual's choice realize self-centred welfare. If we accept the above reformulation of self-welfare goal, we may conclude that self-welfare goal is neither violated nor realized, and this is not the same as realizing this characteristic of privateness. So we have not met the conditions of combination five but have at least steered clear of a violation of self-welfare goal; instead of fulfilling all three of the requisite conditions, we have met the realization of self-centred welfare and the violation of self-goal choice, but instead of the realization of self-welfare goal, we have rendered self-welfare goal not violated. Like a ruling of 'not proven' in Scottish criminal law, 'not violated' is perhaps a poor substitute for 'realized' in the case of self-welfare goal, and, following Walter Scott's description of 'not proven' as a 'bastard verdict' (Barbato 2005: 546), perhaps we have achieved a 'bastard fulfilment' of the conditions in combination five. This, I

*Self-goal choice* 129

submit, is the nearest one can come to fulfilling the conditions of this combination if one's aim is to have the realizations and violations of the characteristics of privateness manifest themselves in a concrete choice.

**Combination six (realization of SCW; violation of SWG, SGC)**

For this combination, the same example will be used, but this time a violation of self-welfare goal is sought. Violating self-welfare goal, according to the capability-theoretic interpretation, as we argued in Chapter Seven (Section I), is to be interpreted as endowing a person with the capability to make commitments. And so, according to the choice-theoretic interpretation, we seek a choice which activates this capability, one which is based on commitment. Making a choice based on commitment, we have also established before, is to pursue a goal – as given by one's commitment – which is one's own goal. This, however, conflicts with the violation of self-goal choice which requires that a person not pursue her own goal in a given choice. The same problem between realizing self-welfare goal and violating self-goal choice which we met in combination five above confronts us here with the violation of self-welfare goal; for whether a choice realizes or violates self-welfare goal, the agent's choice is goal orientated. To ameliorate the problem, one can avail oneself of the reformulation of violations of self-welfare goal given under combination five. The reformulation states that a choice which violates self-goal choice neither realizes nor violates self-welfare goal. This might be comforting for combination six in that one avoids a realization of self-welfare goal, but the non-realization of this characteristic does not imply the violation which we require, and so the conditions of combination six are not met, as the status of self-welfare goal remains indeterminate – neither realized nor violated. This is as near as one can come to fulfilling the violation of self-welfare goal whilst simultaneously violating self-goal choice. As for the realization of self-centred welfare required in combination six, the same applies as it did for its predecessor: as long as a person remains unaffected by any changes in the welfare of others which her choice brings about, self-centred welfare is realized. Neither the violation of self-goal choice nor the indeterminate status of self-welfare goal get in the way of this realization of self-centred welfare. Cyrilla, then, lowers the blind and derives no sympathetic welfare from the concomitant increase in Paul's welfare. Her choice is goalless in the sense that we have interpreted the violation of self-goal choice. Because her choice has no goal, she neither realizes self-welfare goal (the realization of which would require her goal to be welfare maximization), nor does she violate it (which would require her to act on a goal given by her commitment). This is as close as one can come to fulfilling the conditions of combination six.

**Combination seven (realization of SWG; violation of SCW, SGC)**

We noted in Chapter Seven (Section III) that one way of violating self-centred welfare at the level of choice would be through a choice as based on sympathy. This would require that the person strive to increase his welfare sympathetically through such choices. Since the acquisition of welfare is, by definition, his goal, when he makes a choice based on sympathy, such a choice cannot violate self-goal choice. We must therefore look to a different way of violating self-centred welfare if the conditions of combination seven are to be fulfilled. A different way can be found by conceiving a choice through which the person derives welfare sympathetically but does not make it his goal to do so. This was how the violation of self-centred welfare was secured in combination four of the previous chapter and it corresponds with a case discussed in Chapter Three (Section V) under the heading of altruism, whereby an agent, $A$, derives welfare from his own action which increases the welfare of another person, $B$. The increased welfare experienced by $A$ results from of his ability to feel contemplative sympathy; but his enjoyment of this welfare was not the goal which motivated him to act. Consequently, $A$ can violate self-centred welfare without making a choice based on sympathy in Sen's understanding of the term. In combination seven, we also have to juxtapose the realization of self-welfare goal and the violation of self-goal choice, and, as we discovered when discussing combination five, these two conditions are mutually incompatible. We can, however, avail ourselves once again of the reformulation of realizing self-welfare goal stated under combination five. This would allow us to say that self-welfare goal is 'not violated' again.

When Cyrilla lowers the blind, then, she derives welfare sympathetically because she increases Paul's welfare thereby. But deriving this welfare is not the goal of her action; rather it is an unintended consequence of her lowering the blind and is therefore a purely contemplative derivation of sympathy. This means that self-centred welfare is violated in and through the fact that Cyrilla feels contemplative sympathy with respect to her choice. Self-welfare goal is not properly realized by this choice of action, as discussed, for its realization would require that Cyrilla make a choice through which she pursues the goal of maximizing her welfare. This cannot be the case for Cyrilla's choice if it is to violate self-goal choice. Her choice therefore leaves self-welfare goal neither violated nor realized. This is as close to fulfilling the conditions of combination seven as we can come. Something about Cyrilla's derivation of welfare in the example fails to ring true, however. Without this assumption, the violation of self-centred welfare would be impossible, but as Sen portrays the occupant of the window seat, she manifests nothing but disgruntlement and exasperation toward her neighbour, and deriving welfare is apparently not something she does. But since she is required to violate self-centred welfare, she must derive welfare as a result of the increase in her neighbour's welfare. Assuming this might appear to be a little *ad hoc*, but it is necessary for the fulfilment of the conditions in combination seven.

### Combination eight (violation of all three characteristics)

The violation of both self-welfare goal and self-goal choice required in combination eight means mirroring the strategy used in combination six for this juxtaposition of conditions. The relevant choice must be goalless (hence violating self-goal choice) and, because it has no goal, the choice neither realizes nor violates self-welfare goal. The violation of self-centred welfare must be conceived, as it was in combination seven, not in terms of a choice based on sympathy but of a choice through which the person who makes the choice derives welfare sympathetically without, however, having made this the goal of her choice.

To vary the example, let us plunge ourselves into the world of fruit, to which Sen is obviously rather partial if we are to judge from the many carposian examples in his work (see 1983c: 398–9; 1993a: 129; 1997: 161, 167–8, 180–1). So partial as he obviously is in this respect that I will make him the star of the example. Sen is being pampered at an afternoon garden party in the grounds of a private college. He fears that the party has been organized for the purpose of getting him to make a donation to the college which is to name a lecture theatre after him. At one point a fruit bowl is thrust in front of his nose, whereupon he hears the words of the college president: 'do help yourself, old sport'. Feeling not only 'sporty' but peckish, Sen peruses the fruit bowl to see that it contains two apples and a mango. Whilst being a fan of apples, Sen does not consider them 'party food'. Mangos, on the other hand, most definitely are, and if he were to pursue his goal of maximizing his welfare, he would make a dash at the mango. But Sen does not know whether there are further mangos with which to replenish the fruit bowl, and nobody seems to want to 'force' the mango on him (Sen 1997: 161) so he takes an apple, the smaller of the two to boot. This choice is based on his adherence to a social norm – 'leave as good and enough for others' – which forbids him from maximizing his welfare. His choice not only lands him with a small apple but also violates self-goal choice, for Sen neither pursues his own goal (eating a mango) nor does he replace this goal with another person's goal which he pursues instead. To be sure, there are plenty of people at the party who would gladly devour what might be the last mango in town, but Sen does not leave the mango in the fruit bowl *in order* to help other would-be mango eaters to pursue their goals; rather propriety admonishes him to relinquish his goal, act on a social norm and take an apple. Neither, we may add, is Sen's goal to act in conformity with the aforementioned social norm, for although his choice does conform to the norm, this is not his goal. Being goalless, Sen's choice of apple does not deliver us the required violation of self-welfare goal. Consequently, self-welfare goal is, once again, neither realized nor violated. Finally, we may say that Sen is a good-natured sort of chap who is much less curmudgeonly than Cyrilla to whom we could only grudgingly ascribe the derivation of sympathetic welfare after she had lowered the blind in the previous combination. Consequently, Sen feels better off in the knowledge that, because he has adhered to a norm and chosen an apple, somebody else can enjoy the mango. This is an expression of contemplative sympathy. Sen's choice of apple was not, however, motivated by the prospect of deriving welfare sympathetically, for he is principled enough to adhere to the social norm without the carrot of sympathetic welfare or indeed the stick of fearing that he might acquire a bad reputation if he made a direct assault on the mango.

Before we conclude this section, there is a further possibility to be addressed, one suggested by some of Sen's remarks of self-goal choice. The fulfilment of self-goal choice means that an individual's choice is 'not restrained by the recognition of other people's pursuit of their goal' (Sen 1985b: 214). The realization of self-goal choice is categorical; it rules out *any* consideration of others' goals. Self-goal choice, by implication, is violated when the person restrains her choices in recognition of other people's goals. But this violation might be caused, as it were, by a small bit of such recognition or by a great deal of it. In the combinations considered in this chapter, the violation of self-goal choice has been unqualified – the goals of the person depicted were negated *in toto*, hence the description 'goal-negating' for the commitment involved. But Sen also adverts to the possibility that a person's choices can be '*partly* disconnect[ed] ... from the pursuit of self-goal' (1985b: 216 emphasis added). For the sake of completeness, an example of a self-goal-choice-violating commitment is required, whereby a person's choice is partly restrained by her recognition of others' goals without thereby negating her own goal completely. Such a case would represent a partial violation of self-goal choice and would therefore involve one's tempering the pursuit of one's original goal through a recognition of others' goals. In such a case, the person acts on her original goal *to some degree* whereby the extent to which she does not act on this goal represents the extent to which she violates self-goal choice. As an example, a variation on Cyrilla's choice in the aeroplane illustrates the case. Let us imagine that Paul has just made the request that Cyrilla lower the blind. Cyrilla's reasoning which issues in the action described below is as follows:

> Here I am, quietly minding my own business, enjoying a bit of sun, having finished the *New York Times* (barring the sudoku puzzle which I am saving until later when the boredom of the flight gets too much). I'm damned if I'm going let some loathsome young whippersnapper spoil my fun just so that he can play his mindless game. However, being someone who generally adopts a live-and-let-live attitude to others (even to those whose asininity reaches the depths of the person in the aisle seat), I am willing to compromise, and so I will pull the blind down halfway (in an ostentatiously grudging way, exuding, whilst I do so, an audible sigh).

Cyrilla certainly restrains the unbridled pursuit of her own goal with this choice, but by pulling down the blind half way, she does not negate her goal, as she does when she pulls the blind down completely; rather, she acts on her goal to a limited extent. Her choice represents a compromise between adopting a live-and-let-live attitude towards others and maintaining some integrity toward her own goal of enjoying the sun.

Having, then, completed the second test of Sen's independence claim, this time using the concrete act of choice as our locus of analysis, the results are mixed. The first four combinations of realizations and violations of the three characteristics of privateness were successfully accomplished in the previous chapter. The last four, however, were not, and the sticking point, in each case, was the need to combine a violation of self-goal choice with either the realization or the violation of self-welfare goal. With a little initiative, which some might deem to be a little too *ad hoc*, these combinations could be approached more closely through the reformulation of self-welfare goal first introduced in combination five. The problem is that a violation of self-goal choice renders self-welfare goal – both its realization and violation – inoperable, for a violation of self-goal choice implies that a person not pursue a goal through her choice, and this implies that self-welfare goal can be neither realized (which requires an agent to pursue the goal of welfare maximization) nor violated (which requires that the agent pursue a goal which is derived from her commitment). There is a high degree of independence between realizations and violations of the characteristics of privateness, but not enough, when these realizations and violations are predicated of choice, to warrant the claim that they can be used in any combination.

## III Violating self-goal choice: an assessment

Sen's critics find the idea of violating self-goal choice hard to swallow, and the idea of a goalless choice, if that is indeed an accurate description of what Sen means by this violation, does strike one as peculiar. One hurdle to accepting Sen's characterization of violating self-goal choice is that a goalless choice is at odds with both our ordinary and philosophical understandings of human action. A typical description of the latter is as follows:

> An action is an event which has an object – an object at which the agent is directing the action's performance; and this object is what motivates the action's performance, being the goal at which the agent is aiming, and which he is using the action to attain. This goal-directedness, this property of being done by its agent as a means to an end, is something which all actions have in common.
>
> (Pink 2008: 158)

Sen's interpreters make similar points about human action in their exegeses of the violation of self-goal choice. After outlining Sen's understanding of this violation, Pettit, for example, writes that Sen's view is 'highly implausible', for we act intentionally, Pettit claims, when 'we try to advance certain goals in a way that is sensible in light of the apparent facts' (2005: 31–2; cf. Cudd 2014: 43; Schmid 2005: 217–18). Sen gives no indication that a violation of self-goal choice involves an agent doing something which does not answer to the name of performing an *action*, and therefore, in contrast to even his sympathetic

134  *Self-goal choice*

critics, he entertains the possibility that rationality does not demand that 'you must act only according to your own goals' (Sen 2007: 348). Sen's critics appear to accept this statement only if, instead of acting on her own goals, the agent be conceived to act on some other goal. This interpretation, though, would not involve a violation self-goal choice.

In determining whether people like Cyrilla pursue a goal when they perform norm-abiding actions, one may agree with Sen (2007: 352) that to contend that the person is pursuing the goals of others is 'not at all a good description of what is actually happening', and Sen is right to eliminate the potential goals discussed in Section I above that might be ascribed to such a person. Sen's claims regarding violations of self-goal choice, however, are not quite as other-worldly as his critics think, at least, if one refrains from conceiving a choice that violates self-goal choice to be one which is made by a person who chooses entirely without aim or purpose; for Sen insists that norm-abiding choices, though they pursue no obvious goal, are made with *reason*. For instance, when arguing that the decisive issue with such choices is not whether they be in the person's self-interest, Sen writes that the 'point to ascertain is ... whether one has reason enough to follow that rule' (2009a: 182 footnote). 'We can *reason* our way', he also writes, 'towards following decent rules of behaviour that we see as being fair to others ... and which can restrain the unique dominance of single-minded pursuit of our own goals' (2009a: 192 emphasis added). These passages are in keeping with the role which Sen accords to reason or reasoned scrutiny in the concept of personhood. In Chapter Four (Section IV), I argued that reasoned scrutiny stands above preference or desire in Sen's understanding of a person's identity, and the current discussion of self-goal choice suggests a further relationship in which reason stands, between reasoned scrutiny and goals: not only can reason temper a person's preferences and guide her away from the pursuit of self-interest; it can also regulate a person's goals and guide her away from the pursuit of her own goals. Consideration of others' ability to pursue their goals and of the existence of social norms which facilitate this ability of others to pursue their goals is what gives a person reason to curtail the pursuit of her own goals.

Stating the relationship between reason and the pursuit of goals like this gives us cause to qualify a statement made in Chapter Three during the discussion of Sen's more inclusive definition of commitment. According to that definition, a person's reason for choosing was deemed decisive to the nature of choices based on commitment, whereby choosing for a non-welfare-related reason is a necessary and sufficient condition for endowing choices with a committed status. In that discussion, I argued that the terminology of 'goals' could substitute for that of reasons for choosing; to say that a person chooses for a non-welfare-related reason is equivalent to saying that her goal is independent of concerns about her own welfare. But goals and reasons are only equivalent in this way when it comes to the first, self-welfare-goal-violating, type of commitment discussed above, that is, for those in which the agent acts on her own goal. Of the second, self-goal-choice-violating, type of commitment one may not substitute the term 'reason' with 'goal', for the agent whose choice violates self-goal choice does not act on a goal but nevertheless acts with reason. The distinction between acting on a reason (with a definite article before the noun) in the first case, in which one pursues a goal, and acting with reason (without a definite article) in the second, in which one does not pursue a goal, is of import here. Acting without a reason (that is, without a goal) is something Sen entertains as a possibility; acting without reason, however, though also possible, has no place in a theory of *rational* choice.

The foregoing description will not, I suspect, endear Sen's critics to violations of self-goal choice sufficiently that they embrace the idea; for reasoned scrutiny cannot substitute for goals in the depiction of rational choice, and it is goals, not reason, which Sen's critics miss when they express aspersion towards violations of self-goal choice. But even for those who are more amicably disposed to this violation, a problem remains. To see what it is requires that we return to the discussion in Section I of this chapter in which I analysed violations of self-goal choice which are accomplished by a person who follows rules of behaviour which she considers to be of instrumental importance. In that discussion, the agent was depicted to follow a rule of behaviour for the reason that adherence to a general rule would allow everyone to pursue their own goals more efficaciously than they would were the general rule to be discarded. Even when, in a given instance, adhering to the rule would be to the agent's immediate disadvantage (judged in terms of the lower degree of welfare she would derive compared to that she would derive from breaking the rule), she persuades herself to adhere to the rule in the name of allowing all to pursue their goals better. She does not, however, pursue others' goals, as we established in Section I of the current chapter with the discussion of Cyrilla; nor does she make following the rule her goal, for the assumption that the rule be of instrumental import to her excludes this. This is how Sen eliminates the possibility that she pursues any goal at all with her choice. The problem which arises for violations of self-goal choice, here, is that the instrumental significance of the rule is interpreted to lie in the fact that it is beneficial to all (instrumental to their pursuit of goals), including to the individual who adheres to the rule on those occasions when rule following thwarts her attempt to pursue a goal, for example the maximization of her welfare. But the question arises: does the individual follow the rule with the pursuit of her own long-term advantage in mind? Her reasoning, that is, might be thus:

> If I wish to maximize my ability to pursue my goals in the long term, it would be prudent to restrain my teleological proclivities and instead follow the rule on those occasions when rule following is to my disadvantage if such restraint will be to my advantage in the long run.

If this train of thought represents her reasoning, the individual is prudently sacrificing immediate gain for a higher future gain, and this seems to be a goal-orientated exercise, whereby the goal is long-term gain. This is the suspicion which we have not been able to banish since the discussion of acting on an as-if ranking in Chapter One. Sen might retort that, for a particular case in which the individual's short-term gain would be greatest if she were to break the rule, she is not pursuing a goal if she decides nevertheless to follow the rule. Hence her choice violates self-goal choice. But looked at in the context of her long-term calculus, goals are very much part of her reasoning. Sen asserts that the action of the person in the window seat of the plane 'is not a corollary of any general pursuit of well-being' (2007: 349). This is perhaps just another way of saying that the rule to which she adheres when she lowers the blind – 'let others pursue their goals' – is of no intrinsic import to her because she need not care one jot about or otherwise value the goals which others can pursue when she adheres to the let-others-pursue-their-goals norm (and, in fact, she thinks on this occasion that the game player's goal, being 'plainly silly', is of no value, either to herself or to the game player or to the wider aspirations of humanity). But if adherence to the rule by all will redound to her benefit when it comes to her ability to pursue her goals unhindered by others, *and this is the reason for her adherence to the rule*, the occupant of the window seat can be reasonably conceived to have and be acting on this long-term goal.

One should note that the assumption made in the previous paragraph, *videlicet*, that the agent's goal lie in the pursuit of welfare is only an assumption. Any goal can be substituted for this one, including those based on commitments of the sort which violate self-welfare goal. This is why Sen sometimes describes the violation of self-goal choice in terms of a person relinquishing 'goal-maximization' (1985b: 217). What he means is that violating self-goal choice involves restricting the pursuit of one's goal in each and every act of choice, whether those goals are self-interested (and therefore welfare orientated) or broader in nature and encompassing of concerns which transcend self-interest. But regardless of the content of one's goals, if a 'noninferior outcome' (2002a: 216) can be brought about by the general pursuit of a rule of conduct, it is an open question whether the individual, for whom that rule of conduct is of instrumental value only, follows it as a way of pursuing her goal of long-term goal fulfilment. Sen interprets such cases in terms of 'obligatory behaviour towards others in the community', and this is certainly a possibility whereby a person simply upholds the rule – perhaps habitually – without concern for her own long-term gain. But one can also uphold such a rule with an eye to the gain to oneself in terms of one's general ability to pursue one's goals without let. Relinquishing the opportunity to rebuff the likes of Paul by refusing his request to lower the shutter does indeed mean that Cyrilla forgoes the chance to pursue her immediate goal of basking in the sun, but if she does so in the hope that doing so will reproduce a rule of conduct which will, in future, redound to her ability to pursue her goals when the latter might meet opposition from those around her on whose forbearance the successful pursuit of these goals depends, it is not apparent that her choice is goalless and therefore the choice does not ostensibly represent a violation of self-goal choice.

## Conclusion

In this chapter, I have subjected Sen's independence claim to the second part of the more rigorous test which was begun in the previous chapter. The claim passed the first test, in which realizations and violations of the characteristics of privateness were conceived at the level of capability, with flying colours. Its success in passing the second test, for which the realizations and violations were conceived at the level of choice, is patchy. One might argue that the second test was unreasonably stringent, and it is true that, when Sen discusses self-centred welfare, self-welfare goal and self-goal choice, he often does so in general terms and in abstraction from concrete choices. But he elucidates the violation of self-goal choice, which he explains in the greatest detail, with a concrete choice. This leads us beyond the mere capability to make non-teleological choices and suggests that the various realizations and violations should be applied to choices.

Whilst exploring how Sen understands a choice which violates self-goal choice, I have argued that his critics have misunderstood him, for the textual evidence from Sen's work indicates that such a choice must be goalless. This conclusion followed from an elimination of possible candidates for a goal which an agent, whose choice violates self-goal choice, might be pursuing. In assessing Sen's conception of violating self-goal choice, I have questioned his success in banishing goals from choices which allegedly violate this characteristic of privateness and suggested that, on some occasions, the individual who relinquishes his immediate goal and acts instead on a rule of conduct may be conceived to be acting prudently, that is, with the goal of increasing his future ability to pursue his own goals.

## Note

1 Despite similarity of terminology, what I call goal-negating commitments differ from Hanisch's (2013) attempt to make sense of violations of self-goal choice, which rests on the idea of 'negative goals'.

# Conclusion

The examination of Sen's concept of commitment has traversed many terrains on which it has led us into encounters with a host of themes and concepts to which commitment has some relationship or relevance. These include sympathy, altruism, meta-ranking, weakness of will, agency, personhood, social norms, rights and agent relativity. It would be an exaggeration to aver that the concept of commitment is the unifying category in Sen's *oeuvre*, for there are important aspects of his work which are largely independent of his work on commitment, for example his analysis of poverty and famines, his capability approach to well-being and his contributions to the theme of equality and inequality. Nevertheless, commitment binds much of Sen's *opus* and it is a central concept of his work.

Having traced the development of the concept of commitment in roughly chronological form in Sen's work, it has transpired that he actually develops two concepts of commitment, or at least a concept which divides commitment into two distinct types. This first time this becomes explicit is in 'Goals, Commitment, and Identity' (1985b) in which Sen writes that a violation of self-goal choice 'reflects a type of commitment that is not able to be captured by the broadening of the goals to be pursued' (1985b: 219). The 'broadening' of goals allows for the first type of commitment, whereby the goals a person pursues are broadened from the narrow confines of self-interest to wider, non-welfare-related concerns. This broadening represents the type of commitment which violates self-welfare goal but not self-goal choice and it can be traced to the analysis in 'Rational Fools' (1977a) of a person who makes a choice for a reason independent of her concern for her welfare. This is how Sen first introduces commitment by name. The other, self-goal-choice-violating, type of commitment is actually of an older vintage than its self-welfare-goal-violating counterpart, and it has its roots in Sen's 'Behaviour and the Concept of Preferences' (1973) with his idea of acting on an as-if ranking. Sen does not, however, identify it as a type of commitment until 'Goals, Commitment, and Identity'.

Summing up the content of 'Rational Fools', Sen writes that the 'main issue is the acceptability of the assumption of the invariable pursuit of self-interest in each act' (1977a: 105). He criticizes this assumption from many angles, and it is worthwhile, in concluding, to review how some of his central claims relate to this assumption.

Let us begin with sympathy which, if admitted to the conceptual canon of choice theory, allows a person's welfare to be influenced by her knowledge of other people's welfare. That a person can feel sympathy in itself tells us nothing about her egoism or ability to transcend it because sympathy, as a contemplative phenomenon, has no connection to the agent's action and is therefore independent of self-interest. Only with active sympathy, as we saw in Chapter Two, does the connection to action become relevant. One's ability to perform actions based on sympathy poses no challenge to the assumption of self-interest because it simply extends the sources whence a person may derive welfare as a goal of her actions. A sympathetic person, whilst not being self-centred, may be perfectly self-interested.

One way of combating the assumption of self-interest is by reconceiving the concept of 'preference' to release it from the clutches of self-interested. This is what Sen suggests, if fleetingly, in his essay 'Behaviour and the Concept of Preference' (1973) when he explores the idea of 'ultimate preferences'. By encompassing all of an individual's interests and concerns under the term 'ultimate preference', one would drive a wedge between choice and welfare by breaking any necessary connection between preference and welfare maximization. People would still be able to act self-interestedly but acting on their preferences would not entail that they always act egoistically because the normative relationship between preference and welfare, as I called it in Chapter One, would be abrogated. The causal connection between preference and choice would, however, be universally upheld, for all choices would be generated by one's ultimate preferences. Non-self-interested choices based on one's ultimate preferences would not be counter-preferential, and this perhaps explains Sen's reluctance to pursue the idea of ultimate preferences, for a proponent of revealed preference theory, Sen's object of criticism in 'Behaviour and the Concept of Preference', would be able to maintain that choices based on an individual's ultimate preferences reveal that individual's preferences in every act of choice. Sen, however, seeks something which creates greater difficulty for revealed preference theory, namely, choices which abrogate the aetiological relationship between preference and choice.

Sen's critique of self-interest begins properly with the concept of commitment. Commitment, as Sen first introduces it in 'Rational Fools' and which subsequently becomes the type of commitment which violates self-welfare goal, is a further way of escaping the assumption that the individual's motivation be exclusively self-interested. By basing choices on a reason of one sort or another, which, by virtue of being derived from a commitment, is independent of concerns for his own welfare, an individual's choices are counter-preferential. The welfare effects of such choices for the individual are open, but self-interest plays no role in motivating the choice because his goal is not to derive welfare. This type of commitment drives a wedge between preference and choice because the choices in question are not causally based on one's preferences.

The second type of commitment, conceived such that it violates self-goal choice, is a further way in which the assumption of self-interest can be negated. By making non-teleological choices, a wedge is driven between choice and goals. Such choices are also counter-preferential, for they cannot be based on the goal of welfare maximization, nor on any other goal which the agent pursues through her choice. Self-goal-choice-violating commitments do not pose any restrictions on the configuration of welfare which ensues for the agent from making such choices, though the agent cannot pursue welfare through her choice, because the pursuit of welfare is inconsistent with a violation of self-goal choice. The terminology with which Sen describes violations of self-goal choice are strikingly similar to the terminology with which he depicts acting on an as-if ranking. In 'Behaviour and the Concept of Preference', Sen writes that people act on 'traditional rules of good behaviour', 'moral rules of behaviour' or on a 'moral code' (1973: 64–5). When, over two decades later, he describes violations of self-goal choice, he mentions that a person's choices can be influenced by 'rules of conduct' (1985b: 214, 217), 'voluntary rules of behaviour' and 'social norms' (2007: 348–9; 2009a: 193). Sen also describes the violation of self-goal choice in terms of a person's recognition of other people's goals (1985b: 214; 2005a: 19), but this, too, is expressed in terms of following a 'norm of good behaviour' which may take the form of 'let others do what they really want' (2009a: 193). This can leave little doubt that, what he refers to as a second type of commitment in his post-1970s work, is what he described with the terminology of as-if rankings in 1973.

I left the discussion of as-if rankings in Chapters One and Four with a lack of clarity about the goal of the agent who acts thus. Sen, it will be recalled, states that a person who acts on certain as-if rankings in prisoners' dilemma situations stands to do better than he would if he and his counterpart both chose the non-cooperative strategy. Mutually cooperative players, Sen stresses, would do better according to their 'true' (self-interested) preferences by acting on a moral rule of behaviour. This led to the suspicion that an agent who acted on such an as-if ranking might have a solely welfare-orientated ulterior goal for following a norm, and this would make a choice based on that goal incompatible with commitment. The discussion of self-goal choice in Chapter Eight indicates that this suspicion might be misplaced; for a violation of self-goal choice implies that the agent does not act on a goal, whether a welfare-pursuing, an other-regarding or a welfare-independent goal. If, then, acting on an as-if ranking is the conceptual relation and forebear of a violation of self-goal choice, the person who acts on an as-if ranking is similarly not pursuing a goal through her choices. She *has* goals, just as Cyrilla has a goal in the aeroplane encounter with Paul; the goal might consist, as Sen assumes in his analyses of the prisoners' dilemma, in the maximization of her welfare which is represented by her 'true', 'actual' or PD preferences. But when she makes choices based on an as-if ranking, she refrains from pursuing this goal and does not pursue another in its stead. Sen rejects the ascription of a goal to the agent which underlies her choices, be that goal the pursuit of her welfare, the pursuit of another person's goal or the goal of acting according to a social norm. Although the agent's choice of action will inevitably have an impact on her ability to pursue her goals as well as the ability of others to pursue theirs, this impact is a consequence of her choices but has nothing to do with the goal which underlies these choices. At the conclusion of Chapter Eight, I cast doubt on the success of Sen's endeavour to argue that choices can violate self-goal choice in the way described, for the agent whose choice allegedly violates self-goal choice can be conceived to pursue a long-term goal of securing the social conditions under which she will be able to pursue her own goals most effectively.

# References

Anderson, Elizabeth. 2001. 'Unstrapping the Straitjacket of "Preference": A Comment on Amartya Sen's Contributions to Philosophy and Economics'. *Economics and Philosophy* 17(1): 21–38.
Aristotle. 1985. *Nicomachean Ethics*, trans. Terence Irwin, Indianapolis: Hackett.
Arrow, Kenneth J. 1963. *Social Choice and Individual Values*, second edition, New York: Wiley.
Aubrey, John. 1975. *Brief Lives*, edited by Richard Barber, London: Folio Society.
Baker, Jennifer. 2009. 'Virtue and Behavior'. *Review of Social Economy* 67(1): 3–24.
Barbato, Joseph. 2005. 'Scotland's Bastard Verdict'. *Indiana International and Comparative Law Review* 15(3): 543–581.
Batson, C. Daniel. 1991. *The Altruism Question: Toward a Social-Psychological Answer*, Hillsdale, New Jersey: Lawrence Erlbaum.
Batson, C. Daniel. 2011. *Altruism in Humans*, Oxford: Oxford University Press.
Becker, Gary S. 1996. *Accounting for Tastes*, Cambridge, Massachusetts: Harvard University Press.
Bicchieri, Christina. 2006. *The Grammar of Society: The Nature and Dynamics of Social Norms*, Cambridge: Cambridge University Press.
Binmore, Kenneth. 2009. *Rational Decisions*, Princeton, New Jersey: Princeton University Press.
Bowles, Samuel and Herbert Gintis. 2011. *A Cooperative Species: Human Reciprocity and its Evolution*, Princeton, New Jersey: Princeton University Press.
Bratman, Michael. 1987. *Intentions, Plans, and Practical Reason*, Cambridge, Massachusetts: Harvard University Press.
Bratman, Michael. 1996. 'Planning and Temptation'. In *Minds and Morals: Essays on Cognitive Science and Ethics*, edited by Larry May, Marilyn Friedman and Andy Clark, pp. 293–310, Cambridge, Massachusetts: MIT Press.
Brennan, Geoffrey. 2007. 'The Grammar of Rationality'. In *Rationality and Commitment*, edited by Fabienne Peter and Hans Bernhard Schmid, pp. 105–123, Oxford: Oxford University Press.
Broome, John. 2013. *Rationality Through Reasoning*, Malden, Massachusetts: Wiley-Blackwell.
Clecak, Peter. 1969. 'Moral and Material Incentives'. *Socialist Register* 6: 101–135.
Coleman, Jame S. 1990. *Foundations of Social Theory*, Cambridge, Massachusetts: Harvard University Press.

Cudd, Ann E. 2014. 'Commitment as Motivation: Amartya Sen's Theory of Agency and the Explanation of Behaviour'. *Economics and Philosophy* 30(1): 35–56.
Cudd, Ann E. 2017. 'Commitments and Corporate Responsibility: Amartya Sen on Motivations to do Good'. In *Wealth, Commerce, and Philosophy: Foundational Thinkers and Business Ethics*, edited by E. Heath and B. Kaldis, pp. 401–419, Chicago: Chicago University Press.
Davis, John D. 2007. 'Identity and Commitment: Sen's Fourth Aspect of the Self'. In *Rationality and Commitment*, edited by Fabienne Peter and Hans Bernhard Schmid, pp. 313–335, Oxford: Oxford University Press.
Drèze, Jean and Amartya Sen. 1989. *Hunger and Public Action*, Oxford: Clarendon Press.
Edgerton, Robert B. 1985. *Rules, Exceptions, and Social Order*, Berkeley: University of California Press.
Elster, Jon. 1979. *Ulysses and the Sirens: Studies in Rationality and Irrationality*, Cambridge: Cambridge University Press.
Elster, Jon. 1989. 'Social Norms and Economic Theory'. *Journal of Economic Perspectives* 3(4): 99–117.
Elster, Jon. 1992. 'Intertemporal Choice and Political Thought'. In *Choice over Time*, edited by G. Loewenstein and J. Elster, pp. 35–53, New York: Russell Sage Foundation.
Elster, Jon. 2000. *Ulysses Unbound: Studies in Rationality, Precommitment, and Constraints*, Cambridge: Cambridge University Press.
Fehr, Ernst and Klaus Schmidt. 1999. 'A Theory of Fairness, Competition and Cooperation'. *Quarterly Journal of Economics* 114(3): 817–868.
Fehr, Ernst and Urs Fischbacher. 2002. 'Why Social Preferences Matter – The Impact of Non-Selfish Motives on Competition, Cooperation and Incentives'. *Economic Journal* 112(478): C1–C33.
Fehr, Ernst and Urs Fischbacher. 2003. 'The Nature of Human Altruism'. *Nature* 425(6960): 785–791.
Fehr, Ernst, Urs Fischbacher and Michael Kosfeld. 2005. 'Neuroeconomic Foundations of Trust and Social Preferences: Initial Evidencee'. *American Economic Review Papers & Proceedings* 95(2): 346–351.
Feinberg, Joel. 1971. 'Psychological Egoism'. In *Reason and Responsibility: Readings in some Basic Problems of Philosophy*, edited by J. Feinberg, pp. 489–500, second edition, Encino and Belmont, California: Dickenson Publishing Company.
Frankfurt, Harry G. 1971. 'Freedom of the Will and the Concept of a Person'. *Journal of Philosophy* 68(1): 5–20.
Gandhi, Mahatma. 1996/1927. *An Autobiography, or the Story of my Experiments with Truth*, trans. Mahadev Desai, Ahmedabad: Navajivan Trust.
Gintis, Herbert and Rakesh Khurana. 2008. 'Corporate Honesty and Business Education: A Behavioral Model'. In *Moral Markets: The Critical Role of Values in the Economy*, edited by Paul J. Zak, pp. 300–327, Princeton, New Jersey: Princeton University Press.
Goldfarb, Robert S. and William B. Griffith. 1991. 'Amending the Economist's "Rational Egoist" Model to Include Moral Values and Norms. Part 2: Alternative Solutions'. In *Social Norms and Economic Institutions*, edited by Kenneth J. Koford and Jeffrey B. Miller, pp. 59–84, Ann Arbor: University of Michigan Press.
Goodin, Robert E. 1980. 'Making Moral Incentives Pay'. *Policy Sciences* 12(2): 131–145.

Güth, Werner. 2002. 'Interview with Werner Güth'. In *Experimental Economics: Financial Markets, Auctions, and Decision Making*, edited by F. Andersson and H. Holm, pp. 19–28, Dordrecht: Kluwer.

Hahn, Frank and Martin Hollis. 1979. 'Introduction'. In *Philosophy and Economic Theory*, edited by Frank Hahn and Martin Hollis, pp. 1–17, Oxford: Oxford University Press.

Hands, Wade. 2013. 'Foundations of Contemporary Revealed Preference Theory'. *Erkenntis* 78(5): 1081–1108.

Hanisch, Christoph. 2013. 'Negative Goals and Identity: Revisiting Sen's Critique of Homo Economicus'. *Rationality, Markets and Morals* 4: 157–172.

Harsanyi, John. 1955. 'Cardinal Welfare, Individualist Ethics, and Interpersonal Comparisons of Utility'. *Journal of Political Economy* 63(4): 309–321.

Hausman, Daniel M. 2005. 'Sympathy, Commitment, and Preference'. *Economics and Philosophy* 21(1): 33–50. [Reprinted in *Rationality and Commitment*, edited by Fabienne Peter and Hans Bernhard Schmid, pp. 49–69, Oxford: Oxford University Press, 2007. Page numbers in text refer to the reprint.]

Hausman, Daniel M. 2012. *Preference, Value, Choice, and Welfare*, Cambridge: Cambridge University Press.

Hédoin, Cyril. 2016. 'Sen's Criticism of Revealed Preference Theory and its "Neo-Samuelsonian Critique": A Methodological and Theoretical Assessment'. *Journal of Economic Methodology* 23(4): 349–373.

Hirschman, Albert O. 1982. *Shifting Involvements: Private Interest and Public Action*, Princeton, New Jersey: Princeton University Press.

Hobbes, Thomas. 1968/1651. *Leviathan, or the Matter, Forme, & Power of a Common-Wealth Ecclesiasticall and Civill*, edited by C.B. MacPherson, London: Penguin.

Hobbes, Thomas. 1994/1650. *The Elements of Law Natural and Politic*, edited by J.C. A. Gaskin, Oxford: Oxford University Press.

Homer. 1967. *The Odyssey of Homer*, trans. Richmond Lattimore, New York: Harper Row.

Jolls, Christine, Cass R. Sunstein and Richard Thaler. 1998. 'A Behavioral Approach to Law and Economics'. *Stanford Law Review* 50(5): 1471–1550.

Kant, Immanuel. 1907/1793. 'Die Religion innerhalb der Grenzen der bloßen Vernunft'. In *Kants Werke, Kants gesammelte Schriften* volume VI, edited by Die Königlich Preußische Akademie der Wissenschaften, pp. 1–202, Berlin: Georg Reimer.

Kant, Immanuel. 1974/1786. *Grundlegung der Metaphysik der Sitten*. In *Immanuel Kant: Werkausgabe*, VII, edited by Wilhelm Weischedel, pp. 7–102, second edition. Frankfurt am Main: Suhrkamp Verlag.

Klamer, Arjo. 1989. 'A Conversation with Amartya Sen'. *Journal of Economic Perspectives* 3(1): 135–150.

Lenin, Vladimir Illych. 1921. 'The New Economic Policy and the Tasks of the Political Education Departments'. www.marxists.org/archive/lenin/works/1921/oct/17.htm, accessed on 30. 1. 2019.

Llorente, Renzo. 2018. *The Political Theory of Che Guevara*, London: Rowman & Littlefield.

Milligan, Tony. 2013. *Civil Disobedience: Protest, Justification, and the Law*, London: Bloomsbury.

Nagel, Thomas. 1970. *The Possibility of Altruism*, Oxford: Clarendon.

Narveson, Jan. 2001. *The Libertarian Idea*, Peterborough, Ontario: Broadview Press.

Nozick, Robert. 1974. *Anarchy, State, and Utopia*, New York: Basic Books.
Peacock, Mark S. 2010. 'Starvation and Social Class: Amartya Sen on Markets and Famines'. *Review of Political Economy* 22(1): 57–73.
Peter, Fabienne and Hans Bernhard Schmid. 2007. 'Rational Fools, Rational Commitments'. In *Rationality and Commitment*, edited by Fabienne Peter and Hans Bernhard Schmid, pp. 3–13, Oxford: Oxford University Press
Pettit, Philip. 2005. 'Construing Sen on Commitment'. *Economics and Philosophy* 21(1): 15–32. [Reprinted in *Rationality and Commitment*, edited by Fabienne Peter and Hans Bernhard Schmid, pp. 28–48, Oxford: Oxford University Press, 2007. Page numbers in text refer to the reprint.]
Pink, Tom. 2008. 'Intention and Two Models of Action'. In *Reasons and Intentions*, edited by Bruno Verbeek, pp. 153–179, Aldershot, Hampshire: Ashgate.
Poundstone, William. 1992. *Prisoner's Dilemma*, New York: Doubleday.
Riskin, Carl. 1973. 'Maoism and Motivation: Work Incentives in China'. *Bulletin of Concerned Asian Scholars* 5(1): 9–24.
Rousseau, Jean-Jacques. 1973/1762. The Social Contract. In *The Social Contract and the Discourses*, trans. G.D.H. Cole, London: J.M. Dent.
Runciman, Walter Garrison and Amartya Sen. 1965. 'Games, Justice and the General Will', *Mind* 74(296): 554–562.
Samuelson, Paul A. 1938. 'A Note on the Pure Theory of Consumer's [sic] Behaviour'. *Economica* 5(17): 61–71.
Samuelson, Paul A. 1948. 'Consumption Theory in Terms of Revealed Preference'. *Economica* 15(60): 243–253.
Schefczyk, Michael and Mark S. Peacock. 2010. 'Altruism as a Thick Concept'. *Economics and Philosophy* 26(2): 165–187.
Schmid, Hans Bernhard. 2005. 'Beyond Self-Goal Choice: Amartya Sen's Analysis of the Structure of Commitment and the Role of Shared Desires'. *Economics and Philosophy* 21(1): 51–64. [Reprinted in *Rationality and Commitment*, edited by Fabienne Peter and Hans Bernhard Schmid, pp. 211–226, Oxford: Oxford University Press, 2007. Page numbers in text refer to the reprint.]
Sen, Amartya. 1961. 'On Optimising the Rate of Saving'. *Economic Journal* 71(283): 479–496.
Sen, Amartya. 1966. 'Labour Allocation in a Cooperative Enterprise'. *Review of Economic Studies* 33(4): 361–371.
Sen, Amartya. 1973. 'Behaviour and the Concept of Preference'. *Economica* 40(159): 241–259. [Reprinted in Sen 1982a, Chapter Two, pp. 54–73, page numbers in text refer to the reprint.]
Sen, Amartya. 1974a. 'Choice, Orderings and Morality'. In *Practical Reason*, edited by S. Körner, pp. 54–67, Oxford: Basil Blackwell. [Reprinted in Sen 1982a, Chapter Three, pp. 74–83. Page numbers in text refer to the reprint.]
Sen, Amartya. 1974b. 'Reply to Comments'. In *Practical Reason*, edited by S. Körner, pp. 78–82, Oxford: Basil Blackwell.
Sen, Amartya. 1975. 'Comment'. In *Altruism, Morality, and Economic Theory*, edited by Edmund S. Phelps, pp. 225–227, New York: Russell Sage Foundation.
Sen, Amartya. 1977a. 'Rational Fools: A Critique of the Behavioural Foundations of Economic Theory'. *Philosophy and Public Affairs* 6(4): 317–344. [Reprinted in Sen 1982a, Chapter Four, pp. 84–106. Page numbers in text refer to the reprint.]
Sen, Amartya. 1977b. 'Rationality and Morality: A Reply'. *Erkenntnis* 11(2): 225–232.

Sen, Amartya. 1981. *Poverty and Famines: An Essay on Entitlement and Deprivation*, Oxford: Clarendon.
Sen, Amartya. 1981–2. 'Plural Utility'. *Proceedings of the Aristotelian Society* 81(new series): 193–215.
Sen, Amartya. 1982a. *Choice, Welfare and Measurement*, Oxford: Basil Blackwell.
Sen, Amartya. 1982b. 'Rights and Agency'. *Philosophy and Public Affairs* 11(1): 3–39.
Sen, Amartya. 1983a. 'Evaluator Relativity and Consequential Evaluation'. *Philosophy and Public Affairs* 12(1), 113–132.
Sen, Amartya. 1983b. 'Liberty and Social Choice'. *Journal of Philosophy* 80(1): 5–28. [Reprinted in Sen 2002a, Chapter Five, pp. 381–407. Page numbers in text refer to the reprint.]
Sen, Amartya. 1985a. 'Well-Being, Agency and Freedom'. *Journal of Philosophy* 82(4): 169–221.
Sen, Amartya. 1985b. 'Goals, Commitment, and Identity'. *Journal of Law, Economics, and Organization* 1(2): 341–355. [Reprinted in Sen 2002a, Chapter Five, pp. 206–224. Page numbers in text refer to the reprint.]
Sen, Amartya. 1985c. 'Rationality and Uncertainty'. *Theory and Decision* 18(2): 109–127. [Reprinted in Sen 2002a, Chapter Six, pp. 225–244. Page numbers in text refer to the reprint.]
Sen, Amartya. 1986a. 'Prediction and Economic Theory'. *Proceedings of the Royal Society of London. Series A, Mathematical and Physical* 407(1832): 3–22.
Sen, Amartya. 1986b. 'Rationality, Interest, and Identity'. In *Development, Democracy, and the Art of Trespassing: Essays in Honor of Albert O. Hirschman*, edited by Alejandro Foxley, Michael S. McPherson and Guillermo O'Donnell, pp. 343–352, Notre Dame, Indiana: University of Notre Dame Press.
Sen, Amartya. 1987a. *On Ethics and Economics*, Oxford: Basil Blackwell.
Sen, Amartya. 1987b. 'The Standard of Living: Lecture II, Lives and Capabilities'. In *The Standard of Living: The Tanner Lectures Clare Hall, Cambridge, 1985*, edited by Geoffrey Hawthorn, pp. 20–38, Cambridge: Cambridge University Press.
Sen, Amartya. 1988. 'Property and Hunger'. *Economics and Philosophy* 4(1): 57–68.
Sen, Amartya. 1989. 'Economic Methodology: Heterogeneity and Relevance'. *Social Research* 56(2): 299–329.
Sen, Amartya. 1990. 'Welfare, Freedom and Social Choice: A Reply'. *Recherches Économiques de Louvain* 56(3–4): 451–485.
Sen, Amartya. 1991. 'Public Action to Remedy Hunger'. *Interdisciplinary Science Reviews* 16(4): 324–336.
Sen, Amartya. 1992. *Inequality Reexamined*, Oxford: Clarendon.
Sen, Amartya. 1993a. 'Internal Consistency of Choice'. *Econometrica* 61(3): 495–521. [Reprinted in Sen 2002a, Chapter Three, pp. 121–157. Page numbers in text refer to the reprint.]
Sen, Amartya. 1993b. 'Positional Objectivity'. *Philosophy and Public Affairs* 22(2): 126–145.
Sen, Amartya. 1994. 'The Formulation of Rational Choice'. *American Economic Review Papers & Proceedings* 84(2): 385–390.
Sen, Amartya. 1995a. 'Is the Idea of Purely Internal Consistency of Choice Bizarre?' In *World, Mind, and Ethics: Essays on the Ethical Philosophy of Bernard Williams*, edited by J.E.J. Altham and Ross Harrison, pp. 19–31, Cambridge: Cambridge University Press.

Sen, Amartya. 1995b. 'Rationality and Social Choice'. *American Economic Review* 85(1): 1–24. [Reprinted in Sen 2002a, Chapter Eight, pp. 261–299. Page numbers in text refer to the reprint.]

Sen, Amartya. 1996. 'Rights: Formulations and Consequences'. *Analyse & Kritik* 18(1): 153–170. [Reprinted in Sen 2002a, Chapter Fourteen, pp. 439–460. Page numbers in text refer to the reprint.]

Sen, Amartya. 1997. 'Maximization and the Act of Choice'. *Econometrica* 65(4): 745–779. [Reprinted in Sen 2002a, Chapter Four, pp. 158–205. Page numbers in text refer to the reprint.]

Sen, Amartya. 1997/1973. *On Economic Inequality*, enlarged edition, Oxford: Clarendon.

Sen, Amartya. 1999. *Development as Freedom*, Oxford: Oxford University Press.

Sen, Amartya. 1999/1987. *Commodities and Capabilities*, Oxford: Oxford University Press.

Sen, Amartya. 2000a. 'Consequential Evaluation and Practical Reason'. *Journal of Philosophy* 97(9): 477–502.

Sen, Amartya. 2000b. 'The Discipline of Cost-Benefit Analysis'. *Journal of Legal Studies* 29(S2): 931–952. [Reprinted in Sen 2002a, Chapter Nineteen, pp. 553–577. Page numbers in text refer to the reprint.]

Sen, Amartya. 2000c. 'The Reach of Reason'. *New York Review of Books*, 47(12), 20 July. [Reprinted in Sen 2005b, Chapter Thirteen, pp. 273–293. Page numbers in text refer to the reprint.]

Sen, Amartya. 2001a. 'The Many Faces of Gender Inequality'. *New Republic* 225(12): 35–40.

Sen, Amartya. 2001b. 'Symposium on Amartya Sen's Philosophy: Reply'. *Economics and Philosophy* 17(1): 51–66.

Sen, Amartya. 2002a. *Rationality and Freedom*, Cambridge, Massachusetts: Harvard University Press.

Sen, Amartya. 2002b. 'Open and Closed Impartiality'. *Journal of Philosophy* 99(9): 445–469.

Sen, Amartya. 2004. 'Social Identity'. *Revue de Philosophie économique* 9(June): 7–27.

Sen, Amartya. 2005a. 'Why Exactly is Commitment Important for Rationality?' *Economics and Philosophy* 21(1): 5–14. [Reprinted in *Rationality and Commitment*, edited by Fabienne Peter and Hans Bernhard Schmid, pp. 18–27, Oxford: Oxford University Press, 2007, page numbers in text refer to the reprint.]

Sen, Amartya. 2005b. *The Argumentative Indian: Writings on Indian History, Culture and Identity*, London: Penguin (Allen Lane).

Sen, Amartya. 2006. *Identity and Violence: The Illusion of Destiny*, New York: W.W. Norton.

Sen, Amartya. 2007. 'Rational Choice: Discipline, Brand Name, and Substance'. In *Rationality and Commitment*, edited by Fabienne Peter and Hans Bernhard Schmid, pp. 339–361, Oxford: Oxford University Press.

Sen, Amartya. 2009a. *The Idea of Justice*, Cambridge, Massachusetts: Harvard University Press.

Sen, Amartya. 2009b. 'Economics, Law, and Ethics'. In *Against Injustice: The New Economics of Amartya Sen*, edited by Reiko Gotho and Paul Dumouchel, pp. 39–54, Cambridge: Cambridge University Press.

Sen, Amartya. 2014. 'Justice and Identity'. *Economics and Philosophy* 30(1): 1–10.

Sen, Amartya. 2017a. 'Reason and Justice: The Optimal and the Maximal'. *Philosophy* 92(1): 5–19.

Sen, Amartya. 2017b. *Collective Choice and Social Welfare: An Expanded Edition*, Cambridge, Massachusetts: Harvard University Press.

Shiell, Alan and Bonnie Rush. 2003. 'Can Willingness to Pay Capture the Value of Altruism? An Exploration of Sen's Notion of Commitment'. *Journal of Socio-Economics* 32(6): 647–660.

Smith, Adam. 1982/1790. *The Theory of Moral Sentiments*, sixth edition, Indianapolis: Liberty Fund. [Reprint of the 1979 version published by Oxford University Press.]

Vanberg, Victor. 2008. 'On the Economics of Moral Preferences'. *American Journal of Economics and Sociology* 67(4): 605–628.

Watkins, J.W.N. 1974. 'Comment: "Self-Interest and Morality"'. In *Practical Reason*, edited by S. Körner, 67–77, Oxford: Basil Blackwell.

Watson, Gary. 1975. 'Free Agency'. *Journal of Philosophy* 72(8): 205–220.

# Index

actions based on sympathy 4, 26, 29, 31, 32–5, 36, 37, 48–9, 52–5, 77, 78, 87, 114, 116, 119, 129–30, 131, 139
aetiological relationship 3, 7, 13–14, 15, 17, 19, 20, 21–2, 23, 44–5, 49, 69, 82, 139
agency 2, 29, 85–6, 89–91, 138
agent-relativity 2, 5, 76, 85–91, 138
altruism 2, 4, 25, 27, 28, 38, 40, 51–6, 57, 82, 130, 138; psychological conceptions of 4, 52–3, 56, 57; through sympathy 27, 52, 54
Anderson, E. 34
apples 76–81, 94–5, 131
Aristotle, 4, 59, 66–8, 73, 84, 102
Arrow, K.J. 18, 62
as-if rankings 2, 3, 4, 7, 15, 18, 19–23, 45, 55, 58, 59, 62, 63–6, 69, 70, 74, 76, 81, 136, 138, 140; *see also* meta-ranking
Aubrey, J. 119n1

Becker, G.S. 26, 36, 106
behavioural economics 82–3
Bowles, S. 12
Broome, J. 102
Brown J. 48

China 20, 63, 67, 69
Circe 94
commitment *passim*; goal-displacing 127; goal-modifying 108, 123; goal-negating 127, 132, 137n1; pure versus impure commitments 51; Sen's initial definition of 39, 40–3, 45, 46, 48–50, 57, 89; Sen's more inclusive definition of 39, 40–3, 45, 46, 49, 50, 57, 114, 134; Sen's official definition of 43, 89; welfare-maximizing type 40–7, 50, 56, 64, 67–8, 69, 102

continence 4, 66–7, 102
counter-preferential choice 1,2 , 4, 5, 39, 43–7, 49, 57, 62, 64, 68, 79–82, 86, 91, 92, 103, 139, 140
Cudd, A. 28, 122, 124

Drèze, J. 99
duty 12, 20, 23, 42, 51, 89–90, 117

Edgerton, R. 103n2
Edgeworth, F.Y. 75
egoism 11, 12–13, 22, 25, 26–8, 29, 33–5, 37, 47–9, 51, 54, 55, 57, 75n1, 139
Elster, J. 94, 97
enkratic choice 68–9, 74–5, 85, 102

famine 99, 138
Frankfurt, H. 73
Frisch, R. 91n1

Gandhi, I. 99
Gandhi, M. 96–7
general will 18
Genghis Khan 25
Gintis, H. 12
goalless choices 6, 104, 108, **109**, 110–12, 115, 137, 140
Guevara, C. 24n2
Güth, W. 82–3

Hanisch, C. 122, 137n1
Harsanyi, J. 61–2
Hausman, D. 13, 17, 27, 61, 92–5, 97, 100
Hédoin, C. 34
heterodox economics: Sen as representative thereof 5, 76, 91
Hirschman, A. 70
Hobbes, T. 93, 95, 116, 119–20n1

identity: personal *see* personhood
incontinence *see* weakness of will
independence claim 5–6, 104–5, 108, 109–113, 115–19, 121, 127–33, 137; *see also* privateness; self-centred welfare; self-goal choice; self-welfare goal
India 98, 99
internal consistency: as criterion for rational choice 3, 7, 8–10, 11

Kant, I. 41–2, 51, 117
karoshi 22–3
Ku Klux Klan 48

Lenin, V.I. 24n2
libertarianism 2, 96–7, 99, 103n1
Lincoln, A. 120n1

Maharashtra 99
maximization 36–7; *see also* welfare maximization
meta-ranking 4, chapter 4, 138; *see also* as-if rankings
moral norms *see* social norms
morality 3, 4, 15, 17, 18, 20, 21, 22, 23, 24n2, 39, 42, 47–50, 56, 57, chapter 4, 76, 87, 89, 90, 93, 94, 96–102, 124, 140; as a graded phenomenon 4, 62, 66
morals *see* morality
motivation 10–14, 19–20, 22–3, 27–9, 32–5, 37, 40–1, 47, 50, 51, 53, 55–7, 63, 75n1, 88, 93, 105, 122, 139

non-teleological choice *see* goalless choices
norm following *see* social norms
normative relationship 3, 7–8, 13–14, 15, 17, 19, 21, 23, 44, 139
Nozick, R. 5, 96–100, 102–3, 103n1

Odysseus 92, 93, 94
optimization 38n1
outcomes: comprehensive versus culmination 86, 89–90, 91n2, 96, 98, 100, 101, 103

personhood 2, 4, 59, 69–74, 101, 134, 138
Peter, F. 27–8, 34, 47
Pettit, P. 27, 38, 40, 54–5, 108, 123, 127, 133
preference *passim*; ultimate 3, 8, 17–18, 21, 23, 44, 61, 139; *see also* aetiological relationship, normative relationship, reasons for choice, reasoned scrutiny
prisoners' dilemma 3, 4, 7, 14–19, 20–2, 23, 58, 59, 62–5, 66, 69, 74, 126, 140
privateness 5–6, 104–8, **109**, 111–13, 115, **115**, 119, 121, 127–9, 133, 137; *see also* independence claim; self-centred welfare; self-goal choice; self-welfare goal

rational choice: orthodox conceptions of 1–3, 5, 8, 12, 13, 14, 16, 18, 26, 28, 35, 36, 43, 44, 61, 69, 74, 79, 82–3, 105, 106; *see also* internal consistency
rational fool 61, 72
reason *see* reasoned scrutiny
reasoned scrutiny 59, 72–4, 134, 134–6; *see also* personhood
reason(s) for choice 4, 39, 40–3, 45–51, 53, 56–8, 64, 66–9, 72–4, 75, 81–3, 88, 90, 107, 108, 117, 134–6, 138, 139
reason-based aetiology of choice 49, 50
revealed preference theory 8–10, 13, 15, 20, 23, 70, 139
rights 2, 71, 96–102, 138; Nozick on 5, 96–7, 102, 103n1; Sen on 5, 92, 97–102, 103
Rousseau, J.-J. 18
rules of conduct, 15, 18, 63, 66, 76, 79, 81, 124; intrinsic versus instrumental importance thereof 124–6, 134–6, 137, 140; *see also* social norms
Runciman, W.G. 18–19

Samuelson, P.A. 8–9
Schmid, H.-B. 27–7, 34, 47
self *see* personhood
self-centred welfare 5, chapters 7 and 8
self-centredness 15, 36, 52, 55, 100, 116, 127; *see also* self-centred welfare
self-goal choice 5–6, **115**, chapters 7 and 8, 138, 140–1
self-imposed constraints 80, 81–5, chapter 6, 125
self-interest *see* egoism
self-welfare goal 5–6, chapters 7 and 8, 138, 
Sen, A.K. *passim*
Sirens 92, 94
Smith, A. 29
social norms 5, 17, 23, 64, chapter 5, 93–5, 97, 103, 124–6, 131, 134, 138, 140–1; constraint view 92; cost-avoidance model 83, 84; internalization view 84–5
sympathy chapter 3; active 4, 26, 30, 31–5, 37, 40, 53–5, 87, 89, 90, 106, 139;

contemplative 4, 26, 29–33, 35, 37, 53–5, 87, 89–90, 106, **109**, 119, 130, 131, 139; epistemological conditions for 26, 30, 37; Sen's offical definition 32, 90, 106; *see also* actions based on sympathy; altruism through sympathy; welfare maximization

states of affairs *see* outcomes

Tubman, H. 48
Tucker, A.W. 14

uncertainty 26, 29, 30, 31–2, 37

virtuous person 4, 68, 73, 84, 102

Watkins, J.W.N. 64, 67
Watson, G. 70, 73
weakness of will 4, 59, 63, 65–9. 74, 97, 100, 102, 103, 138
welfare maximization 1, 3, 8, 11, 12, 13, 14–16, 17, 19, 21–2, 38n1, 48, 63, 65, 78–9, 80, 81, 83, 84, 85, 107, 109, 111–16, 123, 126, 128, 129, 133–5, 139–40; contrasted with welfare-increasing choices 35, 49, 56–7; welfare-maximizing type 40–7, 50, 56, 64, 67–8, 69, 102; relation to sympathy 4, 25, 26–8, 34, 35, 36–7, 49; *see also* commitment; normative relationship; self-welfare goal